MEMOIRS

*50 Years at the
Courier-Journal
and Other Places*

MEMOIRS

*50 Years at the
Courier-Journal
and Other Places*

John Ed Pearce

THE SULGRAVE PRESS

EXECUTIVE EDITOR   John S. Moremen

EDITOR   Amy Spears

ASSOCIATE EDITOR   Amy Humphrey

PRODUCTION   William S. Butler

Cover Design Double Vision

ISBN 1-891138-26-X

Printed in USA

The Sulgrave Press
2005 Longest Ave.
Louisville, KY 40204

To the girls.

"It is a hard thing for a man to write of himself. It grates his own heart to say anything of disparagement, and the reader's ears to hear anything of praise from him."

Abraham Cowley

TABLE OF CONTENTS

1

Fifty Yards in Fifty Years

A good memory is essential both to liars and those who would write their memoirs, though memory is seldom good enough. It is difficult, if not impossible, to reach back across the gulf of fifty years and reconstruct with reasonable accuracy what was actually felt, said and done at any particular time. Honest recall does not always produce what we seek. Time tends to chip away truth, producing over the years outlines easier for the ego to accept, making the past more pleasant to recall. Even with an effort at honesty, I doubt that I can remember what I felt on that gray, cold morning of December 28, 1946, as I approached the blocky limestone building at the corner of Louisville's Third and Liberty streets that housed the prestigious *Courier-Journal*, where I had just been hired to become the newest and youngest member of the editorial board. It was a post more exalted than I had ever sought or even dreamed of.

Can I remember the feeling? Probably not. I was excited, surely, a little nervous, but not really awed by the prospect as I passed through the revolving doors into the dingy lobby. I could not imagine failure. On the contrary, I was confident, as I took the rickety cage elevator to the executive floor, that the door was opening on avenues that would lead to fame and fortune. At 26, I was not, after all, a virgin when it came to employment. For eleven years I had made my living at a wild array of jobs without once being heaved from the payroll, and felt that, with luck, this one could be handled.

At the time I was not living in the style of a world class journalist. On the contrary, I was living at the YMCA, then at the corner of Third and Broadway, a musty warren that served as overnight shelter for soldiers from Fort Knox, and home for threadbare old shufflers who could afford nothing better. Even so, I was lucky to get it. Some ten million veterans had been thrown into the housing market at war's end, many of them, like me, now waiting for houses or apartments to be built so they could call in wives and children and begin what they assumed would be a normal life. I was typical, having married in the waning days of the war a girl I met at UK, and now having the added responsibility of a 16-month old daughter, a responsibility that seldom left my mind. I was awaiting word from the man at the *Courier-Journal* who assured me that a fine apartment would be ready for us any day.

So scarce was housing that, to get a room at the Y, I had to accept a roommate, a pudgy, coffee-colored man with thick glasses and a twitching, furtive look who wore the same dirty suit day after day and ate in the room. Often, when I came home at night, I would find him crouched by the window, peering through binoculars into the windows of apartments across the street, watching in his lonely lust the tired salesladies collapsing with cigarettes and contemplating empty evenings. When I surprised him at his voyeurism, he would whirl, squint at me and giggle. There was also an elderly gentleman with gray tufts of hair on his chest who seemed to spend an inordinate amount of time in the shower room, smiling shyly and speaking in a soft voice.

I made another discovery at the Y, one that would prove to be the most fortunate of my life. In the rear of the building was a large gym, complete with courts, running track, lockers and exercise and weight rooms. It was not only a fine relief at the end of the working day, but a cheap alternative to the movies along Fourth Street, though I loved Fourth Street. There were good places to eat—the English Grill at the Brown Hotel, the Seelbach, Leo's Hideaway, Kunz's. Proper ladies, the type who shopped at Jenny Lind, ate at the Orchid Room at Stewart's, but we nickle-nursers of the fourth estate, along with young businessmen, lawyers and other unindicted criminals, sought the blue-plate special at the Blue Boar, or crowded into the Colonnade, a famous cafeteria in the basement of the Starks Building, where we battled old ladies for a place in line and the best pie in town, though the old ladies, creatures of temper and elbows, battled back. There were also good bars and movie houses along Fourth. It gave the town a metropolitan tone, a good place to meet friends for dinner or after-work drinks. Fourth and Walnut at Christmas time was as colorful and exciting as New York. When the life went out of Fourth Street, a lot of Louisville's character drained away.

But none of this was foremost in my mid as I rode the elevator up to where destiny waited. My confidence, though, took something of a bath when I walked into the executive lobby and was faced with an imperious female with piled black hair and a barrel torso sitting on spindly legs. I sensed at once the type of female bully who, as a secretary to the senior partner of the firm, takes her resentments out on the junior partners. She sailed toward me behind a balcony of breasts so massive that had she fallen forward, I estimated she would have bounced for an hour.

"I suppose you're Pearce," she said haughtily; not Mr. Pearce, not John Ed, just a condescending Pearce. I admitted as much, she nodded and motioned rather than have to speak to me, and I followed her down a dim hallway to where a door opened into a cranny fit for Bob Cratchitt. She waved me in and left.

I recoiled. Surely, I felt, there must be some mistake. The hovel's sole furniture was an ancient desk with matching chair clunked into the center of the ten-by-twelve room. It was, I was told later, the same desk used by the immortal Henry Watterson. Its top swung upward to reveal a typewriter that must also have been his. Perhaps, I told myself, this is only a strange sort of waiting room; at any moment Barry Bingham or someone of like stature would appear to show me to my carpeted corner office where I would peruse books from the shelves that line the paneled walls, contemplate the city from tall windows or compose editorials that would shake and shape the community.

It was not to be. Instead, after a few minutes, a stout thirtyish man who seemed to have come from instructing a private boys' school history class came down the hall, went into the room next to mine, and shortly came in, smiled and said, "Mr. Pearce, I presume?" in a Southern accent that lent my name the unfortunate but familiar pronunciation. Again I confessed, and he introduced himself as George Burt, whose name I recognized from the masthead. We spent a pleasant and instructive half hour as he proceeded to tell me, in good natured, round tones, the secrets of my new territory. Yes, the damp truth was that this really was an office. More furniture could be found if I demanded it, though he agreed nothing would make it less dreary. Yes, I was early, as the harridan out front had announced. Editorial writers rather set their own schedules as long as they arrived in time for the ten-thirty editorial conference that was usually held in Barry's office. After conference, we would gather in the office of Russell Briney, editorial section editor, and decide who would write what, after which we would go to the library for research materials, or go out to lunch. Deadline was at three. After that, Russell made up the page, we all read it for errors and typos and went home, usually around five. If we were going to be late or leave early we told Russell. The editorial staff of the *Louisville Times*, the *Courier*'s afternoon sister paper, met with us, Burt added, but wrote their own stuff, had their own routine.

Naturally, I wanted to know who decided who wrote what. "Oh," said Burt, "it's pretty routine. We have what you might call specialties if you want to impress someone, areas in which we have experience or have written, and we rather automatically take subjects in our field. Barry, if he has time, takes foreign policy; Russell or I will if Barry doesn't. Russell also likes to write about education and City Hall. Tarleton handles farm topics, I usually do defense. Mark seldom writes unless Barry is out of town; then he leads the conference and writes, especially on foreign topics. You met Grover Page, the cartoonist? You will. A word of warning: Grover insists on coming around and showing us the preliminary draft of his daily cartoon. He'll say, 'Here's a good one!' or 'Here's a funny one.' It is hard to distinguish. If it is one of his funnies, I advise you to laugh. If you don't, he will—strenuously— and in the process cough on you."

Grover was, as I discovered, a bit eccentric, but good humored and kind. He smoked a pipe, or carried one in his mouth, a corncob abomination. He had at one time been an engineer and knew about vitreous pipe, a talent seldom put to use. He also had an aversion to city squirrels, insisting they had intermarried with rats (you can tell by their tails, he said; almost no hair) and mongrelized the breed. Though he worked fast, he spent long hours at the office, kept a bottle of Old Tub Whiskey in his desk drawer, and often smelled strongly at day's end.

As we talked, a lank-haired youth came down the hall, bawling "Paper boy!" which he seemed to consider a bit of high humor, and threw on my desk the morning *Courier*, and the day's first edition of the *Louisville Times*. Burt took his and retired to his office, while I considered through dirty windows the rear of the Starks Building across the alley where trucks roared and men heaved bundles of papers into them from the loading platform. Ideal ruminative atmosphere. But an ironic note here: today, fifty years after that morning, I have an office in the Starks Building and park in the building garage, often in a spot looking across the same alley and at the same dirty windows of the same office. I trust that traveling fifty yards in fifty years is not depressingly symbolic. Actually, it has been better than that would imply.

A few minutes later a studious, dark-suited man with graying hair parted in the middle walked thoughtfully past, then came back and introduced himself. He was, as I had guessed, Russell Briney. He bore not the slightest resemblance to the stereotypical newsman, looking more like a senior editor in a proper publishing house, reading manuscripts and offering in a comforting voice lethal critiques to sweating writers. He welcomed me and said he would see me in conference. Sure enough, on the dot of ten-thirty, Burt poked his head in, said, "Shall we?" and I followed him down the hall and past the Mother of all Mammaries to Barry Bingham's office.

It was an impressive group that gathered in a semi-circle around the throne. Barry sat at a desk, bestowing on us a subdued smile. Mark Ethridge, stout, serious, was to his right. I had not met Ethridge, though I had heard him speak once at the University. He was impressive, widely knowledgeable, articulate, charming, even without his towering reputation. Members of the news staff adored him, partly because he had paid his dues in every phase of the newsroom, partly because of his published opinion that a good reporter, instead of being promoted to an editor's spot as reward, thus removed from reporting, should simply be paid at the editor level. Then came Briney, Burt, Tarleton Collier, a short burr-cut pipe smoker from Georgia, an authority on farm matters; Tom Wallace, gray, with strong, handsome features and a stern, almost lordly expression. Uncle Tom, as he was called behind his back (no indication of his racial views), was actually ahead of his time in his defense of the environment and years of battle with public utilities over their plan to dam the Cumberland River near Cumberland Falls for hydro power; then Jim Hutto, slender, tweedy, with a snorting laugh and a way of smoking in a quick, jerky manner. Then there was Lisle Baker, quiet, conservative secretary-treasurer of the company who had come to the *Courier* from Monticello (Ky.) by way of a Frankfort bank, and told in approving tones of the bank president in his home town who refused on principle to pay depositors interest on their money, feeling that it was enough that he protected their money free of charge. It must have been torture for him to sit and listen to the heresies of raffish liberals. I never saw Lisle in other than a conservative three-piece suit; rumor had it that he wore it in the shower.

Barry got down to the business at hand with a minimum of talk, consulting a pad on which he had written notes on the topics of importance in the news. "Well," he would say, "the Russians aren't making it any easier for us in Eastern Europe. You can see where State's uneasiness over Iran and Turkey stems from. This surely plays into the hands of isolationists in Congress." "It looks as though Chiang is running out of room. I suppose the China lobby in Congress and the Luce bunch will stick with him, but it seems more and more that Stilwell was right about his being a selfish crook." "I hope the president will stick to his guns on public housing. . ."

On each topic, members of the group would chime in with other views, ideas, agreement. Mark, I noticed, offered data but seldom opinion, speaking briefly and from experience. After Barry ran through his lists, he would ask Mark if he had anything to add, and then go around the circle, asking for additional topics. On this, my first day, the discussion was rather desultory and the meeting lasted less than forty minutes.

My initiation, however, was not over. As he put away his notes, Barry turned his smile my way and said, "Well, as you know, I have been hoping to find a young Kentuckian who knows the state and can bring more of a Kentucky flavor to the page, and now we have him. I think most of you have met Mr. Pearce. If not, please make him welcome. We are expecting great things of him."

Let it be said in my behalf that I did not faint, scream or break down in sobs. For one mad moment, I felt an impulse to say, in honesty, "Oh, no. I'm not a Kentuckian. I'm from Norton, Virginia. I came to the University because I got a job there, and I came back to Lexington because I had a job there when I left for the Navy. I took Tom Clark's Kentucky history because it was a requirement, but aside from joy spots around Lexington, I know nothing and care less about Kentucky. Until this moment, of course." But for once, I had enough sense to keep my mouth shut and smile properly around the room. I had read that Arabs forgave a lie to save your life, to flatter a woman, or to complete a deal. For the moment, I was an Arab, dealing. The others smiled in return except for Ethridge, whom I noticed looked at me in a quizzical manner. I had an idea he was not sold on his new expert.

Following conference, we gathered in Russell's office. There was a short period of muttering and light talk and everybody went to his cell. The young authority on Kentucky went to the library and checked out Clark's history and retired for an afternoon of hard reading, amazed at how much he had forgotten in four years of the Navy.

For two days I was given no assignment, but on the third Russell asked if I would like to treat the case of the superintendent of public instruction, who had been accused of some untidy doings, and I allowed I was dying to do just that. For two sweaty hours I addressed the matter of the errant super, wanting to appear fluent without risking the horror of mistake. Nervously I turned in my first effort, that there was much to be said on both sides, and that the superintendent should choose the wise course, with public good in mind. Hard to argue with that. I would have had a much calmer career had I stuck to such lofty reasoning.

There was less socializing among the editorial staffers than I had expected, and I took to dropping down to the newsroom and having lunch with some friends from UK days who had joined the *Courier* before the war, such as Jim Caldwell, a good friend who had edited the campus newspaper, the *Kernel*, and who would, I was confident, run the *Courier-Journal*, given his judgment and management ability. Jim had never been a flaming liberal; our mutual friend Harry Williams used to flay him for conservative editorials. And now he had not only joined the American Legion but married a Catholic. I could forgive the Catholic, a wonderful girl named Ryan, who was an Olympic-class swimmer, a good writer, a reporter on the *Times* and made a fine wife and mother. Lovely woman. But the Legion? Another UK grad who had gotten to the CJ before me was John Carrico, *Kernel* sportswriter of sly wit with whom I liked to play tennis because he was as bad as I, and who once helped me in a prolonged effort to dry out a mutual friend who had essayed, futilely I am sad to say, to drink himself into a state where Uncle Sam would not draft him. Vincent Crowdus and Joe Creason, a campus sportswriter with a perpetual smile and gift for simile who was, as I recall, voted Mr. Kentuckian, or most popular man on the campus, were also good friends.

When pressed for time or money, as we usually were, we would go across Liberty Street at lunchtime to Pryor's Restaurant, a minus-two-star establishment owned, not surprisingly, by a man named Pryor, who charged the printers an exorbitant percentage for cashing their paychecks, and then endangered their health with what was said to be food. The specialté de la maison was a virulent form of chili, a tongue scalding mixture that sported on its surface a half-inch of grease that defied removal. Each spoonful dipped off in vain effort to get to the mysteries beneath was immediately replaced as if by a hidden subterranean grease springs. Nevertheless, Pryor's was a favorite of people from the *Courier* and talent that fouled the airwaves at WHAS, the radio station owned by the Binghams that shared the building with the newspapers. These included a couple of ersatz cowboys who dressed in boots, played guitars and later entertained the kiddies with a show called *T-Bar-V*. There was also a raffish announcer who delighted in making love noises to Bertha, the stolid blonde waitress who stood on the windowside tables and swabbed at the windows, showing in the process a pair of meaty thighs generously endowed with blonde hair.

"Hey, Bertie" the silver-tongued devil would croon, "what do you say you put down that swab and let's so over to the Milner and fuck a while?"

"Oh, I can't do that," Bertha would respond.

"Why not?" persisted the lover.

"Cause I'm on till five," she would whine, her virtue preserved by the clock. Pryor's also served bad coffee. And it was there that I met B.M. "Buddy" Atkinson, whose friendship was one of the most valuable aspects of my years in Louisville. Possibly because we were both small-town Southerners, the products of proud and stubborn Southern parents, public school and state universities, and whose tendency toward loose living conflicted with a Protestant sense of obligation, we took to each other. We were about the same size, both had enjoyed a somewhat rowdy college career, married in the service and collected a daughter in the process, and both were goaded by ambition and determination to find the paths of prosperity. Each morning for years, Buddy would come to my office or I would go by his desk, and we would take time out for weak coffee and mad schemes on how to get rich, at which he proved better than I.

As I began to relax, the writing became a little easier. I was trying hard to make up in a few weeks what I had missed in four years and, of course, I couldn't. But I had an idea of the state's political make-up from my year at Somerset, and I was reading my eyes out trying to put some meat on the bones. In all, it was interesting work, and the weekly paycheck, tossed on my desk by the lobby lady, signaled that I was not on probation, as I had feared, but a permanent fixture. Only one small incident tended to cast a shadow.

I had become very fond of Barry Bullock, the elderly, precise gentleman of the old school who had been in the news department for almost forty years before being given what amounted to semi-retirement as editor of the Point of View letters from readers. It was a tedious, nasty, but important job. Mr. Bullock, as he was known to everyone, had to collect letters to the editor each morning, verify by phone or letter the signatures, making sure the person whose signature appeared on the letter actually wrote it, since it was a hoary trick of smart aleck readers to write a scurrilous letter and sign the name of a friend—or enemy. He would then type the usually handwritten scribble into English, enter it into the record that showed when letters were received, when verified, when published, and possible response or rebuttal. Mr. Bullock went about his crappy job with unfailing good humor, always courteous, always on time, always neat.

Then one morning, as I was talking with Burt in his office, Mr. Bullock came to the door. I hardly recognized him. His face was flushed and swollen. He trembled. Indeed, it seemed he might be having a serious seizure of some sort.

"The dirty bastards!" he quavered. He walked to Burt's desk and flung down a small sheet of green paper. "Forty years and this," he shouted. "Forty years! Not even a gold watch. Didn't have the decency to shake my hand, say good luck. Just 'your retirement will begin as of Monday!' The ungrateful bastards! Never notice that you're a human. Just a name in the accounting department. Like a janitor!"

Neither Burt nor I knew what to say. We stammered the usual terribly sorry, hope you enjoy not having to come in here everyday, etc. Mr. Bullock turned and walked out. I never saw him again. I heard he didn't stop even to pick up his final check.

I couldn't believe it. The *Courier-Journal*, that great paper so revered by idealistic newsmen, Barry Bingham of the elegant courtesy, Mark Ethridge with his support of higher pay and better condition—they wouldn't do a thing like that. I couldn't believe it. But fifty years later I remembered.

2

Inside and Outside Politics

1947 was a strange year, a time of dichotomy and contradiction. The American people, trying to find their balance and discover where they were after the turmoil of war, were at once optimistic and fearful, confident and uncertain, aggressive and cautious, encouraged by an economy that appeared surprisingly strong, afraid that it might collapse into the nightmare of depression again as millions of veterans scrambled for jobs.

But the mood and status of veterans were different from other times. Historically, Americans prefer to give veterans a parade, a bonus and a ticket home. They have little patience with veterans who seek some more material reward, as evidenced by General MacArthur's battering of World War I veterans who marched on Washington during the Depression asking payment of their bonuses. Those who had ducked service in World War II were loudest in their praise of those who served, and first to turn their backs on them. But now, thanks in large part to FDR, there was the GI Bill of Rights. With its help, millions of veterans were going back to college; others were buying homes, while others got "rocking chair money"—$20 a week for 52 weeks—while looking for jobs. For once, they didn't have to depend on public sympathy. This was a great stabilizing factor, and added immeasurably to public optimism.

My life improved, radically and abruptly, not because of the GI Bill, but because the mythical apartment for which I had been waiting materialized at the corner of Woodland and Bluegrass, off Southern Parkway, my wife and 16-month old daughter arrived from Ohio, and we began to settle down. The change made life more normal, and certainly more pleasant, but not necessarily easier. Though the bus stopped at the corner, it was a long haul from Woodland to Liberty. Instead of trudging around the track at the Y after work, I helped my wife with groceries, painted, made shelves and walked with Susie who was, just as I remembered, the smartest, cutest, etc., child in the world. A far, far better thing than the Y.

By happenstance, most of the other families in the ten-apartment complex were Jewish—Alan and Lucy Schneider, Ferd and Mimi Weiss, Bob and Marian Loeb, Sam and Isabel Hellman. There were also Lyman and Mary Everly, and a Miller couple whose name I have forgotten—all the men veterans, lawyers, businessmen, insurance salesmen. With the exception of Bill Snyder, the executive officer aboard ship, I had had little experience with Jews. In Norton, the Cohens were Jews, owned the quality clothing store and were considered good people, especially since they owned the only tennis court in town and let us play on it when they were not using it. My brother Joe had a Jewish friend, Jerry, about whose religion Joe told strange (and totally inaccurate) stories, including a report that Jerry's family was taking him to Knoxville to see if he was Jesus, undoubtedly the weirdest misconstruction of a Bar Mitzvah on record. We couldn't see that Jerry was different from any of the other urchins, and concluded that he had not been found to be Jesus.

***

To our delight, the people in the surrounding apartments proved to be good neighbors, bright, humorous, generous and well-educated. We threw loud, drunken, hilarious parties, played tennis in Iroquois Park, took our children to the playground and watched them play in the sandbox. You want normal America, you've got normal America.

Affairs at the office were not progressing so smoothly. While I was trying to catch up on four years of history by reading old papers and news clippings, events were chasing each other, changing the world situation at a dizzying rate. We were becoming accustomed to referring to Truman as the president, and were unhappy to see him taking a beating from a Congress composed of Republicans and reactionary Southerners of the Dick Russell, Harry Byrd stripe, the same set of cotton-boll conservatives who had set their faces against FDR and stymied the New Deal in the years before the war. Republicans are always resistant to change, largely because they are more comfortable than those who seek it, and they are able to appeal to the fear of change among the poor, who have seldom seen benefit from change.

Editorially, we felt very comfortable backing Truman as he tried to create a Fair Employment Practices Commission, raise minimum wages, bring about the beginning of universal health coverage and make sure that everyone had the right and opportunity to vote. Typically, the Republican Congress blocked him at every turn. Business was more and more in control of things, in Congress and in Louisville. I began to appreciate the difficult role of a liberal paper in a conservative town and state. Louisville had a strong, old-family ownership circle that controlled the banks, the Chamber of Commerce and most of the larger businesses that made up the power structure. I soon saw that the better class did not view us approvingly.

***

In foreign affairs, we faced a trickier course. With the end of the war, the paper, like most Americans, hoped that the wartime allies could continue their cooperation and give the world a real and lasting peace. But many Americans believed the Russians wanted peace only on their terms, and doubted that we could trust the Soviet Union to keep any treaty or agreement. They believed Stalin understood nothing but force (Truman said as much himself), and feared the Russians had dropped their hostility toward the western democracies only while the war lasted. There was reason for such suspicion. The Russians had suffered incredible losses at the hands of Germany, losses that made ours seem minor. They blamed some of the losses on the U.S. failure to launch a second front in Europe sooner and take some of the German pressure off the Red Army. Some Russians charged that we had held back in hope that Russia and Germany would beat each other to death and make easier our job on the Western Front (and a lot of Americans, of course, wished for just that). Further, the war experience convinced Stalin and the Kremlin that they could protect themselves against a repetition only by assuring that nations along their borders were friendly, meaning communist. Wartime allies do not always make peacetime friends.

In editorial conference we discussed continually the fact that Russia had reasons for its seemingly aggressive conduct. With the atomic bomb and our undamaged industrial plant we had no reason to fear Russia. And we believed that Washington, if we were to avoid the threat of war and the constant drain of arms spending, must try to find a way to compromise differences. It was a decent and humanitarian policy, and a handful of Washington newsmen and government officials visiting our conference convinced us that such a policy was defensible. But we realized early on that strong nationalist, anti-Russian currents were running in the country. Both Truman and Congress favored reducing the arms budget, and did cut back the size of the armed forces, but not as much as liberals and peace-firsters wanted. National nervousness grew with Russia's tough talk and brutal actions, and we had to keep in mind that it was possible that Stalin was willing to attack Western Europe with his huge standing army before the West could gather its forces. Though ours was one of the most widely-quoted editorial pages in the country, we had first to consider our immediate readers. We knew we had to mix realism with idealism if we were going to convince readers of our basic reliability. Much as some of us would have liked to take a pacifist stand, events counseled caution. Being considered a pariah was one thing; being thought disloyal was another.

Though I was intrigued with foreign affairs, and hoped that I would be permitted a corner of the policy field, it is probably just as well that I was not. I was incensed when Winston Churchill, at Westminster College, in Missouri, gave the tough speech in which he charged that an Iron Curtain was being slammed down across Europe by the Soviets. I was afraid we were preparing the public for re-armament or actual hostilities, had no desire to go to war again, and his words were almost tantamount to the declaration of Cold War. Whether his was a self-fulfilling prophecy is a pointless question.

***

And Barry made it plain that he wanted me to stick to my state knitting. One task handed me was the selection of bits taken from editorials from other state papers for inclusion in a Monday morning round-up. I would read through the exchanges, snip out interesting, outrageous, intelligent or plain nutty excerpts, write an introduction and a few joining sentences and run them in a fairly long column. It was more popular than you would imagine. The *Courier* circulated in every hamlet and hollow in the state, and people liked to see their local paper quoted in the big-city publication. So did the local editors, as I well remembered. But it was hardly mind-taxing work for a world-famous-to-be journalist.

The position of the *Courier-Journal* in the state, the high regard in which it was held, was intriguing. People might loathe the editorial policies of the paper, and consider it just short of un-American, but they depended on it, were accustomed to it, and were proud, if secretly, of the paper's national reputation. They might refer to it as "the goddam *Courier-Journal*," but they wanted it there on the doorstep every morning, and raised unshirted hell with the poor circulation manager when they didn't get it. Each night, around eleven o'clock, the paper-laden trucks began roaring out of the alley in back of the *Courier* building, regardless of storms, floods or icy mountain roads, heading for Pikeville and Paducah, Pineville and Fulton, taking the two-star edition to the reaches of the state. In my travels around Kentucky, I early on came to believe that two things—the University of Kentucky, and the *Courier-Journal*—were chiefly responsible for holding together the fragmented, dissimilar regions that made up what I called the Disunited State of Kentucky. It gave us on the paper a sense of obligation, and with it a great deal of pride.

Kentucky shared the postwar problems, uneasiness and enthusiasms of the country as a whole, of course. Furthermore, it was gearing up for a race for governor, and there was nothing that Kentuckians liked better. Before television, candidates were flesh and blood people who rode into town behind a bunting-draped sound truck, mounted the courthouse steps or a park bandstand and beat the air and common sense to a bloody pulp, kissing anyone who would hold still, shaking every available hand, calling listeners by name. Trusting his listeners not to read press reports too closely (a safe assumption) and without TV to carry his words beyond the city limits, the candidate frequently promised different things in different towns, knowing he could always duck behind the claim that he was misquoted.

At the time, Kentucky was more a three-faction than a two-party state. There was the Republican Party, usually a weak bunch accustomed and doomed to minority status, and then there were the Democratic factions, wings of the party that invariably fell out prior to elections, fought each other like raving maniacs but usually managed to eat enough of their bitter words to allow a joint effort in the general election. When the split proved too raw to heal, enough malcontents would bolt to the Republicans to allow them to win one of their rare victories. This Democratic love of internecine warfare was not peculiar to Kentucky and was of long tradition. Eighty years ago Mr. Dooley noted that "The dimmycratic party ain't on speaking terms with itself."

That is what had happened in 1943, when the Republicans won with Judge Simeon Willis, a silver-haired, handsome, dignified and apparently honest judge from Ashland. The Democrats had been struggling for cohesion ever since the popular A.B. "Happy" Chandler resigned and turned the office over to his Lieutenant Governor, Keen Johnson, who then appointed Happy to the Senate to succeed Matt Logan, who had died, conveniently for Chandler. Johnson proved an unspectacular but not unpopular governor, but the Democrats were hard put to settle on a successor. They finally lighted on Lyter Donaldson, a hard-working highway commissioner who had been obliged to say no too many times, and whose personality sent shock waves of apathy through the state. Willis won, conducted himself well in office, but could do relatively little under wartime restrictions. The Republicans, refusing to learn from history, then chose a bland, inarticulate man, Eldon Dummitt, whose only evident qualification was a desire for the office.

The Democrats, hungry for the trough, trotted out their usual two candidates, both able and attractive. Harry Lee Waterfield, a Clinton County newspaper publisher and former legislator, was a persuasive speaker and, as a champion of public power for farmers through the Rural Electric Cooperatives, and a supporter of most Roosevelt policies, was considered the more liberal. Facing him was Earle Clements, one of the most intriguing figures in Kentucky political history. From Morganfield, in Union County, Earle had been farmer, sheriff and Congressman, and was now back home ready for higher things. Big, heavy-set, strong—he once played football for the University of Kentucky—there was something almost menacing about Earle, and he was known to lose his temper and shake or hit people. He also liked to hug people, pull them close and slightly off-balance and speak to them in confidential tones. He possessed a wealth of Southern charm when he wanted to use it, and a keen political intelligence, but he was not a good speaker and didn't like to speak. It was said of him that he would rather huddle with someone backstage and win one vote than take the stage and win a hundred. As Harry Lee favored farm co-ops, Earle was reputedly close to private utilities and considered the more conservative of the two men. Partly for that reason, we went with Harry Lee. Barry suggested I see if I could be of help, and I wrote some for Harry Lee, my first taste of campaign flackery. He lost.

This had one strange result. Barry, probably divining that I was not as expert as he had imagined, dispatched me to Frankfort for Clements' first legislative session, to observe, become familiar with the state's political leaders and, when advisable, write reports or editorials. It was a generous postgraduate course, and a pleasant one. But it had its hazards. As a political science student at UK, and as a weekly editor in Somerset, I had acquired a smattering of knowledge about Frankfort, but now I was not in the stands but on the field. Being from the *Courier-Journal* opened doors, but it also hardened a lot of faces. To be regarded so seriously was heady stuff. Being new, I tended, as newsmen do, to see the paper's power, which was considerable, as my own, which was nonexistent.

State editor George Michler sent a large staff to Frankfort, but he demanded that they cover in some detail every bill, rumor or sentiment that surfaced. We had the best Capital bureau possible in Alan Trout and Hugh Morris, and I imagine they could have done a satisfactory job by themselves, but Michler wanted no stone left unreported. Trout, a slender native of Eastern Tennessee, was a fascinating character, a drawling pipe-smoker who affected a rustic pose but was in truth a widely-read college graduate with a love for and skill with the language. Trout charmed the state with a column called "Greetings from Old Kentucky", in which he discussed such momentous questions as why the whangdoodle mourneth its firstborn, or why an old hound runs with his hind quarters slued slantwise, why sticky flies portend rain or why potatoes have to be planted in the dark of the moon. He gave away gourd seeds and buckeyes that reputedly brought good fortune and cured the pains of rheumatism, and in a state that was slowly urbanizing but harbored nostalgia for its rural yesterdays, he was a familiar, comforting symbol. When I was an editor in Somerset, Trout came to town to cover a speech by John Y. Brown, Sr., who was running, futility, against John Sherman Cooper for the U.S. Senate. Trout was a bigger attraction than the candidate. I was awestruck. Hugh Morris, younger, handsome and athletic, had been a carrier officer during the war, had a head for figures, and was a meticulous reporter who could grasp the hidden realities of a budget. He and Trout were expert at good-cop-bad-cop. Morris would bore in, scare hell out of a legislator, and leave him vulnerable to Trout and his deceptively folksy manner.

***

I tried to keep out of the way of the reporters clustered in the crowded *Courier-Journal* bureau, then in a large front room on the third floor of the capitol, and still overhear what was going on. Some of the reporters, unaccustomed to having an editorial writer snooping around, gave me a cool reception, forcing me to pick up information when and where I could. Many years ago, in his duties as publisher, Judge Robert Bingham had employed a former Confederate general and astute political observer named Percy Haley, who was Bingham's liaison with and adviser on matters in Frankfort. There was a rumor abroad that I was training to be Barry's Percy Halen. One evening over drinks Fritz Lord leaned toward me and said, "Pearce, tell me the truth. Did Bingham send you here to spy on me?" The idea was totally wild, but it illustrated the strange way some people viewed me. Still, it was exciting duty.

An important piece of legislation, one that we had been watching for, surfaced early in the session. Known as the REA Bill, it would have removed rural-electric cooperatives from regulation by the Public Service Commission. Farmers, especially those from Western Kentucky, wanted it very much. The KU, Kentucky Utilities, was moving quietly but powerfully to block it. We were encouraged by rumors that Governor Clements, a known friend of KU, had engineered a compromise. So we, like everyone else, were amazed when, during a lunch recess, Earle wandered into the House chamber, saw the REA Bill written on the orders of the day on the blackboard that then stood at the front of the House, stalked to the board and, with a swipe of his big hand, erased it, turned and stalked out, red-faced and furious. It was a totally illegal act, but at the time no one was eager to challenge him.

I had become friendly with Senator Richard Moloney, the stocky, sly-smiling, cigar-chewing Irishman from Lexington, one of the few men I trusted implicitly; when he couldn't tell me the truth, he wouldn't tell me anything, which was clue enough. I went to him and asked him why Earle had done it.

"He had his reasons, John Ed," Dick said. But what were they?

"I can't tell you," he said. "You'd better ask him."

So I did. That afternoon I caught up with the governor as he was walking down the hallway by the Senate, fell into step with him. He seemed in a good mood, put his massive arm around my shoulders and called me partner. The time seemed propitious so I told him that I had asked Moloney why he had erased the REA Bill from the board, and Moloney had suggested I ask him personally. The change in the man was remarkable. Instantly, his big body tensed, his face flushed, the veins stood out on his neck and with a sudden motion he grabbed me by the lapels and slammed me against the unwelcoming marble wall of the corridor.

"You sonofabitch!" he snarled, and with every syllable he slammed me again against the hard wall. "You've been trying to gut me ever since last November! Well, let me tell you..."

Fortunately for me, and the condition of my skull, Joe Ferguson, then attorney general, was standing nearby, talking to a state trooper who was escorting the governor. "Governor!" shouted Joe, "Governor!" The poor trooper stood, staring, not wanting to lay hands on the governor, but not wanting to be witness to a murder by the governor, either. Fortunately for all of us, Ferguson's plea proved sufficient, Earle released me, whirled and stormed off toward his office. My head was ringing prettily, but I found to my relief that I was otherwise sound. Word of the incident spread, and I gained a measure of fame for being the first man Earle Clements ever shook, though not the last. It was a distinction I would willingly have passed up. I looked up Moloney and told him that in the future he could keep his advice to himself. He laughed.

***

Funny thing. Years later, when Earle was running for re-election to the Senate, I was trailing him as he and Clarence Maloney worked Main Street in Madisonville. I was keeping a respectful distance when Earle called me over and introduced me to some network people who were following him, identifying me and then adding: "I'm afraid I did my friend here an injustice some years ago, but to his credit he never held it against me. Always been fair." For Earle, a proud and sensitive man, it was a considerable apology, and I appreciated it.

I always liked Earle, liked to listen to him as he campaigned.

He had enormous energy, would get up at daybreak and get on the telephone, getting people out of bed, asking their help, their advice. At first I considered this poor policy. Wrong again. The people he roused from slumber were actually flattered that a man of Earle's importance wanted to talk with them, get their advice on how to campaign that day. He would then head out, sometimes driving himself, sometimes driven by Emerson "Doc" Beauchamp or Dix Winston. Earle drove like a demon, tearing down the narrow two-lane county roads at 80 miles and hour or better, talking all the time. He had the strange habit of pulling on his right nipple, driving with his left hand. It scared Beauchamp to death. "Goddammit, Earle," he finally rasped out one day, "I'll pull your titty if you'll drive the goddam car." Earle glared at him.

Earle seldom stopped for a full meal unless he was dragooned into a luncheon or barbecue, but would work right through the day and evening, speaking, shaking hands, moving through fair crowds or church picnics. Then about ten o'clock he would stop at a Dairy Dip or the like, get quart of ice cream, go to his hotel, get into a hot tub and eat it, giving orders or reminders to aides who sat taking notes. I was sorry when we later fell out. It was a mistake of the paper.

I also made friends during the legislative session with Tyler Munford, the short, wiry, nattily-dressed editor of the Morganfield *Messenger*. Tyler had been in the legislature and was at the time lobbying for someone, maybe the KU, and we would sit up in the Capital Hotel and argue half the night. He was a great Clements man and a poker-playing friend of Moloney. I once tried to play with them, and Moloney told me that anytime I wanted to sit in he would send a cab to Louisville to bring me to Lexington.

3

Gentlemen of the Legislature

Before development of the Frankfort motels and the Capital Plaza, the Capital Hotel was the center of after-hours activity in the Capital, and during the legislative session something of a zoo. The place had a colorful past. Old-timers could point out where Colonel David Colson and a wayward character named Ethelred Scott settled an old Army dispute by shooting it out in the hotel lobby. It was what you might call an unusual situation. Colson, a sitting Congressman from Middlesboro, had been given an appointment as colonel of a regiment raised to fight in the Spanish American war; Scott asked for and received Colson's help in getting appointment to lieutenant, but then seemed to go haywire, turning against Colson and causing him all kinds of trouble, refusing to obey orders, spending most of his time off-post in bars.

Colson finally had to put him up for court-martial and Scott was convicted. But he went to Washington, obtained a pardon and returned to post. As might be expected, relations between him and Colson were strained, and as they were about to be sent to another station, Scott shot Colson, wounding him slightly. Colson refused to prosecute and returned to Kentucky. On January 16, 1900, Colson was in the Capital Hotel lobby, talking with the famed Eastern Kentucky entrepreneur, John C.C. Mayo, when Scott walked in with a local farmer named Julian. Scott drew his pistol and, using Julian as a shield, started shooting at Colson. Colson returned fire, but hit and killed Julian. Scott, deprived of his shield, ran, Colson shot him in the head and killed him. Colson was shot in the elbow, but lived for four more years.

Another untidy episode occurred when William Goebel, governor-elect, was shot, also in the early days of 1900, and carried into the hotel. A mob of people tried to jam their way through the front door, and in the crush, an unfortunate black man was pinned against the wall. He was also pinned against a white man who took affront at this inter-racial familiarity, and snarled, "Get away from me, you damn nigger." The black man tried to explain that he could not move, but the white man, unsatisfied with this evasion, simply pulled a pistol and shot him dead. It took him some time to hit the floor. No one paid any attention.

In my postwar salad days, no one made great issue of such nebulous questions as ethics. Lobbyists, legislators, and newspapermen were free to mingle as tastes dictated. In a corner room on the second floor of the Capital, the liquor lobby had its hospitality suite, commonly known as the Snake Pit. Free to all, a healing stream, it was run by Big Ed Prichard, so-called to distinguish him from his distinguished son Ed, Jr., or Sonny, as he was called, and a man named Tucker. The Pit was open 24 hours a day, for all practical purposes, and some of the more hedonistic lawmakers took advantage of it. Sometimes a weary salon would become too full of hospitality to make it to his room and simply fall on a handy sofa, to remain until one of his fellow legislators needed his vote and arrived to revive and rush him off to the Capitol.

A few enterprising ladies usually could also be found around the lobby or bar of the hotel, some of them there on honest lobbying chores. For a while in the late forties, members of the Assembly felt the need to protect their constituents from dangerous barbers and operators of beauty parlors and would introduce bills to regulate these sensitive industries. One year they would introduce a measure to outlaw beauty-parlor permanents. Naturally, this would draw horrified beauticians to Frankfort in good numbers to protest this invasion of their emporiums of loveliness. The ladies would lobby, the bill would never get out of committee, and everyone would enjoy the exercise in direct democracy. The next year some wag would introduce a bill to outlaw home permanents, and the ladies would rush to encourage passage of this progressive move to protect women from dubious lotions. Again, the girls would lobby, the bill would die before seeing the light of day, and everyone would register satisfaction.

The most famous of these episodes occurred before my time, so I can only pass on what was told me on good authority and, as far as

I know, never denied. It seems that Frederick "Fritz" Lord, towering, craggy-featured political reporter for the *Louisville Times*, and a photographer named Absher or something of the sort, were loafing in the Capital lobby one evening when they were approached by two of the female lobbyists.

"Are you two gentlemen with the legislature?" asked one.

"Oh, yes," said Fritz, who was not behind the door when they passed out quick wits. "I am Senator Lord, and this is Representative Absher. What can we do for you charming ladies?" Things were off to a fine start, and after a drink or two in the bar, both couples retired upstairs to discuss issues one-on-one, so to speak. But only a few minutes had elapsed when the door to Fritz' room flew open and his lady burst out, clad only in her underwear. Down the hall she ran, beat on Absher's door and shouted, "Mary! Mary! If you ain't done it, don't do it! That sonofabitch is with the *Courier-Journal*!" Fritz only chuckled when the *Courier* lads complained that they got none of the game and all of the blame.

***

But perhaps the most colorful character of those days was the Senator from Harlan County, Nick Johnson. I did not believe some of the stories I heard about Nick until I got to know him. Then I became satisfied that Nick really did not give a damn what he did or what people said. A dark-haired, flat-eyed man of medium height and stocky build, Nick sported a deep scar across his forehead and a stitched line of scar across his belly, wounds, he said, from World War II machine-gun bullets.

"Hell," he said. "I don't give a damn what happens. I'm living on borrowed time, anyhow." Some said that Nick got the battle scars from an angry husband, but I tended to believe Nick's version because, had the husband legend been correct, Nick would have been the first to admit, indeed claim, it.

Nick apparently dispensed a good measure of charity from his insurance office on Harlan's courthouse square. Richard Harwood, later of the *Washington Post*, and I were once in Harlan on some unlikely errand when we discovered to our horror that the place was dry. Following instinct, we dropped by Nick's office, to find him berating a seedy, part-time primitive preacher. Nick was not happy with this member of the Lord's anointed.

"Dammit, preacher," he bellowed, "you're lazier than a nutted dog. I gave you ten dollars last week, here you are again. What about that job up Kenvir I got you?"

The man pulled a pathetic face, swore that he had been working every chance he got, but needed money to help some of his flock. Nick was not impressed.

"Your flock? Both of them? Here, here's five dollars. That's it. Now get out of here."

The servant of the Lord took his benison and bowed out.

"Pretty good old boy," said Nick, smiling. "Can't let him get used to putting the bite on me, though."

Harwood asked Nick whether, in the absence of legal drinks, Harlan offered the services of a bootlegger.

"Do we have bootleggers?" asked Nick. "Does a hog have a asshole? What do you fellows want?" He picked up the phone and dialed an obviously familiar number. "Lester," he said, not bothering to identify himself. "Bring me a white and a red, okay?" Two minutes later, a taxi stopped out front, and Lester came in, not attempting to hide the fifth of bourbon and fifth of vodka he was carrying. We had a drink.

Nick got into a fight one night with a black janitor-elevator operator in the third-floor hallway of the Capital Hotel. The black man, about twice Nick's size, tried to avoid combat but finally took offense at some of Nick's language and advanced on him in a threatening manner. Nick didn't budge, and gave as good as he got. Finally he grabbed a fire hose hanging on the wall, beat the black man with the nozzle until he fled and then turned the hose on the hallway, wetting down some indignant roomers. This was too much for even the tolerant management, and Nick was banned. Unperturbed, he rented a large, comfortable house on the Kentucky River, invited some girls from home, and set up quarters.

"Hey, Nick," said one of his friends, "wasn't that your wife I saw you with last night?"

"Yeah," said Nick resignedly. "First time this session I didn't get laid."

Sad to report, I am told that Nick later moved to Florida and became conservative and conventional, an upstanding citizen.

***

We had some stout drinkers in the Assembly, most of them, it seemed, from Louisville or the mountains. At the pre-legislative session at Kentucky Dam Village, one senator from the hills never quite made it back to his cottage under his own power, and tourists and other law-makers would stand by astonished as two state troopers, one at either end, bore him to his cottage and deposited him like unclaimed luggage on the porch. Another, named John something or other, wore sunglasses during House sessions. His friends said it was to keep people from seeing that he was bleeding to death through his eyes. The same friends, incredulous at hearing one day that John had quit drinking, looked on in astonishment as John walked into the House and put down beside his desk a quart milk carton from which he occasionally took a healthful pull. Sadly, they found that the carton contained half and half—half milk, half vodka.

***

But the major issue that year was the Presidential race. Truman had progressed from a tentative, self-effacing man struggling under the lingering shadow of Franklin Roosevelt to become a feisty, stubborn, no nonsense leader, champion of most liberal causes, doing what he thought his predecessor would have done. But he was scorned by the ultra-liberals following Henry Wallace, who wanted a softer line with the Soviets, less spending on defense and more attention to social problems. And his efforts at social legislation were often stymied by a Republican Congress whose members were feeling their oats after years of minority under the New Deal. They despised Truman as a political accident, and were twitching in anticipation of getting him out of the White House and getting their man in. Their man was former New York Governor Thomas Dewey, a proper but bloodless conservative who had made a reputation prosecuting gangsters. All polls indicated that Dewey would win in a landslide; he was already announcing some of his cabinet selections.

Those who clung to belief in the New Deal as vision of the future as well as shaper of the past, had little hope. Our editorials correctly pointed to the country's unexpectedly strong recovery and warned against the Republican calls for tax and spending cuts and curbs on labor, whose improved wages were fueling the economic resurgence (plus ça change, le plus c'est la même chose). The polls dripped gloom for us, and in Republican words of confidence and joyful anticipation, on the street and at parties as well as from Washington, the mood of GOP victory and our downfall was unmistakable. Democrats were ridiculed, Truman written off as a former and future nobody.

We worked, raising money, writing letters, bringing in speakers, trying to find wisps of encouragement from Truman's gutsy "Give 'em hell, Harry!" whistle-stop campaign. But as the election neared, no pollster gave Truman a chance, and one even stopped polling, so positive was he that it was all over but the formal announcement of Dewey's victory. Dewey himself, seeming surprised and slightly disapproving of Truman's immoderate conduct, was said to have his suit pressed for the inauguration.

We all voted, then sat up that night, hoping against hope as commentators complimented Truman on a courageous effort, but steadily predicted a Dewey sweep. We went to bed forlorn, then woke the next morning to a chilly rain and the incredible news that Truman had won. I remember Ferd Weiss running down the sidewalk between our apartments, his face upturned to the rain, shouting "We won, John! We won!" A heady day. At editorial conference we looked at each other, grinning stupidly, trying to determine what had happened, and pondered editorial comment that would express more than amazement and gloating. But we felt a great relief. We had a strong Democratic governor, and now a strong Democratic president who could look forward to working with a less obstructionist Congress than the "do-nothing" Congress against which he had campaigned so vigorously.

***

And big things were happening within the company. In the summer of 1948 we moved from the crowded mausoleum at the corner of Third and Liberty to the new building at Sixth and Broadway. It was a massive disappointment. The new building was not pretty. It was not stately or dignified. With its curiously rounded front it seemed —and still seems, I think—awkward, ill thought-out. A visiting architectural critic dubbed it "neo Greyhound bus station."

The interior was no better. Inside the Broadway doors lurked a dim and cavernous lobby, dominated by a lighted globe of the world. (Its support appeared flimsy and many would not walk under it.) The wall to the right held a massive mural featuring what we assumed to be a panorama of Kentucky—a man resembling Henry Clay, people working tobacco, steamboats on the river, and some strangely clad, blonde girls bearing a curious likeness to the Bingham daughters, prominent teeth and all. We could hardly believe that people of such excellent taste as Barry and Mary Bingham could have devised or approved such a mishmash. But they had.

Our offices were no better. The third-floor executive lobby was impressive—dark paneling, soft overhead lighting, tasteful plants in brass holders and a stark, elegant reception desk. But once outside the lobby things went downhill in a hurry. Editorial writers' offices were cozy cubicles of opaque glass walls and linoleum floors under neon tube lighting, graciously furnished with gray metal desks. The offices lined both sides of a neon-lit hallway leading to the purchasing department, whose denizens were inclined to stare in at us as they passed on the way to the elevators in the lobby. On the other side of the lobby the executive offices were better. Much better. A soggy beginning. The editorial conference room was elegant, with a long, polished table, comfortable chairs, thick carpeting and fabric-lined walls, with a large oil painting of Judge Robert Worth Bingham, Barry's father, dominating the room from the far wall. At least we were to be allowed an hour of dignity each day before being scourged to our dungeons. My office was depressing. I never did like that office.

Two events benefited our department during 1948-49: Weldon James and Molly Clowes joined the editorial staff. Molly had come from England as a child when her father came to Louisville to install the Bertillon method of criminal investigation in the local police department. Before the war, she had been a reporter on the old *Herald-Post*, had married Willy Walch, a towering Frenchman with a dark scar across his forehead, a reminder of his service in World War I, when he became the first man to sink a German submarine from the air, and had moved with him to Chicago, where he was French consul, or consular agent. Now they were back, Willy took a job teaching at the University of Louisville, and Barry welcomed Molly to the paper. They bought one of the new-fangled Lustron metal homes at the end of Dover Road, off Lexington Road, where they entertained often, Molly being an enthusiastic cook, just as Willy was an enthusiastic eater. I did not take to Molly immediately. Of medium height and solidly built, with dark hair and blunt features, she had about her a no-nonsense air that was something of a put-off. Wrong again. She was one of the best, kindest, most thoughtful, as well as the most intelligent people I would ever meet.

And then there was Weldon James. A South Carolinian by way of the world, Weldon carried himself with the air of someone who was what he had been—a magazine writer, Marine officer and foreign correspondent. If Weldon could have had just a bit more money, or status, he could have been a magnificent stuffed shirt. He had been a United Press correspondent in China when the conflict with Japan became nasty, and was aboard the American gunboat USS Panay on the Yangtse River when Japanese planes, through either error or arrogance, attacked and sank it. Weldon escaped unscathed, waded ashore, made his way to a telegraph office and wired in one of the year's top stories. He stayed on to do his usual good job and was rewarded by being made a member of the first class of Nieman Fellows at Harvard, no small distinction. He then joined *Collier's* magazine, one of the country's top weeklies, only to have his career cut short by WWII. That did not faze Weldon. He managed to get a commission in the Marine Corps and landed not on Tarawa or Iwo Jima, but in London, as Marine attaché and public relations officer. Not only that, but he shared an office with a young Navy lieutenant commander, Barry Bingham, a top-notch chap from Kentucky. Weldon also met and married Lady Margaret somebody or other, whose late husband, a pilot in the Royal Air Force, had been lost in the Battle of Britain. As luck would have it, Weldon was traveling across the United States for *Collier's* in days after the war, when he happened to drop in on his old friend Barry, who insisted, or so Weldon said, that he become an editorial writer on the *Courier-Journal*. Margaret, an English beauty, was happy to settle in a pleasant, roomy old house out on Westport Road, have a husband at home for a change, and to be accepted by the Binghams.

Weldon soon made it clear that he was not to be regarded as were others. And in this I think he was justified. Barry welcomed us so excitedly that it hardly seemed he was talking about a job at all, but about a company of good fellows who dropped by, wrote an editorial or two and then went about the important things in life, such as writing for national magazines. This probably saved Barry money in the meager salaries that went with these jolly jobs, but it also created some misunderstanding among the staff members. Regardless of who was favored by the publisher, others had to busy themselves with getting out an editorial and op-ed page every day. While we were supposed to be cheerily dashing off bits of wisdom, someone had to edit the wisdom, select columns, edit and write heads for same, approve cartoons, order and approve illustrations and grapple with letters to the editor. Vance Armentrout, an aging former Frankfort reporter, handled the dull letters chore, but after he retired, it fell to whomever was on hand. I hated letters to the editor, published in a column titled Point of View. They were usually illiterate as well as ignorant, and putting them into publishable prose tore the nerves.

Weldon managed to dodge these mundane duties. He invariably showed up for conference three or four minutes late, took his seat and chuckled appreciatively at whatever was being said, sometimes laughing with ill-timing at a serious point. After conference he would retire to the company cafeteria, where he would hold forth for a group of female employees who found him charming—as he was—recalling days in the Orient, chuckling in faux self-deprecation and waving about his cigarette, held between first two fingers in a manner absolutely unique. Finally, he would drift down to the department, type out a brief, well-reasoned piece and toss it on the desk of whoever was in charge, about five minutes after deadline. He and Margaret threw nice parties.

Weldon was so pleasant that it was almost impossible to dislike him, but my increasingly good friend Buddy Atkinson dismissed him as a con man. Buddy was an extremely hard worker and resented those who worked less. He had started with the *Times* as a sports writer, then a feature writer, and had now graduated to the lofty state of columnist. And just, I gathered, in time. His exploits as a feature writer had become legendary. At one point a hustler had come to town with a wrestling bear and challenged all comers. Buddy ridiculed Old Bruin in print as a toothless hairball, and the hustler issued a well-advertised challenge to Buddy on behalf of the affronted bear. The challenge was, in true Kentucky style, at once accepted. On the appointed night, Buddy climbed into the ring, his 140-pound physique pale under the lights, confident that the bear had been properly coached. An error. At the bell, the bear lumbered across the ring, Buddy punched him, and the bear almost tore his head off. Terrified, Buddy fought to get free, screaming, "Get this hairy sonofabitch off me," and finally, as some-one wrote, did a Shakespeare, exiting, pursued by a bear. The large crowd booed lustily, loving it. Years later I received from Sallie Crimmins, of Avondale, Virginia, a letter telling how she nursed Buddy through some of his more arcane exploits. "I applied the mercurochrome when the bear clawed him, remember when he rode with Lucky Teeter through the wall of flames. It was a joke that he never could have married Anne had I not spent a week sewing on buttons and getting his shoes repaired so he would be presentable when he met the Cooks (Ann's parents)."

On another occasion, Buddy was supposed to interview a famed stripper named Zorima, who had promised to doff her FULL LENGTH MINK COAT—a rarity then—and plunge into the icy Ohio. Sadly, Buddy had looked upon the wine the night before, overslept and, when his Cherokee Road landlady awakened him, went into a Chinese fire-drill, screaming, trying to run and put on clothes at the same time, and finally getting into a taxi which deposited him on the Fourth Street wharf just as Miss Z was opening her coat to reveal her famed good-ies. Buddy misjudged the icy paving stones, his feet flew out from under him, and poor Zorima looked on in horror as this creature zoomed down upon her, clipping her shapely underpinnings neatly from under her and plunging them both into the icy Ohio. Zorima dragged herself and her FULL LENGTH MINK COAT dripping from the river, flail-ing and screaming at Buddy, while cameras flashed and Z's managers looked on helplessly. Buddy tried to explain that he was there to inter-view the star, but the star was there to beat Buddy over the head. He made a strategic retreat.

There was also the Sunday when churchgoers walking through Cherokee Park heard strange cries coming from somewhere above, and looking up saw this frightened creature clutching a limb of a huge beech tree, thirty feet above the ground. "Help me!" cried Buddy. Fire-men were called, ladders were extended as to a cat rescue, and the rescuer said to him, "I'll get you down on one condition—you tell me how the hell you ever got up here." The tree was at least fifteen feet around, the lowest limb fifteen feet above ground. To this day no one ever figured out how he got up in that tree.

But in the meantime he had married the very prim, proper New Englander Anne Cook, they bought a small house in St. Matthews, had four children and settled into the postwar pattern. Buddy took to the straight and narrow, straying only infrequently. He was a brilliant writer, with a fine sense of humor. He later landed in Hollywood, and would have been highly successful had he not spent his energy, physical and emotional, on battles with himself. He had, like so many creative people, a demon. Sober, he was the sweetest, kindest, gentlest and most generous man I ever knew. But once the bottle was opened, he became a raving maniac, that's all there was to it, Jekyll and Hyde (I always suspected that Jekyll's potion was nothing more than good, 90-proof booze).

Buddy began writing a humor column for the *Times* entitled Downdrafts, a thing of huge popularity. But it paid little better than bear-fighting, and Buddy began writing fiction. And selling fiction. He got an agent, Lurton Blassingame, who sold his short-short stories to *Collier's*. Hardly a month went by that Buddy did not have a one-page howler. His rates went up. He moved his family into a bigger house across from Cherokee Park. I writhed in envy.

And with reason. My home life was not as smooth as it could have been. Our friends were leaving apartments one by one for houses, homes, most of them out in the east end of town, the better addresses. We were caught in the bind of a salary that remained at $100 a week while inflation climbed upward. My wife was not happy with this, and I could not blame her. Instead of being envied because of my supposedly lofty job, we were being regarded with something approaching condescension.

4

Everybody Has a Family

Perhaps no word is more laden with emotion, more redolent of nostalgia and memories than home. I have not lived in Norton for almost sixty years, no member of my family lives there, no friends. The things and places that were the framework on which my boyhood was draped are gone—the schoolhouse, the corner store, the drug store, the park and swimming pool. Even our house is hardly recognizable, so old and battered. I was never very fond of it, anyhow. Yet when I think "home," I think Norton.

I was born in a house the Baptist church now stands, the first son and fourth child of a strange and rather pleasant family, four girls, three boys. My father, tall, slender, dark-haired and blue-eyed, was a Kentuckian (although I think he was born in Tennessee and would not admit it) the son of John Quincy and Gertrude Pickens Pearce. He graduated from Georgetown College and took a brief whirl as a circuit revival preacher—Baptist—and it was on one of these soul-snatching missions in Tazewell, Virginia, that he met short, stocky, blonde Susan Leslie, who became my mother. Mama was the daughter of Joseph Alexander and Ella Bland Leslie. They were also Baptists (Lord, it's a wonder I turned out as well as I did). Indeed, Grandpa came to Tazewell shortly after the Civil War as the first minister of a Baptist church, but gave up the cloth (do Baptists have cloths?) and bought the *Clinch Valley News* from a man named Kelly. It remained in the family until the 1960s when, the men of the family having all died, it was sold.

***

I loved to visit Grandma and Grandpa. The Leslies were proper, middle-class Southern Protestants of English and Scotch descent, tending to be short and stocky. Grandma Leslie, a Bland whose people had come down from Pennsylvania, I think, was a wiry little woman who reminded me of a steel bird, barely five feet tall and weighing about ninety pounds. I never heard her laugh, but she had a quick smile and a soft Southern voice that issued gentle commands that were never questioned. She called Grandpa Mr. Leslie. He was also short, but stocky, and seldom changed his placid expression. Each evening he would alight from the straw-seated streetcar, move solidly into the parlor, where he read the paper and smoked his pipe under the fringed floor lamp until time for dinner, or supper as it was called, protected from intrusion by Grandma, who decreed that "Your grandfather is not to be bothered." Grandpa also presided over the table. No one spoke until thanks had been returned and everyone was served (and there was precious little talk after that, though the atmosphere was by no means grim, and the food was delicious). Grandma was a good cook, aided by an aging drudge named Mrs. Burch. (Grandma would not allow black help in the house.) Grandpa insisted that we chew each bite 40 times; we didn't.

The three men of the family were respectable but unremarkable, with the exception of Uncle Joe, who became the editor of the Norfolk newspaper, a trustee of the University of Richmond, and married well, as his wife let it be known; her family was close to the Byrds. Uncle Bland took over the *Clinch Valley News* after Grandpa died, and Uncle Franklin succeeded him. Bland caused a stir, and sparked Grandma's disapproval, by marrying a divorced woman, a delightful school teacher known throughout her life as Miss Rhudy.

The Leslie girls did less well. Mama married Daddy, who played the guitar, mandolin, violin and piano, and of whom no great things were expected. Isabelle, Mama's sister, married a man from Wisconsin named Gard, and was considered lost to decent society. Eventually she was allowed to visit and bring her strange-talking Yankee husband with her, but he was always referred to as Mr. Gard. Aunt Nancy, short, plump and pretty, had Grandma's sweet smile, but not her flinty disposition. She taught music in a studio on the second floor of a downtown building, smoked cigarettes and had a plant growing out of a skull. When she did not have students she would play for me, such things as Debussy's Arabesque or Golligogg's Cakewalk. She had studied in Chicago, where she knew Percy Grainger. She later shocked the family by declaring that she hoped to live long enough to meet Franklin Roosevelt and Harry Belafonte, whom she described as the best-looking man ever born. Fortunately, Grandma was by this time dead; she did not consider "niggrahs" as men and would probably have turned Nancy's picture to the wall had she heard her. After Grandma died, Nancy also took over the job of henpecking poor Uncle Frank who lived all his days in the white frame house on Tazewell Avenue and ran the Linotype in the news office. Each evening when he returned home, he was expected to get out the car and take Aunt Nancy for a drive before dinner. But in his forties, he formed an attachment with a girl down in North Tazewell (goodness knows how), and one evening violated ritual by announcing that he wanted the car for himself that night. Aunt Nancy divined what he was about and put a stop to it, telling Frank that he was being ridiculous and that people were talking. He stopped seeing the woman. Aunt Nancy also raised a beautiful flower garden, with pansies, candy tuft, sweet william and bleeding heart. There were golden glow and hollyhocks around the kitchen windows. Aunt Nancy called me Dear Heart, which I secretly liked.

***

I don't know why I go on about this genealogy. I suppose we all poke back into our family roots in hopes of discovering some relative of prominence, or some sort of revelation. I once started a Roots study but became bored.

But I will continue anyway. On the paternal side of the family, Grandpa Pearce was described as a "merchant and owner of Norton's Mountain View Hotel," in his obituary, and had been at one time principal of Pineville, Ky., schools. (I wonder where that Quincy came from? His family may have come down from Boston, a bunch of—gasp, shudder—Yankees.) Grandma Pearce was a Southern lady, went to a female academy, and had a sweet voice. Her father went on the note of a friend who defaulted and gave Great-Granddaddy some slaves in payment. The family was Southern but hotly anti-slavery, and poor Great-Granddaddy was denounced so vehemently that he sold the slaves. That did not solve anything. In an early Catch 22, the outraged family turned on him for dealing in human flesh. Indeed, when his wife died, his sister went down to Charleston, got Grandma and took her to Pee Wee Valley, Ky., where she was reared by an uncle, James Chilton and his wife, in a house across the street from the home of Annie Fellows Johnson, who wrote the *Little Colonel* books. Grandma grew up tall and pretty and fell in love with a railroad man. He was not considered suitable by the family, and she was married off to John Quincy Pearce. They had four sons—John Edward (Daddy) who, I think, was named Jonathan Edwards, after the Yankee preacher, but shortened it; Richard, who lived outside Houston, Texas, worked for a railroad, had five wives (one at a time) and was, according to my mother, "a total rascal who could charm the birds from the trees." At age 60 he could chin himself with one hand. Then there was Clarence Chilton, Uncle Doc, who was an M.D. and reputedly the sweetest man who ever lived. He certainly was as far as I was concerned. I worshipped him. He practiced medicine in Pennington Gap, Va., where I often visited in the summer. He fell in love with a woman in Dryden, a nearby village, but she refused to marry him because he had not served in World War I, and he stayed single until he was dying. There was also Will, who played the violin, got sick and died. People called Will tend to do that. When Grandpa died, Grandma brought out a picture of the railroad man and put it on the dresser.

***

No one understood Daddy. After the love offerings fell off, he gave up the ministry, borrowed some money from Grandpa Leslie and went out to South Dakota to become a rancher. He actually bought a small spread near Rapid City, though my sister Rose said that he never really became involved with cows, but sold insurance in town to get money for a herd. Unfortunately, he tried to break a pair of horses to a buggy, they ran away, he jumped from the buggy and was almost killed. Mama got him to Chicago, where doctors patched him up, put a steel plate in his shattered leg and told him that his cowboy days were over. He and Mama returned to Norton, which was not the Wild West but a rough and bustling mining and railroad town in the mountains of Southwest Virginia. Daddy's father, I gather, was still running the hotel but died almost at once, before I was born, leaving Daddy little or nothing. He may have had an interest in the hotel. But he again borrowed some money from the Leslies and began a newspaper in Norton named the

Coalfield Progress, which became, to everyone's surprise, a huge success. How Daddy managed to put the bite on the Leslies remains a mystery, since Grandpa Leslie had not only the first but last dollar he ever made. But he did, and during the boom years of the twenties, though the crowded streets of Norton were murky with smoke from the clanging railroad yards and coke ovens belching flames and clouds of black smoke at either end of town, we breathed the heady air of affluence.

It could not last, of course. For some again unexplainable reason, Daddy sold the *Progress* for a ridiculously low price, crowded us all into the elegant Roamer acquired with *Progress* wealth, and moved us to Pineville, Kentucky. Thus my early memories of Norton are brief. I do recall trotting about the streets of downtown selling copies of the *Progress*, the sidewalks teeming with miners, railroaders, businessmen, drummers (salesmen), and foreigners (immigrants who came in to mine coal).

Then there was the day when Mama put me into clean clothes and walked with me the block down to the schoolhouse, where she delivered me to Miss Carpenter, a black-clad, stern-faced woman who had launched generations of urchins onto the seas of learning and expected them to follow her charted course and no nonsense. I do not remember much about that year, interrupted by our move to Pineville, except that we were divided into three sections—Bright Eyes, Busy Bees and Workers, a cruel hierarchy established on scant evidence and, I suspect, social standing. I wonder if the Busy Bees worked harder to escape their second-class citizenship, or if the poor Workers were hounded through their school lives by their label of inferiority. Having read from the age of three, and being the son of the local newspaper publisher, I assumed my rightful place as a Bright Eye, giving me the right to show off in front of the class.

I was lucky to come from a family of readers. In the evening, Daddy would read the paper, Mama would peruse the *Good Housekeeping* or *Ladies Home Journal,* and the girls would sprawl on the floor with homework. I yearned to be admitted into the magic circle and was given a volume recounting the adventures of Baby Ray, a tedious bastard who lived in a world of short words: Baby Ray had a cat; Baby Ray loved the cat; the cat loved Baby Ray, ad nauseam. Soon I was nagging my poor mother to explain words in papers and magazines, and became a reader. I often wondered whether the Workers, struggling to make sense of the printed words, hated us Bright Eyes. I also remember the day a girl named Minnie peed in her pants, unable to hold back the criminal tide and not knowing how to ask to be excused. I recall the look of anguish on her face and the shock of those around her as the stream of her disgrace trickled beneath her desk before Miss Carpenter rescued her and towed her away.

I always made good grades and was considered bright, mostly, I think, because I had a knack for memorizing; indeed, I couldn't help it. My mind absorbed words, lines, facts, especially useless facts. Throughout my school years I had managed to avoid embarrassing the family, but I had shown no signs of becoming wildly successful, as my father insisted I would be. I can recite for you the words to songs we sang in the first grade, but I have never seemed able to remember things that might have made me rich. And I did not help matters by going into newspaper work, where even moderate success usually pays poorly.

***

Years later, my choice of a profession was coming back to haunt me. I liked and was proud of my job at the *Courier-Journal*, but was disappointed to find how little my salary bought. Our friends were not only moving into houses but joining clubs, and some were sending their children to private kindergartens. My wife was disappointed and unhappy, and I sympathized with her; she was a pretty, healthy, gregarious, fun-loving woman, and being cooped in a small apartment with two children (we had had a second daughter, Marnie) was not her idea of the good life. Furthermore, I have an idea I was taking her too much for granted. I spent too much time with the children, too many nights trying to make money by writing. We did have great vacations, in Fort Lauderdale and later on Lido Beach off Sarasota, but two weeks do not a year neither make nor compensate for fifty weeks of boredom.

But suddenly it seemed that my efforts would pay off in true all-American style. Buddy Atkinson had been selling short stories. I determined to do as much and cooked up a plot based on Allan Trout, the great *Courier-Journal* reporter. I titled it "Look Homeward, Hayseed," a curtsey take-off on Thomas Wolfe, and Buddy persuaded his agent, Lurton Blassingame, to look at it. I was sitting at the kitchen table one Saturday morning, contemplating the down side of poverty, when Western Union called, and the woman read me a wire from Blassingame: "*SatEvePost* paid $750 for Hayseed. Now let's make some hay." I was stunned. My first short story in the country's top weekly magazine! I could see the glory road stretching out ahead of me. And for a while it did seem that my fiction might change my reality. I continued to sell to the *Post*, at rising rates, and even rewrote a few stories for television series—*Studio One, GE Theater, Summer Theater*. Rich and famous.

We got another break when Weldon James, living then on Crescent Avenue, took a leave to write a book, and we took his house. It was a marvelous improvement; we had a house with an upstairs, a yard to mess in, neighbors. The girls loved it. We could and did entertain, and were entertained in turn. And that year I got my semi-scholarship (it lasted only a few weeks as I recall) to the American Press Institute at Columbia University. A great time. Montgomery Curtis, director of the Institute, asked me to lecture on the Tennessee Valley Authority and the federal experience with regional authorities. I knew a little about the subject and pretended to know more, luxuriating in the realization that I was actually lecturing at Columbia. I also made friends with a *Milwaukee Journal* writer named Bailey, and together we enjoyed New York, spending hours downtown, during which we fulfilled an old ambition bred of years of *New Yorker* ads, of owning a Brooks Brothers suit. I also went to Lord and Taylor and bought dress-up dresses for the girls, an audacious act which turned out well. But—and this was possibly an unheard alarm bell in the night—I did not bring my wife any substantial gift.

***

It was at that importunate juncture that I received the letter from Katherine telling me that Joe and Daddy were in trouble in Albany, Georgia. Joe had moved to Belmont, North Carolina, with Mama when she left Norton. He had become a devout Episcopalian (can Episcopalians be devout?) and through the church made good friends in North Carolina. He had always shown an ability to play the piano, and continued, though Mama did not encourage him, as I think she should have ("One musician in the family is enough," she said). But after high school, Joe had no way to go to college, though his music might have gotten him a scholarship had he been counseled properly. He later got a Julliard scholarship and composed for the movies in Hollywood. He began drifting, eventually drifting to Atlanta, where he fell in with a literary crowd and became something of a protégé of Margaret Mitchell. She let him occupy a store-room of sorts behind her home, and he seemed to be doing well when Daddy showed up.

Daddy had been in Texas, where he and Uncle Richard failed, again, to get rich. But he had saved some money, had bought a new car, and now insisted that Joe come with him to Albany, where he was going to get rich, again, building concrete houses that could be poured into a plywood mold in one process. Joe didn't want to go, but he was basically afraid of Daddy, as we all were; it was something in his preacher voice and that blue-eyed stare. So he went. The scheme collapsed, of course, and then they were broke, Daddy owed money to the bank and, worse, he was sick. Old, broke and sick. I had no choice. I got the address from Kat, told her that I would see what could be done.

My wife had some things to say of a critical nature. Daddy had all but deserted the family, Mama had divorced him while I was at UK. Through college and afterward, I had never heard from him. And now, when we needed money so clearly, I was being asked to deprive my family to bail him out. I couldn't argue with that. Still, he was my father, and I was the eldest boy (was that a Southern thing?). And we had to do what we could. So I got into the car and drove to Albany, Georgia.

I dreaded the encounter. Family matters are always delicate, involved affairs, and the father-son relationship is perhaps the most difficult of all. At one time I had worshipped Daddy, then feared, then hated him for letting the family down and embarrassing us children in the eyes of our peers just when we needed the support of pride and position. But in the end, when I thought of him at all, it was with a weary pity and a desire to be free of depressing memories of the years of family decline. As my wife said, I had made my own way and was at a critical point in that effort. But he was still my father, still family. And I had to try to help Joe, whatever happened. He had endured so much and gotten so little from his part in family life.

Albany, Georgia, is a pretty town of graceful homes and many trees. Signs of prosperity were all around, except for the ragtag neighborhood where I drove around until I found the address Kat had given me, a shabby, rambling boarding house on a dusty street. A mean-eyed slattern came to the door and said, none too kindly, that yes, Joe and Daddy were there, and led me down a moldy hallway to a dim room, already hot in the morning summer sun. And there was Joe.

"Bud!" he said, and I recalled then that both Mama and Daddy had sometimes called me Bud or Buddy or, worse, Brother. We hugged, and it hurt, the touch so full of family memories, hope and good times, trouble and laughter. "What on earth?" he asked, and I explained Katherine's message, and asked how he was, and where and how Daddy was.

"Oh, I'm all right," he said, "but Daddy is in pretty bad shape. I don't think he's so much physically sick as he is just sort of, sort of collapsed, given up." I was afraid of that. Joe said that Daddy was about broke and owed the bank for a loan on which he had given the car as collateral.

We talked for a few minutes. It was good to see Joe. He had always been a pleasant, humorous boy, slender and blonder than the rest of us, with more talent than the rest of us. I hated to see him caught in a situation like this, wished that I could help.

We went into this sunny but untidy room, and there on the rumpled bed, asleep, his face unshaven and gray as his wispy hair, his mouth sagging half-open as if prepared to weep, lay Daddy. My father. And I put aside all thoughts of the past in order to deal with the moment, turning my mind to this remainder of the handsome preacher, the romantic musician, the would-be rancher, the editor, the buyer of fancy cars, the architect of impossible schemes, now a frail old man being dashed in the rapids of life's turbulent stream.

"Hi, Dad," I said, and he opened his eyes and looked at me, and for a moment I braced myself, thinking he was about to cry. But he didn't.

"Buddy!" he said, and reached an unsteady hand toward me, and I took it, wishing foolishly that things might have been different, that we could go back to the lovely house in Rutherfordton, North Carolina, where we had moved when we left Pinevile, and be a family, wishing that I was rich, and could wave my checkbook and make things right. "How in the world? How did you know?"

"I heard you were feeling low," I said, trying to keep my tone light. "Thought I'd better come down and see about you."

"Oh, Buddy," he said, sitting up, the protruding collar bones stark under flimsy underwear. "I hate for you to see me like this." He looked around as if wanting something to hold to. "I've had some bad knocks lately, Buddy. I guess you can tell that. But I'll be back. I just need a little time to get on my feet again. They haven't busted my hull yet."

We talked in words of pretense for a while, and then I told him I would be back in a few minutes, and Joe and I went out. At the door the harridan called to me and said that Daddy owed her fifteen dollars in rent. I paid her, gave her another five and told her to take him something to eat. At the sight of money she became Mother Mary, smiling a nasty simper.

Joe and I went to the bank where we found, to my surprise, a sympathetic and tolerant banker. I gave him a check for Daddy's outstanding loan and promised to take care of payments on the car, if necessary. Daddy was going to need that car. The banker told me not to worry about it, that he knew this must be an awkward time. We went back to the boarding house, I told Daddy what we had done, and gave him some money. Again, he seemed near tears.

"I'm ashamed," he said. "I haven't even asked about you. Do you have children?" I told him I had two girls, and he shook his head. "Think of that, two granddaughters I haven't even seen."

"Don't worry," I said. "You will," knowing he never would.

"Well," he straightened up, "I'll be back. I just need a little time. You'll see. Don't count me out."

He walked out with us, and I told him that I thought I had better take Joe with me, that I didn't want him to have to worry about him. He seemed resigned to it. We embraced. His mouth trembled.

"Oh, Buddy," he said, "I wish it could have been different."

"Don't worry," I said. "It will be."

We waved. He lifted his hand, brushed it across his face as he went back inside. I drove Joe to Charlotte, and then drove all night to get to Louisville. My wife was still hostile. She would have been more so had she known how much of our bank account I had spent. But to this day I feel I had no choice. Family ties are ties of love and comfort, but also of obligation. I think this is especially so among Southerners. And he was still my father.

As you might expect, Daddy's troubles did not end there. Less than a year later, I got a letter from him, asking for a small loan until he could get back on his feet. He was in Roanoke, Virginia, living God knows where or how. I had an idea that he needed more than a little loan, and a letter from my brother Don affirmed my doubts. Don was sending him money. So did I, ten dollars here, ten dollars there, five dollars when that I was all I had. It was hard to think of him alone and lonely, tired and sick, as he had been when last I saw him in Albany. But there came a day when I had no money left in the bank, and no way to get more on short notice. Don was in the same shape. Shortly Don wrote saying that Daddy had died, and that he was having the body shipped back to Norton for burial. I went to Norton, and we buried him in the family plot in the cemetery on the hill above our old house, where Don and I would later sit and listen to the country people wailing and hollering and carrying on as they faced the inevitable. I tried to get out of Don what expenses he had incurred, but he said that he would let me know when they were all in. He never did.

This was so much like Don, not only a good man and brother, but the one on whom the family could depend when I was off pursuing my own interests. He had always been stronger than I, younger but tougher. When we were little I tried to get him to go with us on the mountain, but he kept to his own friends. I felt protective toward him because he was two (or three) years younger. One time a tough little bastard from Wallsend beat up Don, pulled out some of his hair. I waited until I saw the kid riding on a wagon-load of coal, jumped on and beat the holy hell out of the kid, making sure I pulled out some of his hair, too. The mule-driver turned around and laid his whip on us, leaving a stripe across my back, a badge of honor. And there was a time when, as we were leaving school for lunch, Don fell down the front steps. I knew immediately that he was hurt; he was, he had broken his arm. I picked him up and ran with him until I realized that I didn't know where to go. Then Emory Province got his car and took us to the hospital. I was almost hysterical. Don tried his best to calm me.

When the war came, Don was in Milligan College, in Tennessee. Unlike his brother, the family's designated coward, he went down and tried to join the Marines. He was turned down because of a congenital hernia, borrowed some money and had it repaired, went back and was accepted. Wounded on Saipan and Okinawa, while his brother was trying to find a way to avoid danger, he ended the war in North China, came home to college, married Judy Skeen, from Wise, four miles from Norton, and became a professor of English. He also became as Golden Gloves boxer, whereas my career in the squared circle consisted of two interfraternity bouts, the second of which ended ignominiously. Don wound up at the University of South Carolina, where he abandoned the pursuit of English and joined the administration, ending as director of federal programs. He is simply a good man, a good brother, a good and loving husband and father to his two daughters.

I felt that I had let Daddy die and had not done much to help Don. I hadn't done much to improve relations with my wife, either. But a short time later I did do something, something I still find hard to believe, that pleased my wife very much. Since we could not afford a country club, I started one. I do not joke. Alan Schneider, my neighbor who was working for Mayor Charles Farnsley, and I often drove down River Road on our way to work, and noticed that, on the corner of Zorn Avenue and River Road, the old Jewish Country Club was going to pot. The Jews had built better digs out in the county and abandoned their old club, letting it go back to the city, from which they had leased it. So we decided to refurbish it and open it to nice, middle class couples such as ourselves who were on their way up but not yet there. Alan approached the Mayor, who encouraged us with a dirt-cheap, ten-year lease, eager to get the thing off the city's hands. We sent out word that we would enroll, for $100 each, three hundred couples willing to work and help salvage the place. We were overwhelmed with applicants and, a happy if ignorant mob, we tore into the tottering hulk and made a club of it, with golf course, swimming pool, tennis courts. Now the girls had a place to swim, play golf and tennis. We had terrific dances.

That was a mad summer, but not all for the good. There were too many parties, too many late nights, too many wretched mornings. I felt guilty because everyone else was having great fun while I was dying to get home and to bed. And I didn't think it was such a good idea for the girls to hang around the club so much. And things got out of hand. A left-wing liberal, I was elected president of a club composed of proper young hustlers, most of them Republicans, Chamber of Commerce types. I found that while I had enjoyed the job of organizing the club in the face of discouraging odds, I really didn't care much for country club life. And, ironically, it did not improve our marriage. On the contrary, my wife became somewhat involved with another club member, and eventually decided she wanted a divorce. I was furious at the time, my pride bruised, but later had to admit that I couldn't blame her. She was such a pretty, shapely, high-spirited thing. I was becoming a rather dull, confused man, not happy in marriage, frustrated when my dream job did not yield dreams. I realized early on that my wife and I had had no earthly reason for getting married, so different were we in backgrounds, tastes, temperament. Like so many wartime alliances, we had been ready for sex, not for the work and responsibilities that went with it. The incident forced me to take a closer look at myself. Because of my voracious sexual appetite, I suppose, I had thought of myself as something of a rake. I wasn't. I was basically a small-town Southern boy growing older, liberal in politics but personally conservative and relatively conscientious, wanting to do the right thing if it didn't cost too much.

The brightest spot in my life was my daughter Susie. We played golf; it got so that I did not feel at home in the pool without her clinging to my neck or demanding that I watch her as she dived and splashed about. Many nights, when I was working late, I would come home to find her, in her sleepers, sitting by the window in her little rocker, waiting for me. "Shhh!" she would warn, "Mama's asleep," and she would take my hand and we would tiptoe to the kitchen, where she would make toast and I would fix cocoa. Then we would sit at her little table and smile at each other. "Now," she would say, "tell me about your day," and I would fight down the rush of emotion, not realizing that I was transferring to and receiving from her the love I should have been giving to and getting from my wife. I have neglected much mention here of Marnie, significantly, I fear. She was a pretty child but moody where her sister was sunny, and I found it hard to get close to her. To this day I can't tell you why.

My wife and I patched things up, but it was a temporary patch. She borrowed some money from her father and we bought a comfortable little Cape Cod model out in Beechwood Village, off Shelbyville Road. Say what you will about look-alike subdivisions, but Beechwood Village was a wonderful place for a young family, full of kids, dogs, cats, cute moms who congregated, drank coffee, smoked and gossiped, and daddies who caught the bus or swapped rides to work each morning, burned backyard steaks and threw noisy parties. But, to make a dull story as short as possible, it was no use. My wife and I were divorced. She got a job in New York and left, and I faced the unexpected task of rearing two girls, eight and ten. I suspect that few divorces are entirely the fault of one party. At the time I felt wronged and bitter, but I can see now where I deserved a lot of the wreckage. It was at about that time that George Burt told me that I was the most self-centered person he had ever known; it hurt because I respected him and his opinion, but when I confided this to Buddy Atkinson, he said that "Burt's full of it. You're the most giving man in the world." I wonder where truth lay.

***

One more diversion I must inject here. Buddy and I were still determined to write our way into the big time, clawing away at our typewriters at night, trying to devise plots and characters in the cafeteria by day. Just before my troubles with my wife came to a boil, Buddy proposed that we beg a week or so off and go fishing down in Fort Myers, Florida, where he had been spending a lot of winter time. (He could write his column as easily from the beach as from Cherokee Road, or so he thought for a while.) At first our trip proved less than a smashing success. It rained. The fish did not bite, the mosquitoes did. The room a friend of his had arranged for us was a damp, dilapidated mess. I proposed that we leave and go to Sarasota, where I knew the shelling was good (I had become a total sea shell nut while on Lido Key). Buddy agreed, but suggested that before we started north we go out to Sanibel Island, supposed to have the best shelling in the world. We took the ferry from Punta Rassa, and—I swear—the moment we drove off the ferry landing and down the shell road leading between rows of pines, the sun came out, and we had ten of the most beautiful days in my memory. We found an inexpensive room and gourmet meals at the Beach House, run by Mrs. Christine Jenkins, a reedlike Christian Scientist with two attractive daughters and two aching feet that kept her hobbling about, trying to get her weight off one foot without putting it on the other, all the while smiling, pretending she felt no pain.

Buddy and I roamed the island all day and far into the night, wallowing in the gentle gulf surf, fishing by night from the clattering wooden bridge between Sanibel and neighboring Captiva, finding shells I had never seen before. Nearly all the roads were of sand, there were two phones on the island then, one belonging to the only doctor, a grocery store, no street lights, and miles of empty beach. I was bewitched. The thought of going home was almost unbearable. When I did get back and faced the looming *Courier* building, I felt sick. When my wife proposed divorce, I had a wild moment when I imagined that she would take the children and free me to chuck everything and get back to Sanibel.

***

Instead, I found myself trying to do my job, take care of the house and be a single parent to two girls. That was in 1953, and fathers who kept house for small children were as rare as virgins and witches. A weird experience, but educational. Ever since, I have felt sympathy for single mothers. It's a rough job. Long hours, heavy lifting and no sex.

I would stagger out of bed, rush through the bathroom, call the girls, clump downstairs and fix breakfast, while the girls got ready for school and put things on the table. That was the theory. In practice, I would invariably have to send Susie up to jar Marnie to life. Marnie did not face the day with a song. Socks had a strangely catatonic effect on her. She would pick up a sock, gaze at it as if wondering what it was doing there in her hand, what she was supposed to do with it, why God was doing this to her, why she couldn't turn back to the bed womb. But finally we would survive the ordeal of breakfast, I would wash the dishes while the girls collected their things, and see them off to the bus at the corner. I would throw dirty clothes into the washer, turn it on and drive to work, arriving an hour before everyone else, justifying, at least in my own mind, leaving early to greet the girls on their return from school. Each day we would clean one room, so that the house would get a cleaning a week, and give us Sunday off. Then I would have a couple of hours to take care of the yard before we started dinner.

In an effort to give the girls a normal home life, we gave a party, inviting all their friends. One by one, the girls trooped in, accompanied by their mothers. I would direct them to the merriment and stand talking to the mamas, who after a few minutes would ask where Mrs. Pearce was, expressions altering radically when I admitted that there was no Mrs. P. Gradually, though, they came to accept me as one of them and not a child molester, and would come in for coffee and cigarettes, doing my starved glands no good, a couple of them being prime sexual material. I kept a roiling groin but a straight face. On summer weekends I got into the habit of taking my troop on trips—to the Falls of the Ohio, Bernheim Forest, Mammoth Cave. I am amazed now that their mothers entrusted them to my inexpert care, but they did. The kids loved it, the mothers saw me as a free babysitter and, I must admit, I rather enjoyed it. I was getting so righteous that dogs wouldn't bite me. I became expert at making pies, and often took half a pie over to the Fikes, who lived next door. This did not impress Mason, Mrs. Fike. "You know," she told me at a party sometime later, "I thought you were queer, making those damn pies. Thought maybe that's why your wife left."

I couldn't have done it without my neighbors, Julia McClenahan and Louise Griffin, who watched for the girls when I was kept at the office. And I surely couldn't have managed without Susie, who was calm and competent in all things, good at household jobs, popular with neighborhood children and good in school. Marnie tried hard, but missed her mother greatly and, she told me later, was afraid of me. I still don't know why, though I was afraid of my father with, I suspect, little more cause. At Marnie's wedding, in the summer of 1996, Susie told me that she remembered the years we kept house as probably the happiest of her life.

***

One more note and we will draw the curtain, gentle reader, on the happy family. I had decided that I should take the girls to Sunday School. During my Navy years I had given up all pretense of religion, and was no more enamored of it now, regarding Christians as those who recommended the teaching of Christ to others, ignored its essentials, and found justification for hating those who did not accept it. After Sunday school, we would also go to church. To my surprise, the girls liked it. I rather liked it myself. I was trying my best, within the confines of radicalism, agnosticism and lust, to be a proper parent.

And I must confess that I still wish sometimes that conventional religion was a part of my life. I am certainly not opposed to religion, as such, though I find its literal teachings a little silly, the Papacy preposterous and the Catholic Church an institution of questionable value. People, or most of them, seem to need and want religion, seeking a way to God, I suppose, hoping he will take them to heaven, afraid he'll ship them off to hell. And it helps to keep the great common folk humble and clean on Sunday. If the untidy masses did not think they would get a reward in heaven, they might get uppity and demand a better break on this side of the grave. Capitalists have reason to recommend church.

And it seems to be a comfort to some folks. Lonely old ladies croon that Jesus walks and talks with them, and tells them they are his own, which is better, I guess, than nothing. My sister Rose was a devout Baptist, and as she approached death she was placid, almost happy in the thought that she was going home to God and Jesus, and would see Mama and all her loved ones.

I believe in God and the wonder and mystery of the creator, and would love to have known Jesus whom, I feel, is libeled by the Bible. But every time I bump into the Jesus myth, I recoil. I cannot for the life of me believe that God came by the earth, got a Jewish girl named Mirim pregnant, then sent an angel to talk Joseph into marrying her, and that Joseph and Mirim, though supposedly knowing how it all began, were still surprised when their son was not like other kids in the neighborhood, walked on water, died but came back to life after three days in the tomb, and rose in a burst of light to heaven, wherever that is. It must have occurred to most of us that the biblical heaven would be a tedious bore, and that the idea of hell is ridiculous. Every time I run into the Jesus myth, virgin birth, resurrection and all that, I fear that most of what we call Christianity was the invention of Paul, a narrow, intolerant man whose teachings have made it rough for women ever since. Isn't it strange that people of most religions vow that their creed is based on love and a desire for peace, even as they hack the heads off those who don't agree with them that theirs is the only way to heaven? Mahalia Jackson had a fine old spiritual that said there are so many ways that all of us pray, but to one God, so many paths winding their way to one God, so many children calling to him by so many different names, but one father, loving each the same. Poor wise, mild, humorous Jesus would be sick if he could see the gaudy churches, the mean-eyed armies calling themselves Christians, the massive financial network of religions based on the opposite of the humility and kindness that he preached.

I would love to believe that everything will be revealed on the other side of death, but I fall short. Oh, me of little faith. Still, I believe in God as the creator of all things; who else? I truly like the Bible and think it contains some of the most beautiful prose in the language. I now pray, although I am not sure why. Maybe it is just to have someone to talk with at the end of day. If, as David declared in Psalm 139 (one of my favorites) God knows "my down-sitting and my uprising... and knoweth my thoughts afar off.." then he knows what is on my mind, what my thoughts and hopes are, and there is no sense boring him with what he already knows. On the other hand, if he is not aware of me, he won't hear me if I do pray. And if God simply mixed the chemicals that created the big bang and sent the process on its way, it is pointless to ask him to alter the process to grant me mercy or help. I am thankful to God for my life in this world, hoping he will hear me and be tolerant. I think that unlikely, but there's no harm in trying.

Anyhow—one day I was finishing off the patio in the rear of the house when Dr. Olaf Anderson, minister of Harvey Browne Presbyterian Church, where the girls and I had been washing our souls, came around the corner of the house and sat down. I dreaded what was to come, but he did not charge me with transgression or offer to snatch my soul back from the flames of hell. He said, in effect, "I have been watching you and your girls. I know a bit about you, and I want you to take over our young married couples' class. We need you."

Friends and neighbors, if you want to humble and make a disciple of a man who has just been rejected by a wife, neglected by friends and overloaded with duties, don't say a word about tomorrow or forever. Just say those three little words—We need you. I became a Sunday school teacher. The girls seemed proud of it. People smiled at us. I was horny but holy. I don't think there was an unmarried woman among my flock.

But I still drew back from church religion. I notice that the Bible begins in paradise and ends in Armageddon, not a persuasive commercial. And I find its negativism depressing, all those 'thou shalt nots'. If God didn't want Adam and Eve to use their sexual organs (the tree of life), why did he give them the happy little things? Of course, it's metaphorical; God was creating an example for social conduct. "Okay, come on out; I know what you've been doing. If you're old enough to screw, you're old enough to leave home and make your own living. Out you go."

I wish the Bible didn't harp on dying. I'd rather not. I wish I could stay around for another century. Or do it all over again, especially if I could be a kid in Rutherfordton. Or even a boy in Norton, hard licks and all. I think I'd opt for a return if I could be fifty. Maybe I can get myself cloned.

5

The Blind Hog Finds an Acorn

Proving the old adage that a blind hog will find an acorn if he roots long enough, I made, in 1948, two sound decisions, indeed, two of the best decisions of my life (forgive me if I jump about from one decade to a previous one, but I had neglected this exciting era of my life): I joined the YMCA and the Navy Reserve. The Y decision was routine; I had been going down Broadway to Third Street each afternoon as soon as I got my editorial written, paying fifty cents to spend an hour or so trudging around the track and trying to develop a recognizable physique. It cost no more to become a regular member, with a locker and all, and when the Y built its new palace on Second Street and became the playground of young women in lycra and moms dunking their babies, I joined the Y's 555 Club, a place of bright colors and muscle building gadgetry.

When women move in, they tend to take over (remember what I tell you, son) and it was only a short while after women started leading exercise classes before shirtless attire was banned, and signs appeared saying, in effect, cut out the dirty talk. It was sad to watch the reaction of the old jocks to the new order and it caused a lot of dirty talk. The men howled when the women took over one end of the basketball court for aerobics and jumped around to loud music. They glowered as shapely young things loped past them on the track and hogged the machines in the Nautilus room, but when girls appeared in the weight room, defeat was in the air. Grudgingly, the dirty-sock and old jock strap crew cleaned up their act. In fact, most of them started appearing in sharp attire, reflecting the fact that many of the female invaders were young and shapely.

I loved the Y. I have always liked exercise. There is no better feeling, this side of love, than the happy weariness after a tough workout. I got into the exercise class run by Paul Schmitt, a handsome and likable young man with muscles who smiled and put us through sadistic calisthenics, ran us up and down a flight of stairs for cruel minutes and then ordered us onto the running track. I got pretty trim. In fact, and I say this with no breath of modesty, when Paul was to be absent, he sometimes asked me to lead the class. It was never as much fun after Paul left to start Milestone, his own fitness club, out in St. Matthews. Good man.

The Navy decision was probably no more important—I truly doubt that I would be alive today had it not been for the Y—but my re-entry into the Navy was far more involved. My feelings for the Navy were always confused. My outrage at being torn away from the blue-grass life I loved in Lexington was ridiculous, though somewhat understandable. It pulled me apart and warped me, and kept me for the first time in my life from doing as good a job as I could have done. There was something massively unfair in the government's saying, in effect, "All right, you sweated out high school, the hardship of Swift & Co., and four years of college. So now that you've managed to make it through, we propose to take you out and kill you, in defense of a capitalist state that has starved half our people to enrich a handful. Now, do you want to volunteer, or do we have to come and drag you out, like a sniveling coward?" Had I been a true volunteer, I think I would have done well in the Navy. As it was, I loathed most of it, lived to escape, and once out found that I missed it. Not the soul of consistency. Little wonder that I later fell in love with a woman who changed men as casually as she changed pantyhose.

So a few of us went over to Standiford Field, where we found the usual number of men shuffling paper and a commanding officer as arrogant and impersonal as if he were a regular. It was as uncomfortable and stupid as the real thing. I felt at home again. We signed up for the Reserve and were shortly told that we were a public relations company. We got credit for all years between the time we entered and 1949, so I had almost seven years of time to my credit already. (Before it was over I had served almost thirty-one and howled like a soul in hell when they retired me.) I refused to join Jim Caldwell in the American Legion, or to become a Rotarian, but I was trying with some sincerity to be a model daddy. Parenthood makes hypocrites of us all, even to the point of becoming patriots.

***

    And parenthood loomed large in those years between 1948 and 1955. Though we tend to look back now on the fifties as a placid decade of Ike and prosperity, Ozzie and Harriet, they contained some rough times for me, in the marital arena, and to a degree at the *Courier*, though these, the Bingham-Ethridge-Pope years, were the paper's glory years. Our coverage of Frankfort was thorough, crisp and fair, our coverage of the Bluegrass —indeed the entire state—was clear, full and objective. The editorial pages were perhaps too obviously liberal, but were also literate, interesting and often humorous.

    I have said, and will say, relatively little about the *Louisville Times* because I knew little about it. By design, there was little contact between us. Company policy also discouraged contact between the third floor (editorial) and the fourth (news). I don't think this made much sense; we needed constant association with reporters, who knew things we needed to know. I don't know whether management feared that we would corrupt newsmen into slanting the news in favor of editorial policy, or that we would be contaminated by association with fact. And we were almost forbidden to visit the second floor, the lair of money-grubbing ad salesmen, where the advertisers might try to buy our pens. I might say in this respect that in more than twenty years of editorial writing, no one ever tried to bribe me. Once a man from the Armory liked something I wrote and sent me a fifth of bourbon, pretty good bourbon, too, but I don't drink bourbon, and I asked Barry what to do with it. He said I should give it back. I padded down to the Armory, found the man's office and tried to explain to his secretary why I wanted to give back a fine bottle of whiskey. She kept looking at me nervously. And once, when I was writing for the *Magazine*, a state legislator from Western Kentucky commented that he liked a profile I had written on John Y. Brown, Jr. and said he would give me a country ham if I would write one like it on him. I thought to myself that I didn't mind so much being regarded as a whore, but not as a cheap one. I was surely worth more than a ham. I'm afraid Kentuckians are cheap when it comes to bribery. Lobbyists once bought a whole slab of legislators for about $400 apiece.

Objectivity in journalism is discussed in reverent tones, but it is a relative thing. No newspaperman is without his own beliefs, biases, possibly prejudices. The current managing editor of the *Washington Post* will not belong to a political party, will not voice a political opinion, will not even vote. In my opinion that is preposterous, and I would not hire a man so deluded. Everything from genes to parental influence, to what we read, the opinion of friends and loved ones, the experience of those near us all influence our opinions, our views of life. Whether they incite or suppress conflicts of interests is arguable. On the *Courier-Journal* we were told that we must avoid not only conflicts of interest but the appearance of conflicts of interest; in other words, we must avoid the way others view us, an impossibility. Individuals on a paper cannot escape having reputations associated with their paper. In my years on the *Courier*, we were all considered wild-eyed liberals by many readers, though the staff contained some total Neanderthals. I wonder how much suspicion of staff members reflects self-doubt on the part of management. The liar suspects that everyone is lying.

Mary Caldwell, Jim's wife, was on the *Times*. Mary was unusual in that she adored Al Aronson, *Times* managing editor and one of journalism's great tightwads. A round, sardonic man with a possum leer that newcomers mistook for a smile, he ran a bourbon operation on a beer budget, not because he had to but because he chose to. He seemed to regard a raise as an affront. For years he would allow a reporter mileage only if the story lay beyond the bus line, and refused to approve money for lunch, even though the story kept the reporter out during the noon hour, since "they gotta eat anyhow."

His penuriousness irritated Ethridge. Each year at budget time, Al would come in with money left over and declare smugly that he would need no increase for the coming year. He considered this frugal, Ethridge considered it cheap, and nagged Aronson to give his people raises. Al would consent to a few, as though each was blood squeezed from the top of his head, declaring "They don't need it." It must be said of Norman Isaacs, who succeeded Al, that when he took over he improved both personnel and pay.

***

Barry Bingham took an appointment in 1949 as director of the

Marshall Plan's ECA (Economic Cooperation Administration) in Paris and was gone for a year. The editorial staff had been big supporters of the Marshall Plan, which was undoubtedly a good idea (though I have read that it was not Marshal's idea at all, but Dean Acheson's. I believe that Acheson, accused by McCarthyites and other such trash as pro-commie, was actually a very pragmatic idealist, and the Plan reflected a cool and calculating political mind). Americans have ever since praised themselves extravagantly for their generosity toward their former foes and allies, but it occurred to me at the time that our generosity was leavened with self-interest. We gave them billions with which they bought American goods; they had no alternative, since we were the only major nation able to produce and sell the needed goods with which to rebuild their factories and homes. The Plan sparked our own economic resurgence as well as their recovery.

Mark took over the daily editorial conference, which became more stimulating than when Barry presided, more fun, more argumentative. Mark had also served on a State Department mission to Greece and Turkey and had first-hand knowledge of the men and events that were shaping the Mideast. Being around him was a learning experience.

Before Barry could get back, the paper was confronted with the Prichard case. That was painful. Ed "Sonny" Prichard, of Paris, (Ky.) was a young genius of whom Kentuckians, especially liberal-wing Democrats, expected and hoped great things. He had finished first in his high school class, first in his class at Princeton, and had been welcomed with great expectations when he entered Harvard Law. After graduating with honors, he became clerk to Justice Felix Frankfurter and soon wound up in the White House as advisor to Franklin D. Roosevelt. Naturally, when he came home, everyone was watching, expecting him to become governor, senator, perhaps even president.

Instead (to condense a long and tragic story), he was accused of stuffing some ballot boxes in the elections of 1948. Election cheating was certainly nothing new to the Bluegrass. The party that was in power voted dead people and absentees and stuffed marked ballots into ballot boxes before the voting began. The outs did likewise where possible, screamed fraud when the votes were counted, and finally accepted the verdict of the people. The case of Ed Prichard was unusual only in the prominence of the accused and might never have come to trial had it not been for Cassius Clay, of Paris, a railroad attorney who seemed determined to put Prichard behind bars. A courtly but hot-eyed zealot, Clay haunted the *Courier*, demanding that we do more to bring Prich to justice, and in a trial that tore friends, firms, and towns apart, Prich was found guilty and sentenced to two years in prison. Like a sparkler dropped into a water bucket, the Democrats' brightest flame went out.

This was especially painful for me. I had not known Prichard well but admired him, his intellect and his liberal principles highly. His wife, the former Lucy Elliott, was also a friend from college days, when we ran in the same crowd and often went on parties together. She was a bright, artistic woman, if eccentric, and good company. But the newspaper was not injured in the process. We had covered the investigation and trial fully and impartially and had called for justice, though hoping for mercy, in our editorials.

But then came the case of Alger Hiss, with far more serious implications. Congress was already throwing off toxic fumes from the House Committee on un-American Activities. Senator Karl Mundt bellowed daily that Communists and homosexuals (he found them interchangeable) controlled the White House, while Senator Patrick McCarran suspected anyone who did not grab a club and wait at the water's edge to beat back immigrants who sought entry in order to destroy their haven. And there was the young California Congressman Richard Nixon, already perfecting his skill at character assassination, questioning the patriotism of any and all opponents.

The Right had never quite forgiven Roosevelt for having gone to war on the side of the Russians, and now doubted the patriotism of anyone who proposed that we try to get along with them. Most of the Right would have been glad to scrap Freedom of Speech and toss into prison anyone who could spell communist. HCUA began calling up writers, actors, federal officials, artists, displaying them like circus animals for public contumely. For writers of a liberal editorial page, this was frustrating, especially since the conduct of Joseph Stalin was making it increasingly hard to ask the United States to exercise patience and understanding. And then the Hiss case broke. Alger Hiss, in case you have forgotten or were too young to remember, was a bright, handsome, well-connected young New Dealer and advisor to F.D.R. at the U.S.-Britain-Russia conference at Yalta, where Roosevelt and Churchill conceded hegemony over Eastern Europe to Russia (since it was already there with the world's biggest army and not about to get out until thrown out). The Yalta agreement did not sit well with conservatives, who thought FDR should have stood up to Russia even if he had to stand alone.

Then, in testimony before the House committee, Whittaker Chambers, a former Communist turned informer, swore that Hiss had also been, and was still, a Communist spy. Though Hiss immediately and consistently denied the charge, the case shook the liberal establishment. Chambers was a strange, furtive, shifty-eyed man, squat, fat and disheveled, and his testimony included incredible details of mysterious typewriters and papers hidden in a dumb waiter and in pumpkins on his farm. Still, there was a worrisome ring of truth in much of what he said, and we worried about the stand we should take. Eventually, his appearance and conduct drove most of us to dismiss Chambers as a kook, one of several admitted ex-Communists who were coming forward to confess and earn celebrity and money for squealing on their former comrades. Most of us on the editorial staff wanted to denounce him outright, but Mark, wisely, decreed caution, which left us wiggle room when Hiss was indicted and then convicted, not of spying, but of perjury in testimony before Congress. It was a disturbing episode. Whether or not Hiss was guilty, his conviction wounded liberal forces and opened the hell-gates of suspicion, through which charged the dogs of hate and revenge, howling for blood.

***

Such matters had little effect on the *Courier-Journal*, already suspected of Red leanings by conservatives but still at the peak of its popularity and influence among the general public, and regarded as one of the nation's top papers. One reason for the popularity was the Sunday *Magazine*, a colorful, well-written section general in scope but Kentuckian much in content and flavor. Begun by Ethridge, it was largely uncontroversial, a relief from the serious news of the rest of the paper. Cary Robertson, a grinning, vague, absent-minded professor type, seemed a strange one to be tying together the many and disparate facets of a magazine but did it with a deceptive skill. Cary wore brightly colored sweaters, gnawed furtively at random bits of food stored in his desk drawers, rode a bicycle to work from his home in Anchorage, a distance of some twenty-five miles, and played the violin in what he called his studio. This was the loft of a barn behind his house, to which, it was rumored, his wife Priscilla, a firm-willed lady and a writer of some note, had banished him and his violin. It was a rat's nest and a fire trap. Clothes were hung or piled everywhere, along with books, magazines, pictures, papers, bits of furniture, all surrounding a large pot-bellied stove from which fell hot ashes that threatened to set the place on fire at any moment.

Cary's vagueness occasionally became a problem. We once had a convention of Nieman Fellows in Louisville, and one afternoon Cary announced that we would all go to his home in Anchorage for drinks. We piled into a half-dozen cars and followed him as, to our puzzlement, he drove through the winding roads of Cherokee Park, which was not on the way, and suddenly stopped. After a few minutes, we walked up to his car, to find him, head back, sound asleep. "Said he was sleepy," said his bemused out-of-town passenger. At this, Cary awoke, smiled and led the way again. We arrived at his home, to which Cary could not find the key, knocked and were confronted by an irate Priscilla, who had not been warned of our plans, said as much and firmly closed the door. "Guess we ought to go back to town," said Cary, shrugging, which we did. We bought a lot of drinks and tried to explain to the visitors that this was not typical Kentucky hospitality.

But Cary managed a beautiful publication, full of Billy Davis's aerial photographs, Harold Davis's and Tommy Miller's color pictures of Kentucky seasons and scenery. Joe Creason and Paul Hughes were capable writers; so was Jim Morrisey, who had the good sense to marry an enterprising young woman named Kay who was establishing Weight Watchers in our region, enabling him to quit writing and lead a decent, wealthy life, evidence of the soundness of the publisher's credo that it does not pay to pay a newsman well; the minute he gets a taste of money he will probably quit.

And there was Cissy Gregg, already famous as food editor. Each week Harold Davis would shoot color pictures of Cissy's food layout, and each one would bring in hundreds of letters and requests for Cissy to speak to some club or other. No matter what people thought of the *Courier*, they loved Cissy Gregg. And Cissy was not what you might expect of a food editor, Betty Crocker or fat old Mammy with flour all over. Cissy weighed just enough to keep her on the ground. It is a wonder a strong wind did not pick Cissy up and deposit her in Virginia. She moved at a trot, had a perpetual smile for everyone, and wore pretty clothes hung on a skeletal frame. After hours, Cissy was a little too fond of drink. It probably hastened the end of a lovable human being.

***

But, then, many people on the paper seemed to drink. Buddy Atkinson seldom drank in those years, but when he did he went totally into the bag. For that reason, he felt fellow sympathy for a reporter named Tom something or other, a former Nieman Fellow, a good writer with an expansive personality who became depressed when he drank, and drank when he was depressed. Buddy would be whacking away at his typewriter when the phone would ring and Tom would be mooing in drunken self-pity. "I wanted you to be the last one, Buddy. Wanted say good-bye. Going to kill myself. Gonna jump."

"Oh, God no, Tom! Where are you? All right, hold on. Don't do anything till I get there." Down the stairs Buddy would rush, tear down Broadway, into the Brown Hotel and up to the room on the fifth floor where Tom was standing by the window, ready for take-off into eternity. Buddy would grab him, wrestle him back to reality, and plead the case for living; you're a good man, good reporter, everybody loves you, great future ahead. And eventually Tom, red-eyed and repentant, would consent to live.

A few weeks later Buddy would again be working away when the call would come from Tom, again threatening to give himself up to thin air and hard sidewalk. Again Buddy would make his salvation dash, again pull Tom back from the high board, again paint for him a future rosy beyond the bounds of credibility. I was standing by his desk one day when Buddy took a call too far. "Are you really going to jump, Tom? You are? Well, I'll tell you what. You go ahead and jump, you stupid, cheap-whiskey, cotton-patch bastard, but do the world a favor and don't hit anybody when you land." Tom didn't jump.

City editor Alec McNeil drank a bit, too, until his wife, in leaving him, got revenge for the money he had spent on booze by running up hideous amounts on their charge accounts before departing, leaving Alec too little to drink on. And then there was Buck Weaver, bulbous, jovial, popular sports writer and race-horse expert, who wrote a column titled Foto-Finish. Good column, though Mike Barry, acerbic editor of the *Kentucky Irish-American*, and self-appointed world's greatest handicapper, once snarled in a column, "Weaver, you couldn't pick Whirlaway out of a herd of dairy cows." Buck just chuckled. Buck often came into the office of a morning under a hard drive, face puffy, gaze inverted, not speaking until he reached a stall in the men's room and pulled a reviving bottle from his pocket. Blub-blub-blub would come the sounds of rejuvenation, and a minute later Buck would saunter, good-natured and hail-fellow back into the newsroom. "Hiya, fellows, whaddya say?"

In his last years as an editorial writer for the *Times*, Jim Hutto began drinking. Strangest drinker I ever saw, although I never saw him out of control. But Jim would come to work badly the worse for wear, weave, under tight control, to the conference room and feel for his chair, where he would sit in a sort of trance, looking neither left nor right, saying nothing but breathing through his nose in a loud and rather disconcerting whistle. Everyone would act as though everything was normal, and at the end of the conference he would find his way back to his office, Burt would suggest to him a subject and Jim would sit down and write a perfectly lucid, literate, error-free editorial. He couldn't see his typewriter but he could write a beautiful editorial. I never figured that out; if I had two beers I couldn't write my name on the men's room wall. Jim finally retired and moved down to Bradenton, Florida, where he was dry as a bone, happy as a clam.

***

But neither gin nor wine nor cheap blend corn could keep these off-hour rowdies from doing a first-rate job during nine to five. In later years, when the empire was crumbling and the vultures were looking for corpses, book writers, apparently egged on by staffers who had axes to grind, wrote that Mark Ethridge was fired because he drank too much, embarrassing the paper and the Binghams. Mark is long dead, and there is little to be gained by pointing out that this was not true. But it should be said out of fairness to a remarkable man. Neither was it true that Mark quit when Barry refused to sell him stock in the company; that issue was settled when Mark came to the paper in 1936. Judge Bingham told him then that no one outside the family could own stock, but promised to lend him $150,000 (a nice sum in those Depression times) to buy his own paper if and when he chose to quit. He was not fired. He had discussed retiring with both Barry, Lisle

Baker and Molly Clowes months before he announced his decision. He had asked to retire two years earlier, but Barry had asked him to stay on until the Bingham sons, Worth and Barry, Jr., got their feet on the ground.

As for his drinking, no one who knew him would deny that he liked to drink, drank in a happy, relaxed social manner, and occasionally drank too much. The most celebrated case of this, and one that probably griped Barry, was the night Mark was picked up for driving on both sides of the road as he left the Pendennis Club. Taken to jail, he insisted on his one phone call, and called the *Courier* city desk, telling the night city editor what had happened and demanding that he send a reporter and photographer to the jail immediately since it was, as he said, big news. The poor guy on the desk finally sent a reporter down, but by that time the astonished turnkey had discovered the identity of his prisoner and was suggesting that Ethridge accept a ride home and forget the whole thing. Ethridge refused, and the story appeared on page one next morning. As it should have.

'Round about midnight—and afterward—when the spirits were high, Mark loved to sing. He couldn't, but that was of no matter. George Burt could sing—he had had classical training—and Mark would insist that George sing, while he accompanied him, possibly one of history's more bizarre duets. I sometimes tried to sing, myself, until one night Russell Briney said to me in a courteous voice, "John, I have sometimes thought you made a mistake getting into editorial writing, but it was a far, far better choice than had you chosen singing."

I also remember the night when, at a party at the Ethridge home in Prospect, Mark got into a heated argument with WHAS staff members and fired the whole bunch, including his son-in-law, Bud Abbott. The next morning everyone came to work as usual and no more was said about it, but accounts of the Midnight Massacre grew and flourished like the green bay tree. Aside from those instances, I never saw or heard of Mark drinking too much. He would take a drink at lunch, sometimes more if a business lunch dragged, but for five years I delivered the editorial page proof to him in his office every afternoon, and not once did I see the slightest evidence that he was not in cool control. If he ever came to work hungover, as some charged, it never showed at conference, where he was always sharp, knowledgeable and humorous.

It is true that Barry let Mark retire when he reached retirement age, but I have reason to suspect that his action had nothing to do with drinking. I have thought since that both Barry and Barry, Jr. would have done better to let those who knew how run the papers, but it is understandable that they would not. The fact is that Barry wanted to run his own papers. He had named Mark publisher when he went into the Navy in 1942, so that he could be confident of company leadership during his absence. I have heard from several people close to the family that Barry later regretted that decision when he wanted to regain control of the company and clear the way for his sons to take over. Family pride may also have played a part. During the forties the *Courier* and *Times* were often referred to as "the Ethridge papers," "the Ethridge press." When Mark was appointed to the Commission on Greece and Turkey, *The New York Times* referred to him, correctly, as publisher of the papers. When Willie Snow Ethridge wrote books about her travels with Mark, reviews usually mentioned that she was the wife of the publisher of the *Courier-Journal*. This made it awkward, when Barry returned from the war, to ask Mark to resume a lesser title.

In any event, the unfounded reports of Mark's drinking were a terrible disservice to the man who, more than any other individual, gave the *Courier-Journal* its excellence and national stature. It was Mark who chose the new type faces, who adopted headlines below the fold on the front page, the practice of jumping continued stories to the back page for ease of reading, who inaugurated the Sunday *Magazine*, and who was, above all else, chiefly responsible for the skilled personnel and high morale on the news staff that, in the long run, was the major factor in the paper's excellence. It was Mark who brought to the paper George Burt, Tarleton Collier, Allan Trout, Sarah Lansdell, Grady Clay, Jim Pope and Jim Pope, Jr., Buddy Atkinson, and Sam Moss.

***

Mark was a cool head in those years when a cool head was needed, for the Chambers-Hiss case had launched us into the stormy seas of anti-communism, and we would not come out unscathed. Next to the Depression, McCarthyism was the most disheartening era I had known. Politics, instead of being the grimy but essential engine under the bright hood of democracy, devolved into what Ambrose Bierce described as a strife of interests masquerading as a contest of principles.

The Republicans, naturally, saw in the situation a chance to tie the liberals to communism, and Democrats to the liberals. Anyone remotely associated with universities, movies, pacifist groups or churches, civil rights, international organizations or anything that could be classified as intellectual or elitist, was ripe for attack. We were damned as pinkoes or parlor pinks, or accused of being soft on Communism, whatever that meant, terms attacking our patriotism and questioning our right to protection of the Constitution. I had long heard that patriotism was the last refuge of a scoundrel, and now I realized where that old saw got its teeth. We didn't expect our Republican friends to defend us, but we did expect them to avoid outrageously false charges. We soon learned that was a naive hope. When Wilson Wyatt ran against Thruston Morton for the U.S. Senate, the choice was painful for Barry. He was a friend of Thruston's, had been in his wedding, and had supported him for Congress. But Wilson was also a friend, legal counsel for the company, and a tough liberal who we felt would stand against the Red hunters. So we backed Wilson. No one expected this to endear us to Thruston, but we were still shocked when, speaking at the Pendennis, he referred to the *Courier* as "the pinkoes over at the *Courier-Journal*," to the vigorous applause of the gathered businessmen. I am still sometimes struck by the virulence of conservative attacks when they see an opening in the liberal wall. I suppose we must assume that when people stand up for such things as the poor, freedom of speech or the right of Americans to be secure in their homes, conservatives will accuse them of near treason. Real men defend high dividends, not high ideals.

***

Our most painful clash with the Red-baiters, though, came in 1954, with what has since been known as the Braden Case. Personally, I think the Braden Case was a disgrace, and a reproach to Louisville, Kentucky and much of the structure of American justice. I don't think anyone was very proud of the role the *Courier-Journal* played in the terrible episode, but I am not sure that we had options.

Carl Braden was a labor reporter for the *Louisville Times*, a rather bland, smiling, bespectacled man whose only fault—that we could see—was his devotion to working people, especially union members, and to liberal causes in general. Thus it was no great surprise

69

when he was damned by anti-integrationists for "stirring up trouble." He stirred it by buying a house in a white neighborhood of the West End, and then selling it—or at least turning it over—to a black friend, Andrew Wade. White neighbors were furious, rocks were thrown, threats were made. And then, in the fall of 1954, a blast tore off a corner of the Wade home.

And here is the lovely part of the story: instead of launching a hunt for the dynamiters, the police arrested Braden and Wade for blowing up the house to incite racial strife and thus weaken the fiber of American society. Local officials swarmed to the attack. Conservatives drooled at the prospect of catching not only a radical. I doubt that even the brain-dead of the Right really considered Carl a Communist, but he was a pigeon, and a whip with which they could beat the pinko *Courier*. Scott Hamilton, the large, gruff but ordinarily good-natured Commonwealth Attorney, tore into poor Carl with happy ferocity. The newspaper was caught; Barry Bingham did not want to be revealed as harboring a criminal in the event Carl was actually guilty, yet felt that he should not judge or punish him until he had been judged and found guilty. So he took Carl off duty but kept him on the payroll as the witch-hunt clanged on. I suppose that was the best the paper could do, but it appeared to be weak-kneed. Several of us were subpoenaed to appear, Dick Harwood among others. Dick was a young Old Marine who wouldn't back down from the devil himself and was itching to get on the stand and tell Hamilton what a sonofabitch he was. Then Barry, Wilson Wyatt and other members of the law firm got hold of Dick and told him in no uncertain terms to answer yes or no, and say nothing else. And they were right. These people were out for blood, and no victim could make a finer trophy than the *Courier-Journal* and the shady characters who ran it.

Carl was charged with sedition—attempting to bring down the government. That's the truth. Right here in River City. His real sin, of course, was selling a house to a black man, but the jury would have found him guilty of anything this side of barbecuing babies. As some wag said at the time, if Carl was tried by a jury of his peers, he must have been a lunatic. He was found guilty and sentenced to fifteen years in prison. He served almost two years before a Circuit Court threw out the idiocy of sedition, a reversal upheld by the Supreme Court. No one seemed to appreciate that in this crusade of the idiots an innocent man's life had been ruined.

6

God, Smoke, and Elvis

In the days when I considered myself a bona fide threat to the girls of Norton High School, and stood before the mirror each morning trying to coax a wave into my stringy hair, there was a program on the radio called Your Hit Parade. It was sponsored by Lucky Strike cigarettes, and featured an orchestra that played the ten songs that had been most played or requested during the previous week. If you guessed the ten songs and sent your choices in on a Lucky Strike pack, you could win a carton of Luckies. If you picked fewer you might win fifty cigarettes in a flat tin box called, imaginatively, a Flat Fifty. We would stand around at the drug store listening as the announcer shouted, "And now for number four on Your Hit Parade—Moon Over Miami!" Cries would go up, "I got it," or "Oh, God, no!"

I don't recall anyone who won an actual carton, but one week, to everyone's surprise, including mine, I won a Flat Fifty. Unfortunately, like an idiot, I had put my correct address on my entry, and when my prize arrived, Mama found it, and demanded to know why this vile trash had come to me. "How should I know?" I protested, avoiding the outright lie, and then cringed as she threw the nasty things into the trash. I spent frantic minutes that evening, rooting through the garbage in the alley, to find my prize, whereupon I went down to the Norton Pharmacy and stood around the weighing machine nonchalantly flipping open my Flat Fifty.

Today there is much examination of youthful psyches to discover why young people smoke—peer pressure, imitation of elders, enticement of advertising, mental weakness. I began smoking at an early age mainly out of curiosity. I saw older men smoke, they seemed

71

to enjoy it, and it seemed logical to suspect that I would, too. I found some of Uncle Doc's Camels, retired to Tom Tiller's tree house with a few fellow-criminals, and puffed away. According to moral lore, when a boy first smokes, he gets so sick he will not try it again for years. It ain't necessarily so. I smoked, it did not make me sick. On the contrary, I liked it, and soon was smoking anything that could be drawn into young lungs. I didn't smoke long. As soon as I returned home to Pineville I embraced clean living, either because I had no access to the weed, no partners in crime, or no interest. But by the time I got to be a senior in high school I was a fairly steady smoker, when I could get tobacco. I know now that tobacco is the coffin nail we nicknamed it, one helluva hard habit to break, and terribly injurious. In high school I was a cross-country runner; smoking ruined my lungs. But it is too late to do anything about it, and there is no use in sniveling. I was a heavy smoker; no one enjoyed it more, but Lord, it carries a price. I paid for my Flat Fifty. But I should add this: no one forced, or even encouraged me to smoke. Uncle Doc did not leave those Camels in his car to destroy my health. Tom Tiller, TeeDee Pugh and Edsel Stuart did not join me to injure me. I don't recall ever seeing a cigarette ad when I was young. It was purely my fault.

Is there a point to all this? In a way, yes. During the decade of the 1950s, the Eisenhower era, and especially afterward, press pundits took to referring to those years as the Flat Fifties, since in contrast to what followed they seemed so pleasantly peaceful. Peaceful for some, perhaps. What was the Korean War? A Carnival cruise? People are still moaning about the Vietnam mess, and our losses there were about the same as in Korea, and the Korean thing isn't settled yet.

For me the fifties were a time of turmoil, or perhaps that is too stern a word. Certainly, they were not flat. The McCarthy era was a nightmare. Americans have a talent for periodic insanity, but I never thought they would go so far as to follow that obvious nut over the cliff, tearing at each other like hyenas. We seem to have a weakness for maniacs. We moan our worship of freedom but fall down and worship people who would subvert it. Any people with walking-around sense should have seen that J. Edgar Hoover was a certifiable amoeba-brain, but it wasn't until he died that we found the courage to admit that he was a cross-dressing freak and an evil totalitarian. I have a feeling that the FBI is too cautious to repeat today its sins of the Fifties, but we still quiver in fear of the CIA, which is a far greater threat to freedoms, here and abroad, than the FBI. The American people worship freedom until it applies to those they don't like.

Recently, political writers such as James Patterson have resurrected Eisenhower and tried to make him appear a great president, if not a saint (which reminds me of the old saw that a saint is a dead sinner, revised and edited). Ike was a great personality, but I managed to control my enthusiasm for him after he failed to speak up for General George Marshall, the man who picked him out of the litter and gave him command of our forces in Europe, the man who oversaw the war in both Atlantic and Pacific theaters, the man who proposed the Marshall Plan for the rehabilitation of Europe. When Marshall was attacked by Joe McCarthy as a traitor and a living lie, not only did he desert his friend and mentor, Ike refused to repudiate McCarthy, and stood on the campaign platform with that demagogue. No man should want public office that badly.

Ike refused a stay of execution for the Rosenbergs, though now it is pretty certain that Ethel Rosenberg was about as innocent as Ike. The great general also loosed the CIA on the people of Guatemala, overthrowing their elected president because he had bought idle land from United Fruit Company for the prices they had paid taxes on and given it to the poor farmers. The idea of poor farmers having land that United Fruit wanted was too much for Ike, Foster Dulles and his Wall Street advisers, and they put in their own trusted dictator, creating a nightmare that was eased only in 1996. But Americans loved Ike, and cared not if he was not exactly the thinking man's president. And, as in the case of Ronald Reagan, I suppose it is good for the American people to have a likable mediocrity in power now and then, a man who appeals to their lesser biases and fantasies.

***

And the fifties were a rough time for me personally. No sooner had we gotten into the routine of a Naval Reserve unit than the Korean War broke out and the word came down that we should polish our brass. I couldn't believe it, but here came orders to report for duty. Since I had no choice, I became a patriot again and made loud noises about serving the flag, having a pretty good idea that the Navy would discover that I had been married, was blessed with children and would toss me back. Which, of course, it did. With the Chinese coming across the Yalu River, the pressing demand was not for public relations officers.

I had pressing demands of another sort, pressing little girls' dresses. That, friends, is no easy task, but being single parent to two small females, and pinching every penny so that I could hire Marie (our sometime maid) for the summer months when the girls would be home, I was forced into all kinds of degradation. But I was learning. I was learning, for one thing, not to take too much advice on how to rear the girls. George Burt, praised be his name, gave the girls a book—for Christmas or birthday—called *Slovenly Peter*. It was a grim and gory thing. Peter was a rotten kid. His mother told him not to run through the house. He ran through the house. He fell and broke his leg—you could see the jagged bones sticking out through the skin and the blood gushing like Standard Oil. My neighbor ladies insisted I burn the horrid thing, warning that it would cause the girls to have nightmares and warp their egos or ids forever. The girls loved it! "Read us the part about where he keeps sucking his thumb and the big scissors man comes and cuts off his thumbs!" they demanded.

A more serious matter arose one Saturday when my daughters, along with Cherie Ryan were playing back on Ring Road, near the railroad tracks. I didn't worry about it; they knew not to play on the tracks. But then they came home early for lunch, and Marnie was in high dudgeon. A man had come down the tracks, I gathered, and had exposed himself to the girls, Marnie, Susie and Cheri. "He pulled out his THING!" said Marnie, "and put his hand on my shoulder." Susie agreed that such was the case, although she seemed not too upset. "I just told him, 'You get your hands off of my sister. We're going home right now,' and I got Marnie and we left."

Well, now! That was something else. Personally, I was just glad that nothing worse had happened, but Bailey Ryan was ready to kill somebody, and I do not exaggerate. The cops were called, an arrest was made, and a detective showed up at Ryans' with a miscreant, picked up feeling a girl in the Vogue theater. The girls were called in to see the man and perhaps identify him, but it was obvious when they saw him that they didn't recognize him as the culprit. Later, the detective praised Susie for the way she had handled the episode. "She did exactly the right thing," he said. "If she had screamed or run, he might have hurt them sure enough. Usually when kids stand up to them, they back down. Did just right." I felt, once again, very proud of Susie. She could be very grown up.

We talked with the girls, who seemed to have dismissed the entire episode. "What did you think when the man did that?" Emma Ryan asked them.

"I thought, what if a lady walked by with him that way," Marnie replied, rightly offended by this affront to the purer sex and social niceties.

A more important event, though, occurred one day when Susie came to me and asked, very seriously, if we could have a talk. I saw that something was on her mind, so we went into the living room and sat down, Marnie to one side.

"I've been thinking about it," Susie said, "and I think I've gotten too old to spank."

You talk about a thunderbolt! Guilt hit me like a hurricane. All of my mistakes. How could I have done this? I remember how my father had whipped me when I was a boy, and how I lost my affection for him, and it never returned.

And now I had done the same thing. I had no idea what had brought this on; I couldn't remember the last time I had spanked either of them. From the time they were little I had disciplined the girls with a swat across the fanny, accompanied by an angry "No!" and considered it a way to clear the air, erase the conduct blackboard, and get the message across. I remembered that I had one time hit Susie so hard that Ferd Weiss, sitting nearby, said, "Oh, come on, John Ed! That's not necessary." And, of course, it wasn't.

How could I have done this? Hit this lovely little creature so dear to me, on whom I depended more than a parent had a right to, who was such a source of pride? We talked for a few minutes; I asked what I should do if they disobeyed, and Susie suggested they be sent to their room, or not be permitted to go out and play. I agreed, eagerly, gratefully. In the future, we would discuss the matter before any decision was made. Susie seemed relieved, though not a tenth as much as I. Marnie, though, demurred. "Not me!" she said, "I'd rather get spanked than all that talk!"

For some reason, I never apologized to Susie. I should have. But after that day, I never hit a child again. And of all my sins, I think that is the one for which I have never quite forgiven myself, though I have little patience with remorse, which is usually part self-pity. But no child should be hit. It isn't fair. She can't defend herself, and the injustice of it can only store up resentment and bad memories. Childhood is a kind of slavery, anyhow. It isn't easy for parents, either. We aren't trained, prepared for the job. My heart goes out to single parents.

***

It was at about that time, 1954, that the Supreme Court handed down its decision in the Brown vs. Board of Education case, the school desegregation decision. The girls were excited about it and were eager to have blacks in their school. It was no one's fault, just the way society was arranged, that they had had almost no contact with blacks except as servants. Susie, especially, was fascinated with the black woman hired by Lucy Schneider and loved to sit and hug her, asking if she, Susie, would have brown skin, too, when she grew up. And one day Marnie came in and announced that Mrs. Hellman had a "white colored woman." I figured it would do them good to have some association with blacks, live in the real world.

We had a brief brush with the kind of conflict that accompanied integration when Olaf Anderson announced that a Mrs. Breckinridge and her son had proposed to join our church, Harvey Browne Presbyterian. Everyone approved such an aristocratic addition to our congregation until Dr. Anderson let it be known that Mrs. B. was black! A Negro! Consternation! Loud grumbling! One man got up and left the church. Dr. Anderson simply paid no attention and, on the following Sunday before he delivered his sermon, went to the rear of the church and escorted to the front a large black woman and her handsome son, and, smiling proudly, introduced them. Not a murmur, and after church a goodly number of our suburban worshippers stopped to welcome Mrs. Breckinridge and her son. Ah, that every incident could have been handled in such a Christian manner. But, I fear, there are few Olaf Andersons running around. I enjoyed Harvey Browne in the years before we moved from Beechwood Village. Christians tend to be weird, but Presbyterians tend to be less weird than others. I have also known some Episcopalians and a Catholic priest who deserve some leniency on that great gettin' up morning.

But I digress. Again. I guess the biggest reason I wanted to go to church was to give the girls a shot at it, to see if they liked it (they did) and let them feel part of a community. And then they betrayed me. Culture shock! They had begun asking for records when we went to the drug store, and playing them on their cheap plastic player, and one day, to my horror, what should assail my ears but the Beatles and Elvis Presley! What had happened? Here were my nice little middle-class girls, who had been churched and clubbed and indoctrinated with the most conventional and boring middle-class values, hearing Beethoven and Brahms and the occasional moderate popular songs that their daddy played for them, hoping that it would prepare them to accept good music later on, and now this!

Actually, I did not object to the Beatles, though the appeal of their shallow, silly tunes escaped me. "She loves you, yeah, yeah, yeah." And if I did not eagerly embrace Elvis, cuh mawn, bebby, at least I recognized him. He had the same inflection, played the same music that was played and sung by the grease-stained semi-literates who whanged their guitars and bawled what we referred to as—forgive it— white trash music in the side rooms of garages on the outskirts of Norton. But he had a good voice, better certainly than other rock sing-ers, and his songs and gyrations were harmless, if tacky. But here were my proper daughters bopping around to some trashy boy from Tennessee. I was held hostage by rock-and-roll, but shrugged, confi-dent that such bad music would not last. Contemporary music critics say that rock was and is the explosion of emotion and power, chiefly of blacks, who had been oppressed and denigrated by such pap as Perry Como and Patti Page. That did not apply to my generation. We did not yearn for the return of Pat Boone and Welk—we didn't care much for them the first time around. The music that we did like, and for whose return we yearned in the years after WWII, was the music of Goodman and Shaw, Dorsey and Ellington, Basie and Herman, very strong, powerful but disciplined music. We never cared much for rock, except as dance music, because we couldn't sing or hum it. It wasn't exactly white-trash, but it apparently struck a note with the millions of people who escaped the lower classes through the postwar prosperity and education, especially the GI Bill. Suddenly, renters who had rid-den the street car to the factory and sneered at country clubs and golf-ers now owned homes, cars and sometimes boats, and belonged to the clubs they once resented. But we seldom leave home entirely. They were not surprised when their children liked rock, partly because they did not consider it black.

***

Change was taking place at the office, too, a cloud no bigger than a man's mouth, Television! WAVE had been on the air for some time, but now WHAS followed, and a competition began that still takes its goofy course. At first television was chiefly rasslers who bounded about and kicked each other, but it gradually expanded to include, on WHAS, Randy and Cactus (Randy Atcher and Tom Brooks) who lured innocent children into the studio of Saturday mornings, used them as shills and sang songs. And slowly the stations began telecasting what passed for news. It was something of a joke—they mainly read headlines and stories from the papers (even as I had done on the radio in Lexington before the war)—and we on the papers paid them little heed and less respect. If people wanted to watch rasslin', comedies and old newsreels, television was all right. But it was, at best, entertainment. If people were looking for news, information, they still had to come to us. We never suspected that the mouse was slowly becoming a ravenous rat. And we were wrong enough to think that the American people would prefer vital information to sloppy entertainment. We learned. Television not only dived into the entertainment swamp, it dragged most of the press along with it.

After a while television began to become more substantial. There was Dave Garroway, Steve Allen, Ed Murrow and his star crew, *Studio One, Summer Theater* (to which I sold some mediocre plays). We began to see the potential of this new medium, and realized what it could do, not just in rasslin' but in quality entertainment and appealing educational programs if it took the right path. Alas, it didn't.

We were experiencing personnel changes that were to have an impact on quality, as well as morale. In 1952 Norman Isaacs had come from the folded *St. Louis Star Times* to succeed Al Aronson as managing editor of the *Times*. Norman was a blend of raging bull and crafty fox, a man of tremendous and aggressive energy. He changed the design of the *Times*, and let it be known that his hot shot young crew was going to show the stuffy *Courier-Journal* what a newspaper looked like. It promised to be fun.

And then the Bingham boys came home. Worth, the eldest, after helling his way through Harvard and a stint in the Naval Reserve, had cut his journalistic teeth in Washington, California and Minneapolis and was ready to start learning the ropes preparatory to taking command of the family papers. Handsome, careless in dress in a preppy way and self-assured, Worth harbored few doubts. Barry Jr., slender, blonder and quieter, was also a Harvard graduate, a Marine reservist, and had served an apprenticeship with NBC television, working on two well-considered documentaries. It was his father's announced plan that he would take over the radio and television stations, as Worth would take over the papers. Jonathan, the youngest boy, was not ready for officer's school. Jonathan was an easy-smiling, sweet-faced, popular boy, which made it all the more horrifying when, wiring a barn on the family estate with some friends for a fraternity party, he touched a power line and was electrocuted. Barry, Sr. seemed stunned. Mary almost collapsed. She was inconsolable. Jonathan's death, though, was only the first tragic passage in the fateful Bingham saga.

***

I anticipated no difficulty with Worth. What I knew of him I liked. Dick Harwood had worked with him in Washington and approved of him. We were all excited at the prospect of having him take over the papers, even with his lack of experience, since he was said to be brilliant, innovative and energetic, and it was widely thought that he would become one of the great publishers of the country. I had settled into my niche on the paper and no longer felt it necessary to spend time on the road, becoming acquainted with the state. That was bad in one way, for it deprived me of my expense account, on which I could live and save my salary, but it was good in another, since it freed me from the small-town hotels of the day.

Kentucky had a flock of hotels widely considered colorful and seemingly determined to live up to their reputation. The LuRay, of Central City comes to mind; there was some trouble with the Operating Engineers over something or other, and I had been out in the field, getting sweaty and dirty and longing for nothing more than a hot shower, when I checked into the LuRay and asked for a room with a shower. The man at the desk seemed astonished by my request, but finally recovered. "A shower. Well, now." Then he brightened. "Yes. Yessir, we got one. Sure have." And he was right. The shower, indeed the entire bath, consisted of a cast-iron cabinet, aluminum painted, smack in the middle of the room, with a shower head of sorts that dribbled out water either steaming hot or frigid. There was a democratic toilet down the hall, first come. I remembered the LuRay years later when, in Vietnam, I stayed at the Continental Palace when I got down to Saigon. I loved the Palace, with its meandering verandah, where newsmen and writers, whores and military men shared the view of the traffic swirling by; it served breakfast in bamboo booths in the back where the waiters swatted at the prowling peacocks and served fine coffee. I recall sitting on the verandah one afternoon, sharing a drink with Mark Ethridge, Jr., who was there on duty with the Detroit papers, when we were approached by one of the most bizarre whores of the Orient, a skinny, fairly tall young woman with flying, semi-red hair and occasional teeth. She sat down, offered to let us buy a drink, and asked if we would like to sample the delights of her flesh. I thought Mark was going to fall out of his chair. Whores didn't bother me but Mark recoiled as though facing Eden's snake. When we declined her offer of mutual joy, she called over another street dove, a small, dispirited girl who seemed resigned to refusal, and offered us a two-for-one bargain. Or a good deal on some nylons. An entrepreneur. I hope she did well, though I doubt it.

Anyhow, I had a fair room but no bath, and each morning as I opened my door to walk to the potty at the end of the hall, the Chinese guy in the next room would pop out in front of me, grin, bow and leave me doing the full-bladder tango while he grew old in the toilet. No matter how quietly I stole from my bed, eased open the lock and the door and started my mad dash for the facility, that sonofabitch would pop out in front of me, grin, bow.

***

The Kentucky hotels were seldom so colorful. Dr. Thomas Clark, Kentucky's premier historian, can recall the days when, traveling through Leslie County in Eastern Kentucky, he and Beth, his relatively new wife, were welcomed into Hyden's only hostelry by a landlord who lighted them up to the loft with a kerosene lamp, where Beth was taken aback to find a large single room, with clumps here and there on the floor where travelers were making do with a thin pallet and a couple of thin blankets. As you can imagine, a trip to the bathroom was an adventure.

Before the Mount Aire was built outside Harlan, about the only choice was the Lewallen, which wasn't too bad, though it would never threaten the Brown. It was at the Lewallen that the majesty of Harlan law grabbed Theodore Dreiser, when that worthy came to Harlan to investigate and write about the miserable conditions in the coal mines and strike a blow for the striking miners. The aging Dreiser had with him a woman, allegedly his secretary, as well as several newsmen, including Bruce Crawford, of *Crawford's Weekly* in my hometown of Norton, Virginia. Lackeys of the sheriff saw the woman go into Dreiser's room one night, propped match-sticks against the door and, when they were still there next morning, nabbed poor Dreiser and held him for trial, charged with lewd conduct. On the stand, Dreiser scoffed at the charge, while denying that the lady in question had spent the night. "What difference?" he asked, with a shrug. "Everyone knows I've been impotent for years." The shrewd folk of Harlan were not about to be taken in by such city-slicker talk, however, found Dreiser guilty, fined him and ordered him out of the county.

Pikeville's Hatcher Hotel, now of blessed memory, was memorable mainly for its lobby, on the walls of which the elder Hatcher had written pithy sayings and moral dicta to enlighten his clients. "A single man is happier than a married one but it makes no difference since he don't know it." "Never hire a man that smokes cigarettes or wears a belt. He'll spend all his time lighting up or hitching up." And so on. The Big Sandy River, which seemed to flood at least once a year, was a frequent guest in the lobby until a mayor, William Hambley, simply cut a huge slice through the mountain and re-routed the river around the town. But by that time it was too late to save the Hatcher.

Pineville's Continental has a dusty place in my heart, too. In my boyhood it was elegant, at least relatively, a place where coal operators, lawyers, bankers and salesmen sat and smoked cigars in the evening, but time had taken its toll when, years later, I decided to spend the night there rather than throw myself on the mercy of friends. Bad decision. The bedsprings let my back brush the floor, and the blankets reminded that others had been there before me. Next morning I shuffled into a long, narrow room lighted by a single light bulb on a long cord, and was served a runny egg, fat, cold bacon and burned toast by a slattern who sat down, lighted a cigarette and issued what may have been a warning, asking if "that good-looking red-haired girl," had come to my room. No. Well, she said, be careful; she's awful good-looking, but not too bright, and sometimes men take her to their rooms. I assured her my virtue was safe and my bankroll too puny to

81

afford red-haired girls who went with men to their hotel rooms. To this day I don't know whether I was being hustled.

Small towns change, as do any towns, and because they are small the changes seem large. During one summer of my single blessedness, I was in training duty over at the Norfolk Navy base, and at the insistence of my sister Rose decided to leave my girls with her for two weeks rather than hire a maid. On the way to Belmont, North Carolina, where Rose lived, we went through Pineville and I pointed out to the girls the sites of my boyhood glory. They were massively unimpressed, regarding the river, the crowded streets, the muddy lot where our house had stood (it had burned down sometime before) with slightly curled lip. They could not, of course, see it through the eyes of a 5-year old boy to whom it was all a setting of beauty and adventure. They were obviously skeptical when I tried to tell them what a fine place it had been to live.

7

Pineville, KY

In her song "Secret Gardens," Judy Collins sings of driving past her grandmother's house with strangers, knowing that they see only a plain wooden cottage, a patch of brown lawn, a sagging fence, but wishing that they might see what she sees through the eyes of memory, a house warm and lovely, birds flashing in sunlight, a forest of lilies, an orchard of apricot trees.

I shared somewhat her feelings when I showed my girls the place in Pineville where I lived as a boy, and saw them wrinkle their noses at the muddy, littered lot, the single forlorn tree, the remnant stones that had once been a house's foundation. They could not see what my brother Don and I saw when we piled from the family car after the long drive from Norton. We raced around the house and through the yard, everything new and exciting, and finally stood, trans-fixed, at the backyard's edge and looked down the sloping bank at the Cumberland river, green and silent between its tree-lined banks, at once mysterious, tempting and frightening, with railroad tracks on the far side, and beyond them the mountain, its forested slopes broken by gray, brooding cliffs. On one side of the yard stood the low shed where later we kept our cow, Maud, and a storage room with a rotting floor. On the other side a large elm tree spread its branches, to one of which Daddy later affixed a tire-swing. The large storeroom we converted into the world's best clubhouse, where we made tallow-dip candles for light, plotted treasure hunts on the river and forbade entrance to girls. Attached to the clubhouse-storeroom was a garage that in time served as a stall for Fan, the Shetland pony on which I played cowboy before we got rid of her after she kicked Mama in the head.

The house was an unremarkable two-story white frame, with a narrow front porch, four steps leading down to the short sidewalk, and the usual rooms—a small living room, to be dominated by the family's prized grand piano, a larger dining room and dim kitchen, flanked by a latticed back porch. A trapdoor revealed steps from the kitchen to a rock-walled cellar, and stairs led from the living room to three bedrooms and a bath upstairs. My sister Rose later said that it was an ugly, uncomfortable house, but to me it was neither grand nor plain, but just our house, where I slept, ate, rushed in to ask for something to eat and rushed out again before Mama could think of something for me to do better than fishing in the river, digging caves in the soft sand of the bank or, later, paddling to secret fishing holes in the flat-bottom boat Daddy gave me.

I realize that my years there were not as fine and pleasant as they seem now, but it is still hard to fault Pineville as a place for a boy to live and grow, mountains looming on all sides, trails leading up to the rocky summits that looked down on streets and buildings and the river half-circling the town. I don't know how or when I learned—perhaps from Daddy, from books, from older boys—which were maple trees, which buckeye, which elm or oak, pine or cedar, where to find blackberries and Jack-in-the-pulpit, how to catch crawdads for bait, which were sungrannies, which redeyes, how to hull walnuts, where to find chestnut trees, before the blight of the late twenties doomed them. How did I know that it was elder that gave off that sweet, musky smell that lay heavy upon the river in the morning mist? When did I learn to use an ax, hoe weeds, climb a tree, make a slingshot or a rubber gun, how to tell a thrush from a flicker, a hawk from a buzzard, a garter snake from a copperhead, how to sense in the wind that it was going to rain, how to gig frogs, make a lean-to, build a fire, cook sassafras tea, tell rhododendron from mountain laurel? I don't know, but I learned, by instinct, by osmosis, all the things that a boy collects along the way, living in town but close to nature.

***

My mother was far more tolerant and patient than I could have been, letting me roam, patching me up when I came up second best in my contest with the sharp edges of the world. She seem convinced that my neck was made for breaking. "You get down from there before you fall and break your neck." I never fell, though Tinker McCabe and I swung naked through the trees in the hollow above the Low's house at the foot of the mountain, playing Tarzan, and I saw every buckeye tree, no matter how tall, as a challenge. She was right, however, in her warning against leaning against the car door. "That door's going to come open some day and you'll fall out and break your neck." The door did come open, and I did fall out, but instead of breaking my neck I hit my hard head on a fire plug and was gone for a while. To Mama's credit, she never said I told you so. They say that age brings wisdom, but I am not sure about that. I think, actually, that age, if it is kind, brings a recognition of ignorance. And I know that every man of my age that I know would trade a year of old wisdom for one day of young ignorance.

I don't know why I never became a better swimmer, with the river at our back door, and a small lake at the south end of town where the water was cool in the hot summer. We splashed water on the sloping bank behind our house, making a slide into the river. Unfortunately, a broken bottle protruded, and when I went whooping down, it sliced my bottom like a salami. Embarrassing.

And then there was Blue Hole, a deep spot in Clear Creek a few hundred yards above the Asher home east of town, with a diving board held down by rocks and a swinging bridge leading across to the property of Sudie Howard, who came out and drove us away if we went ashore on her side of the creek. The Asher family included three boys, as I recall, and a raft of pretty girls. Doris was pretty, and Babe, whose real name I later discovered was Pauline, was cute, but Ethel was my favorite because one day she said to me, "Boy, you should have been down at the pavillion last night. What a dance!" I, of course, couldn't dance, but the fact that she spoke to me as if I could, as if I were grown up, made me feel big, and I never forgot.

Whenever I think of the Asher home it is always summer, flowers are blooming around the wide concrete front steps and the older kids are laughing and talking on the porch while the hand-cranked Victrola plays and Rudy Vallee sings. I don't know how Minnie Asher, the sweet-faced matriarch, put up with us, but she did, and always with a smile. We would walk out from town, ask permission if anyone was around or otherwise just go into a bathroom and change into bathing suits and walk up the railroad tracks to Blue Hole. Later we would change back into our clothes and go to the kitchen, where there were always ginger cookies and cold milk. Sometimes the big kids would have a party, dancing on the porch, and we would hang around the steps, listening, sometimes allowed to spend the night. One evening I was there at dinner time, and when everyone else trooped into the dining room, I followed. Minnie kept looking around the table, and her gaze kept coming back to me. Finally, she said, "Now you, you aren't mine," and I confessed that I was Brother Pearce. That seemed to satisfy her.

I loved all the Ashers, and still stop and see Babe when I am in Pineville. Tinker McCabe had a crush on Babe, but wouldn't go to see her unless I went with him. The three of us would sit on he hillside behind the house, eat grapes and talk of things we were going to do. On Minnie's one-hundredth birthday, the Ashers let me come back and sit with them on the porch, wondering how we could get Minnie down the long steps for the family portrait and then back up again. Minnie solved the problem by coming to the head of the steps, asking where they wanted her, walking calmly down the steps, smiling for the picture and then walking back again. The Ashers were an old Eastern Kentucky family, descendants of the famed Dillion Asher, and made of stern stuff.

***

When I was a boy in Pineville, religion trailed me like a shadow. For some reason, Daddy got the idea that I could sing, and before I could defend myself he and I were advancing to the front of the First Baptist Church on Sunday morning, where he played the guitar and I shrilled out the timeless Baptist messages - not just "Jesus Wants Me for a Sunbeam," "Brighten the Corner Where You Are," and "I Washed My Hands This Morning," but "I Come to the Garden Alone," and "Where he leads me, I will follow." I grew to enjoy it, became an unbearable little ham, and preened repulsively before the congregation, aware of the approving looks of the church matrons, and the whispers, "Ain't that cute?" etc.

Strangely, I can't recall a moral lesson learned from Sunday School. I do remember one learned at Maggie Broughton's. Maggie ran a green ten by twelve foot store across the street from the school house, selling school supplies and candy, gum, pop and other luxuries. Maggie's pièce de résistance was a candy draw: you paid your penny and got a round, tasty piece of chocolate-covered nougat. The center was usually white; if it proved to be pink, you got a whole bar free, and it was delicious. One day I got a pink center, and the prize bar, but before I stuffed the prized pink into my mouth, the devil entered my heart, and I slipped it into my pocket and the next day palmed the bought piece and made as if to break open the pink piece, which I showed to Maggie. I got another bar, and left, feeling not clever but nasty, unclean, guilty. Almost at once, even before I ate the now-flavorless bar, I wanted to go back, confess my sin and return the ill-gotten prize. There must be a moral in the fact that I have never forgotten that.

School proved to be routine, not unpleasant, made easier by the fact that I read everything I could get my grubby hands on, helped on by subscriptions to *Youth's Companion*, *The American Boy*, *Open Road for Boys* and *Our Dumb Animals*, a publication seeking good treatment of dogs and cats, chiefly dogs, supposedly man's best friend despite their habit of biting people and using the yard for a toilet. The family also splurged to buy a set of *Compton's Pictured Encyclopedia*, an excellent collection that I devoured like candy. In addition to these approved publications we boys managed to collect stacks of such informal literature as *Wild West Weekly*, *Blazing Guns*, *Thrilling Detective*, *Railroad Man's Magazine* and so on. On rainy days we would gather and read, swapping copies, never tiring of the plot that never varied—the hero rides into town, the hero encounters bad guys, the hero kills the bad guys, the hero rides out of town, as the girl says oh, Jack, do you have to go, and her daddy says there'll always be a place here for a man like you.

As a result of all this literary grazing I found later that, to a surprising extent, I had broken the bonds of the provincialism of our small-town culture (although it was not nearly as provincial as outsiders would have you believe). Though I had seen little of America, and less of the world, I had come to know Everest and the Amazon, Paris and merchant ships and green islands of the blue Pacific. When, as a young man, I finally saw them, I recognized at once the dusty plains of the West, Arizona's canyons, New York and the Rockies, for I had been there in my books and magazines and *Compton's Pictured Encyclopedia*, had seen the people and places through the eyes of imagination. I pity children who have television in their homes. Truly.

The same applied to music. Daddy played everything he could

get his hands on—guitar, mandolin, banjo, you name it. I have an idea that he was whaling away on the Gibson guitar when he should have been down at the office collecting bills and selling job printing. Once, when I was away at boarding school, the house caught on fire and Daddy, so Don told me, grabbed his guitar and mandolin and rushed outside. Mama and the girls grabbed the china and silver, pictures and books, and threw rugs over the piano. Whenever Daddy went fortune-hunting, Mama would take over the newspaper, collect and pay bills, straighten up the office and put things on a paying basis. I think that's what she really liked, that and playing mah jong with the girls and the other women in the neighborhood. She taught me how to play. I liked it. She also taught me how to play croquet, which became very popu-lar during those years. She loved flowers, too, and I sometimes went with her to pick blackberries for pies and gather wildflowers at the same time. She was always trying to get Jack-in-the-Pulpit to grow around the yard, but it wouldn't. A love of nature is a fine gift to give a child. It was but one of the many blessings she heaped upon me.

Sometimes at night Daddy would sit on the front porch and play, and neighbors would drift over, some bringing a fiddle or man-dolin, and they would play and we would all sing. We'd sing of how the moon shines tonight on pretty Redwing, whose lover had not come back, or about Buffalo Gals, or Sourwood Mountain. On moonlight nights that was really good, with the clematis on the front-porch trellis smelling good and the girls singing in their sweet voices.

And we had the Victrola, a big cabinet model with a wind-up crank on the side, that played black records a quarter-inch thick, songs about the vacant chair (we shall meet, but we shall miss him), "Yes, We have no Bananas," or "When it's Nighttime in Italy, it's Wednes-day over Here." There was also a record of the Two Black Crows, and one about the little boy who wanted a drink of water after he went to bed. He was a dopey kid who thought little cowboys were calfboys. Mama liked "Listen to the Mockingbird," "Over the Waves," "The Naughty Waltz." We also had Galli Curci and John MCormick singing arias from operas, and orchestras playing the overture from Traviata and Shubert's Unfinished Symphony. I didn't pay much attention to all this, but later found that I recognized much of the classical music to which I was introduced.

***

At school and in the neighborhood, a pecking order was soon established. I was regularly beaten up by stronger boys, and in turn beat up weaker ones. My scholastic career was interrupted when I was ten or so and was packed off to Lee Baptist Institute, in Pennington Gap, Virgina. I never understood why, but was all for it. I loved Pennington Gap. Uncle Doc lived there and had offices over the A&P, with bedrooms to one side. I sometimes went to stay with Uncle Doc in the summertime, when the family apparently figured it was a good time to get rid of us for a while. Uncle Doc would give me half a dollar for breakfast, and I would go down to the cafe on the corner by the railroad tracks and get a quarter's worth of breakfast, keeping the other quarter for wild living. The cafe was a good place. The man behind the counter liked me, I could tell, and gave me just about anything I asked for, and put money in the nickelodeon that played "There'll come a time some day, when I have passed away; there'll be no father to guide you, from day to day." There was another one about a rosewood casket sitting on the parlor stand that I thought was a coffin, and one about how they cut down the old pine tree to make a coffin of pine for that sweetheart of mine. He and the man who worked at the post office and Mr. Sneed at the hotel would get us boys into banana-eating contests in which we had to see how many we could eat in a minute.

Uncle Doc, everyone said, was overworked. I know that he would sit down at night after supper and twiddle the knobs on the radio, getting WLW in Cincinnati, or KDKA in Pittsburgh, but then the phone would ring and he would say, "Oh, all right. Keep her quiet and I'll be there as soon as I can." He would put on his coat, put his pearl-handled thirty-eight in his pocket and head up one of the hollows, to St. Charles or Blue Diamond, Oconita or Stickleyville in that pretty blue Buick. When he got home I'd be in bed, and he'd go over to the dresser and take out a bottle and drink. I asked him what it was and he said it was medicine. I guess, in its way, it was.

Uncle Doc had to do everything. I remember one time when a farmer came into town on a Saturday, driving a team and wagon, and the horses bolted at a train whistle and the man's wife, holding a baby, fell out, hitting the baby's head on a rock. She and her husband came running up the street, hollering like they were going to die, and climbed the long stairway to Uncle Doc's office. He came out into the waiting room when he heard all the commotion, and the woman held out the baby. "Do something, Doc," she wailed. "Oh, God, do something."

Uncle Doc took one look and shook his head. "You've got to get her to a hospital," he said. "She needs a surgeon. I'm not that kind of doctor. You'll have to get her up to Norton."

With that, the howling increased. They all knew that the baby wasn't going to make it to Norton. "You gotta help her, Doc," sobbed the woman. "You just gotta!"

Uncle Doc sighed. "All right," he said, and told his nurse to get the table ready, but turned to the couple. "I don't think I can save her," he said. "I'll try, but I've warned you."

He went back into his office, and was gone a long time, while the farmer and his wife sat, rocking and moaning. Finally he came back, sweating, his shirt sleeves rolled up. "Well," he said, "it looks like she's going to make it. God knows why." With that, the hollering only got louder, and the woman fell on her knees and grabbed Uncle Doc's hand. He looked tired and relieved.

I knew Uncle Doc drank. One time when we lived in Pineville, he came through with his nurse, slurring words, smiling vacantly and scared me to death. I didn't know what was wrong. Later I learned that once a year he would go up to Louisville, where he had gone to medical school, to a convention, and stay drunk for a week. He deserved it. He had a nice nurse named Dora. Pretty. Her sister married the man who invented the Eskimo Pie, and the three of them came through Pineville, driving a big tan Rolls-Royce, and stopped to see us. Dora's sister had on an ermine coat. Everybody in the neighborhood came down to see the Rolls-Royce. Our social standing went up sharply, if temporarily.

When I didn't stay with Uncle Doc I would stay with Grandma Pearce, who moved to Pennington Gap to be near Uncle Doc after Grandpa Pearce died. I preferred to stay with Uncle Doc, but Grandma's was all right, too. She was good to me, let me churn butter and get up early in the morning and go with Mr. Crowell, who lived next door, to take his cow to pasture. Sometimes we would see rabbits, and there were morning glories on the fence. Grandma sang songs about loving Jesus and had a concern for my immortal soul, though that concern ran a poor second to her worry about my bowels (nasty word). I was a healthy little beast, and there was nothing whatever wrong with my digestive tract, but she was convinced that I was a potential victim of the dread constipation. Every day she would fix me with an accusing eye and demand to know whether "your bowels have moved," and every evening, whether or not I had produced, she would shove some concoction down me, Ex Lax, Black Draught, or a pink, chewy candy that went through me with the explosive force of Krakatoa.

***

So I did not mind when I heard I was going to Lee Baptist Institute. Daddy approved because it was a Baptist boarding school, Mama because it was in Virginia, and might cleanse me of some of the stigma of Kentucky. If LBI was supposed to polish my brain or correct my morals, it failed utterly. I had a ball. Uncle Doc gave me quarters when I dropped by his office, and I went to see cowboy pictures or bought candy. Tom Tiller, a town boy, had a tree house, and when Uncle Doc left Camel cigarettes on the seat of his Buick coupe we would steal them and hie off to the tree house to smoke and play cards. When the real thing was not available we climbed the hill behind the dormitory and rolled cigarettes of a silvery leaf that grew on a short stalk and was called rabbit tobacco or life-everlasting. Wrapped in newspaper, it made an inferior smoke, but a smoke.

I had a revelation. One Saturday a group of us went to the picture show. "The Border Legion", was showing, a silent movie, of course, and the man on the piano down front was playing "All Alone By The Telephone," (an Irving Berlin song whose relevance escaped me then as now), when this one guy gets shot with an arrow. They hauled him into the cabin and laid him out on the table. Somebody had to get that arrow out. The man turned to the others and said—the immortal words leapt on the screen and burned into my memory, "Let Pearce do it!" Well, obviously, that was a sign that I was meant to be a doctor, and I emerged from the movie a pint-sized Paul, saved on the road to LBI. I told Uncle Doc about my decision, confident that he would offer to send me to med school, but he just smiled.

LBI was fun. I roomed at first with a boy named Evans, who put brilliantine on his hair and let me use his tennis racket. I starred as the Utility Man in the school play *Down on the Farm*, strutting out on stage with bandanna, straw hat and overalls and cawing in my nasal tenor "Oh, I'm the Utility Man, to please everyone is my plan." Needless to say, I brought down the house. I also had my first chance to dabble in sex, but flubbed it. Two little girls, one of whom claimed to be my girlfriend, took me to the basement of the new dorm and offered to let me see their equipment if I would let them see mine. I demurred, mainly because the previous summer Uncle Doc had given Jimmy Young fifty cents to take me down to the river and teach me to swim, and as I stood knee deep in the clear stream, Jimmy looked at my male organ and said, "Man, that's the funniest looking peter I ever saw," and I was ashamed to let the girls inspect it.

As a result, I had almost no sins to confess when the fall revival came around. That was a major event. A visiting devil-beater was brought in, and for a week we were hounded into the church whenever the doors could be pried open, flayed for our sins and warned of the likely consequences. I recall how, on an innocent Sabbath, I was reading the hair-raising account of Tom Swift and the *Caves of Ice*, which I concealed within a hymnal, when salvation overtook me. Tom and the eccentric professor had built this magnificent dirigible and hangared it in an ice cave (don't ask), when Coach Skaggs apprehended me. "Put that down and listen!" he hissed, and I abandoned poor Tom to his fate to listen to the preacher as he told of the nasty fate awaiting those who did not come forward, confess their sins and give their souls to ever-loving Jesus, who was willing to let bygones be bygones. Just last Sunday, he bawled, Brother Fleenor (all Baptists, I think, are brothers) failed to come forward, and paid the hideous price. "Oh, he sat on the back pew," related our would-be savior, "and the tears ran down his face as he recalled the sins of his life. But he would not come forward and give his soul to God. He hung back," And, as you might guess, on his way home he did not see the freight train backing up until too late. Of course, by the time they scraped poor Brother Fleenor out from under the train, dogs wouldn't have him for dinner, and since he had failed to get right with God, down to hell he went, and the preacher went to gruesome lengths to describe the screams of pain and agony issuing from the fiery pit.

"And now," he yodeled, "as we sing this one last verse from that beloved old hymn, 'Just as I am, without one plea, oh, lamb of God, I come to thee', won't you come? Won't you give your soul, let God wash away your sins and join in the everlasting joy of heaven? Won't you come?"

Hell, yes, I said, seeing the flames engulfing me and my sins, whatever they were, and down the aisle I fled, pursued by Bill and Jack Barton who were rumored to be guilty of real sin; at least Hubie Kirk said Jack jerked off in the bathroom. Jack said he was a damned liar and offered to fight, but we suspected Hubie was telling the dirty truth. My poor peter, the object of ridicule and scorn, was too immature to afford such pleasures, but I figured I could confess the rabbit tobacco if worse came to worst.

"Oh, glory," said the sin-flogger, as we threw ourselves on his mercy, "little lambs come home to God!" And the next Sunday they herded us lambs behind the pulpit and into the baptismal tank, where they put us into what looked like small hospital gowns and flopped us backward into the water. Some salvation! The preacher's hand slipped from my face and I got a nose full. I thought "This sonofabitch is going to drown me," but I survived, and we got dressed and returned to the admiring congregation. Smitty, our Sunday School teacher, gave us each a half-dollar, Uncle Doc added another, and I was rolling in dough. Grandma was proud. When the spring revival came around, we were all prepared to find glory and half-dollars again, but when the preacher hollered for us to come forward and we leaped from the pew, Coach Skaggs cut short our dash for heaven and half-dollars. "Sit down!" he snarled. "You done been saved." So much for purity. And grammar.

We lambs met in Jack Barton's room after our meeting with baptism and near-strangulation and resolved that from that day forward we would pray, read our Bibles, and shun sin. Redemption proved slippery, though, and within a week we were back up on the hill, smoking rabbit tobacco and wallowing in bad thoughts of girls and their organs. Nine or ten years later, I was passing through Pennington Gap on my way to UK and ran into—you guessed it—the girl who wanted an introduction to my equipment. Wow! A babe! Ten years had done good work. I had an impulse to offer her a private showing, but desisted. I think she remembered. She grinned.

***

If LBI was not enough, the next year Daddy took me with him when he went down to Houston, where he and Uncle Richard were going to pursue a scheme (one of a long line) guaranteed to make them rich. No doubt about it, as his name-sake, I was Daddy's favorite, and he was determined to give me the advantages of travel, which was fine with me. I have wondered if there is significance in the fact that I was never homesick a day in my life.

The trip to Houston was great. We stayed in a fancy hotel in Chattanooga, and I saw my first sea gulls and ocean-going ships in New Orleans. Uncle Richard lived out on the prairie, where he worked for the Seaboard Railroad, and though I was enrolled in John Marshall Junior High, I spent most of my days on the prairie, where I slaughtered, with the .410 shotgun they gave me, anything that moved—rabbits, birds, snakes. I became a pretty good shot, too, and, back home, when some boys from Wallsend, across the river, came across in a boat to attack us, I blasted away with my trusty weapon, making a nice noise and kicking up water alongside their attacking boat. They retreated. I suppose it didn't occur to me that I might kill somebody.

It was then, as I recall, that I skipped a grade. Daddy was forever trying to make the school people let me skip a grade, laboring apparently under the illusion that I was bright. I wasn't. I was average. I skipped fractions, and had trouble with them from then on. A couple of other events occurred in Pineville: for one thing, Daddy started whipping me. That was a mistake. I have no idea what I had done (he once threatened to "wear me out" if I brought home another B on my report card, and maybe that was it), but he got a switch and beat the hell out of me, as I screamed in pain and outrage at his betrayal. I hated him for it. The next time he did it—and again, I have no inkling of the cause—I cursed him every time he hit me; the more I cursed, the more he hit, until he finally left off, quivering with anger and astonishment. It was a horrible episode; I never really liked him after that. Some children take to punishment ("My old daddy took me to the woodshed many a time, and I bless him for it,") and some don't. I didn't.

I also shed religion, at least the Baptist version. Like the revival preacher at LBI, Brother Kelly, the Pineville preacher, shook hell in our faces each week without fail, describing in the most vivid terms the endless torment that awaited us on the other side of the grave. I began to have nightmares in which the fire engine would come down the street, siren screaming, warning us that the world was ending, and, sure enough, a hideous wall of flame was leaping over the crest of the mountain beyond the depot, rushing down upon the town and rolling down Virginia Avenue like a river of molten lava, as people fled screaming or were engulfed in the flames. But, as in dreams where I found myself naked on the courthouse square, I was unable to run, and awoke panting and sweating with fright.

A group of us had camped up near Lonesome Pine rock one night, and the next morning I went out to Turtleback (now called Chained Rock) to watch the day break and the fog rise from the town below, rolling down Harlan Valley and Straight Creek, covering the town and creeping up the sides of the mountain until it enveloped me, the rock and the world in a glistening coat of silver. I was awe-struck, caught in the beauty of it, wishing the moment never had to end, and feeling the magnificent gift of the earth that God had given us. Silently, I thanked him, thinking that a god who would give us such a morning could never throw us down into hell and punish us for small sins. All that stuff about sin and hell, I figured, was a bunch of shit, something grow-ups made up.

***

A friend of mine recently asked her son what he thought of his parents when he was ten or twelve years old. He thought on it and finally said he couldn't recall thinking much of anything. I think I was the same way. The world was divided between us and grown-ups. They were mainly providers, people we asked for things, sometimes getting them. Daddies went to work at different things, and mamas took care of the house. It was a good idea to keep away from them; they didn't let you do things, and it was best to go on and do them and hope you didn't get caught. Mine made me do things I didn't want much to do, but gave me stuff, too. It never occurred to me to ask if they loved me. I assumed they did. In fact, I can't recall ever hearing my mother say that she loved me, but there wasn't a day in my life that I was not aware of her love, draped around me like armor.

We boys made money by collecting bottles and selling them to the man at the "nigger" shack, sometimes getting enough for a NuGrape or a Nehi Orange. We collected copper wire, picked blackberries and sold them door to door. Miniature golf was making a big hit, so Jay and Fred Barlow and I built a peewee golf course and charged a nickel to play on it. It was a pretty good golf course, too; I wonder at our skill and perseverance. But then Jay and I got into a fight and tore up the course, each taking a ruined half. I liked Jay. He always fought fair. He is a friend to this day.

Daddy put me to work. I learned how to operate the Chandler and Price job presses, sitting on a high stool, and to melt and pig lead

95

for the Linotype. That was hot, dirty work that required the brains of a dog, but running the job press was something else. I got pretty good at it and was proud of my skill, turning out cards and posters for the candidates who seemed always running for office (Vote for J.L. Sizemore for Jailer. Mrs. Sizemore is a fine cook, and your loved ones will be taken good care of when they run into trouble. Elect Eb Taylor Sheriff. I lost a leg facing the Hun across the water, and I need the job.) The groceries and the town's one movie house also ordered hand-bills describing their offerings, and we would get the job of delivering them once they were printed. This was tedious but easy work, and sometimes paid as much as a quarter. We would put posters in all the cars, stores and offices around courthouse square, and then (shame!) stuff the remainder into a storm drain. But we got passes to the Satur-day afternoon cowboy movie, and the accompanying serial, in which The Green Archer saved the stupid girl who was tied up in a tower where a fuse was burning that was going to set off a keg of gunpowder and blow everything to hell and back. Buck Jones, Hoot Gibson, Fred Thompson—they don't make heroes like that any more.

The office job was not without excitement. One day the print-ers sent me around to Broughton's restaurant for a bucket of near beer, and on the way back I heard a shot and looked across the street to see people standing around a man who was down. They said the victim was a lawyer who had represented the shooter's wife in a divorce suit. Another time there was a mine explosion up at Kettle Island, and they brought four or five dead miners down to town and put them on the sidewalk outside Dr. Wilson's office, across the street from Daddy's office. They were covered with a tarpaulin. We went over to look. One man pulled up a corner of the tarp and showed a man who looked green and black, he had been so burned. I asked Roy Gibson, the printer, why men wanted to be miners, and he said they didn't have anything else to do.

Mining was tough. The operators and miners were always fight-ing because the mines were dangerous and the miners didn't get enough pay to live on. Usually the sheriff and his deputies were on the side of the operators and would beat up the miners and anyone who tried to help them. One time the Red Cross sent in a freight-car load of food for the Harlan miners' families, but the sheriff wouldn't let anybody open it, sent it back. Herndon Evans, who ran *The Pineville Sun*, which was better, I fear, than Daddy's *Cumberland Courier*, sided with the operators and warned that Communists were stirring up trouble among the miners. Daddy didn't take any position on it, though Mama, who ran the paper when Daddy was away getting rich, liked some of the union men. There was one named Peggy Dwyer, so named because he had lost a leg in the mines and had a peg leg. He came down to Pineville from Harlan, where they were having trouble, and stayed in a rooming house not far from the school. Some men hired by the operators came down to kill him and dynamited the boarding house, blew a whole corner off. It was the wrong corner, and Peggy wasn't there, anyhow.

***

There was violence around Pineville, but it didn't bother us. Neither did death. We first came into direct contact with death when Johnny Carter got sick. That didn't bother us much; kids were always getting sick with diphtheria, scarlet fever, flu. But then we saw the doctor and a lot of people going into the Carter's house across the street, and someone came over and said Johnny was dead. Ross Jones said he vomited up shit and died. We said "Jesus!" Brother Carter came over and sat on our porch and cried, and we sat with him, trying to make him feel better. Later we went to the funeral and stood with Brother and came home with him. Then we went down on the riverbank and dug in a cave we were making. Johnny was a good guy, but he was dead and there was nothing we could do about it. I think about that now when something happens at a school and the authorities send out a bunch of counselors to help the kids deal with their grief. We didn't get any counseling, which was just as well. I suspected, as I do now, that you don't deal with grief. You live with it and in time its sting fades and becomes part of memory and life.

The only real drawback to Pineville that I can recall was the river. It flooded. Fifty-one weeks a year it was a pretty, gentle stream where I swam, fished, paddled my boat and hunted frogs. But then, usually in spring, the word would be passed that trouble was on the way. "They had a cloudburst up Middlesboro," someone would report, and everyone would get on the phone to spread the warning. "Awful rain up at Harlan, town's under water. Better get ready," and within hours the river would start rising, turning brown with the topsoil washed down from Harlan or Yellow Creek, laden with debris, trees, lumber, outhouses. Someone would run down to the U-Tote-Em

97

and get groceries, while the rest of us rushed to carry as much furniture upstairs as we could move. Don and I would carry kindling and coal up for the grates that would be our only heat, and fill the bathtub with water for drinking. The girls would usually leave and go to stay with friends who lived up on the hillside streets, and Daddy would go down to the paper to move paper and typecases up on shelves and wrap the motors in axle grease, while at home we braced for the trial.

And then the river, foaming and swirling, would creep across the back yard, roaring as it poured into the basement, and then come creeping down the street. Once Don and I made a raft, and when the water came up to the front yard, paddled away. We quickly found, however, that the water had a mean current, and we were being washed away. We leaped off into waist-deep water and waded back to the house, while Mama, trembling, delivered a talk on youthful insanity. Later Don and I leaned from upstairs window and heaved lumps of coal at rats that were seeking shelter. Mama commented on that, too, pointing out the mental level of boys who wasted precious coal.

But the main battle against the water was waged to save the Knabe grand piano which dominated the living room and was the family pride. All together, we would lift one side, shove a book under a leg, then under another leg, and another, each time raising the piano until it teetered on volumes of *Tom Swift, The Bobbsey Twins,* Greek mythology. Then we would sit on the stairs, lighting candles in the night to watch the water rise on the books and then on the piano legs, praying that it would not get to the keyboard. As daylight broke, we could see that the water was not rising any more. The piano was safe. We gave a cheer.

One time a young woman who lived down at the low end of the street came to stay with us, carrying her baby and worrying about her husband, who had gone off in a boat carrying what could be moved. She must have been no more than a girl, and I remember how she looked as she sat by the window and watched the water rise on her house. As it finally rose over the roof, she put her head down on the window sill and cried.

But if anything was worse than a flood it was cleaning up after the flood. Our river had covered everything with six inches of slimy, sticky, smelly mud, and as fast as the water receded we attacked it, sweeping, hosing, pushing it out of the house, off the porch, across the sidewalk. It was hard work, and never quite successful; for weeks afterward, the house had that moldy smell, and bore high-water marks on the sides.

But nature heals as nature wounds, and soon the river would be back where it was supposed to be, the mud would dry and crack and blow away with the wind and the rain, and we would venture down to the riverbank, subtly changed, to search for treasures left by the raging waters. But my boat was swamped, ruined. We never salvaged it; before we could undertake the task, Daddy announced that we were moving to North Carolina, a town named Rutherfordton. I was horror-stricken. The idea of leaving Pineville, the mountains, the river, the clubhouse, the pasture down River Road where I took Maud the cow, the Asher's house, the swimming holes, all the wonderful things that were life itself, the thought of leaving was like the prospect of dying. On the fatal day I raced around the yard like a crazy child, down to the river, back to the clubhouse, too hurt to cry, wanting to touch everything for a last time. I had no way of knowing that we were heading to the happiest, most beautiful home I would ever know.

8

Madams, Morals, and Harvard

One of the most colorful of the characters who personified the newspapers of "the old days," including ours, was the "newsboy," not the noble youngster who rides around in the cold dawn tossing papers toward front porches, but the oft-bedraggled hawker who stood on street corners selling the last edition of the *Louisville Times* in the afternoon or the first edition of the *Courier-Journal* in the morning to folks plodding to and from work. Journalistic ethics played little part in this branch of the business. "Mayor caught in love nest," one would bellow, waving the sheet above his head, "Fire guts business district." The mayor, of course, had attended a wedding, and the incinerated business usually turned out to be a hot dog stand that had caught fire. Most people paid little attention, but occasionally a reader would complain that the Clark Bridge had not collapsed nor the Highlands been swept by fire, as the creative salesmen had claimed. "There's nothing in the paper about that," the indignant reader would protest.

"Don't look at me," he would reply. "I don't write it, I just sell it."

These raucous merchants of the street have, alas, been supplanted by metal boxes into which we drop more money than the product is worth, another small step in the replacement by machines of the human touch in a world that could use it. They yielded also to that old devil television, which has drawn the people who once opened the evening paper to the squawking screen that gives them snippets of news and commercials that blare at them whether they choose them or not.

But I digress. I have digressed at length, perhaps in part because what I was reporting was nice to remember, perhaps because the late fifties were the time of events some of which I would as soon forget. In 1955, I married again. That didn't work out. My new wife and Susie didn't get along. (Where have you heard that before?) A disaster. It made my first marriage look like the afternoon of a faun. As you may have surmised, marriage has not been among my more successful undertakings. I think it was Fielding who said that in every marriage there was a least one fool. In this one, I think there were two. Bert Combs once said that my greatest failing was a tendency to be erratic; "John Ed will do something brilliant one minute, and then turn around and do something absolutely adolescent." I fear that was correct. Ordinarily my judgment is fair or a little better, but when it comes to women I have made blunders that deserve places in Guinness. And this was one.

I don't approve of the Hollywood habit of making private lives public, and revealing details of one's sexual or love life, things that are cheapened by exposure. Affairs between two people are best left to the two. Still, I suppose I should offer some explanation, if not a full effort at justification. I met my second wife while she was working in the women's section of the *Courier-Journal*. She was a handsome young woman, tall and blonde, one of two daughters of a good Louisville family of some means, with a proper background of Louisville Collegiate School, Smith College and a successful debut, and a flair for music, painting and decor. We went out several times while the girls were visiting their mother in Connecticut, and, being relatively young, healthy and somewhat lonely, I was pleasantly surprised—indeed, astonished—when she began showing a serious interest in me. It occurred to me that she would be good for the girls, instructing them in matters of taste, dress and manners in ways I could not. There may be a clue in that.

She seemed taken with the girls in the weeks after they returned and before we were married, and they seemed fascinated with her. Marnie, especially, was overjoyed to have a woman in the house again. But the mutual fascination did not last long. The new wife knew little or nothing about housekeeping; she was accustomed to preparing smart little dishes for parties, but not three meals a day for a man and two growing girls. She resented it when Susie, who had become handy around house and kitchen, did not like what she cooked and offered suggestions. Susie, who was actually the better housekeeper and had been treated, I fear, somewhat as a helper, bristled at being treated like a small child, and an intrusive one. Both looked to me to put the other in her proper place. I knew I should support my wife and help her establish rules, but the truth was that what she demanded was often unreasonable, while what Susie asked made sense. Like so many men in a similar situation, I was in a corner. And I never really got out.

When our first daughter, Virginia, or Dinny, was born, things came to a head; my wife demanded in no uncertain terms that I send Susie to live with her mother. I was stunned, incredulous that anyone caring for me at all, and knowing my devotion to the girls, my fight for custody and my efforts to hold the family together as a single parent, would propose such a thing. But she insisted. It became a constant tension within the family. In a sense I could understand her attitude. Love between parent and child was not familiar territory for her. Her family was not close; she and her sister argued often and violently with their mother, and their father was sometimes violent toward them. They had never been pushed together, as had my family, by hard times and the need to keep up appearances. And they had never played and worked together as had the girls and I.

But Susie's mother was only recently married, and perhaps not eager to spring two daughters on her new husband. Susie and I grew together as a sort of group within the group, a natural but unhealthful situation. Those first two years were not exactly a prolonged honeymoon. It was hard to reconcile the lovely and charming woman my wife could be when there were only the two of us, and the woman who would propose such a cruel thing to me and, worse, to Susie. I would have tried laying down the law but was afraid it would only increase the tension. And I had little option to trying to make things work. Even had I wanted to, and I did not, though the thought crept in now and then, I could not say so long and walk out. I had three girls to support, no way to support two houses if I took my girls and moved out. The first two years were difficult.

Two years after we married we got a break. I applied for and won a Nieman Fellowship to Harvard, and off we went to Cambridge, Mass. for what was easily among the most gratifying years of my life. In case you are interested, the Nieman Fellowships are awarded each year to ten or twelve journalists, most of them Americans, but with a smattering of newsmen from other countries, who are selected after review of their applications and personal interviews by a board. The few who are chosen are given a year at Harvard, where they are free to take any and all courses they wish, in the hope that this will make them better journalists and the world a better place. The Fellowships were established when Joseph Nieman, publisher of the *Milwaukee Journal*, proposed to give money to Harvard with which to establish a school of journalism. Harvard didn't care to do that, perhaps believing that journalism was not a bona fide profession (they were probably right if they did). Instead, they established the foundation that grants the fellowships each year, with a curator who heads up the program and designs a schedule to make the year even more valuable and pleasant for the Fellows.

A Nieman Fellowship is, in my opinion, the greatest thing that can happen to a newspaperman. Journalists need, as much as other professionals (whether their calling is a profession or a trade is a matter for pointless debate) an occasional sabbatical where they can confer with others of their craft and listen to people of learning and experience, without the pressures of deadlines or daily production. Is this better than a journalism school? Probably. Most journalism schools (about half a dozen are exceptions) waste young people's time and mental energy on trade topics when they should be gaining a broader liberal education and appreciation of the language. I think I learned more from people in the field and my collegiate peers than I did in journalism classrooms before I transferred to a major in history and political science. What knowledge of language I gained came from reading, the single greatest source of knowledge, and from men such as Grant Knight and Willis Tucker, God bless their memories.

The Nieman is a wonderful year. We had a fine group of Fellows, including Tom Wicker, Stanley Karnow, Dean Brelis, Peter Kumpa, Simmons Fentress and Jack Jurey. Barry Bingham, a great believer in the program, had given me a generous living allowance, in addition to my salary and the stipend that goes with the award, so we could live and entertain comfortably. It was total immersion in the world of the intellect. Some people said that I was making a mistake in not concentrating on a particular field of study, and perhaps they were right, but I chose to spend my days listening to lectures in any field that interested me, from economic history to Constitutional law and comparative religion, figuring that I could do the reading when I got home, whereas I would never again have the opportunity to hear Frank Friedel, Arthur Schlesinger, Jr., Robert Woodruff, and the fascinating group of scholars to whom we were exposed. I had a handsome office in Adams House that I shared with Bernard Bailen, now a famed historian. It was better than any office I have had since.

During the first few weeks before my wife and child arrived, Barry and Mary invited me out to their home at Chatham, on Cape Cod, where they lived for much of the summer, and once my dinner companion was Rear Admiral Eliot Morrison, former Harvard history professor, official Navy historian and author of the History of Naval Operations in World War II. I was awed. Fortunately, I had read most of his fifteen volumes on the war and was able to make some feeble conversation. Curiously, Sallie Bingham, still in college, was introduced and drawn into the circle by her father, who obviously was pleased with her, possibly because she was preparing to be a writer, a career I think Barry would have preferred. Barry was a fine editorial writer and took the task very seriously, but he liked more, I think, writing such original things as editorial notebooks. He had a little cubbyhole off his main office, and when he emerged from there with a piece of writing in hand, he glowed. There was really a radiance about him. He loved to write. He wrote a novel in his first year out of Harvard, but deemed it so bad that he would not try again. Unfortunate. Perhaps he should have been poor, and obliged to try again. When the stomach growls, you discover talents.

Dignitaries from government and academe came to dine and talk with the Fellows. In the afternoons we would often gather at a coffee house near the Yard to drink and argue. Henry Kissinger, then a professor at MIT, would sometimes join us, or rather, we would find him sitting there and gather around him. He was delightful, arrogant and articulate, deft at defending policies, with most of which we disagreed, then and later. A few years ago I sat next to Kissinger at a Derby party given by Marylou Whitney at her farm near Lexington, reminded him of our Harvard talks, and admitted that we found him interesting but arrogant. "Oh, I was not really arrogant at that point," he said, chuckling. "I was just learning."

Marnie and Susie went to live with their mother in Connecticut for the year; my current wife and I already had one daughter, Virginia, or Dinny, and another, Betsy, was born while we were in Cambridge. With Dick Harwood's help we found a plain but roomy first-floor apartment in adjacent Arlington, and I caught the Mass Avenue bus down to Harvard each morning. We had a busy social life. One afternoon each week the Foundation sponsored a beer and coffee party to which some member of the faculty would be invited to speak. Sitting in his precise, brilliant lectures, I had gotten the impression that Arthur Schlesinger, Jr. was a rather cold, aloof man, but at the beer busts he was easy, informal and charming, crackling with wit and insight. Once a month we would have a formal dinner, sometimes as guests, sometimes as hosts to publishers or public officials who would address us on national and world topics and then discuss interests with us.

In addition, we entertained a lot within the group. Barry came up, and we had a cocktail party for him. Everyone was intrigued with the publisher of the great *Courier-Journal*, and he showed a great interest in the Niemans. We got tickets to rehearsals of the Boston Symphony for, as I recall, fifty cents, and were welcomed by many of the clubs in town. We also had access to the Harvard gym, and David Lawson, a likeable Nieman from New Zealand, and I went over frequently, both liking exercise. After the snow began, several of us would go up to Stowe on weekends to ski, in the fall we took weekend tours through the famed autumnal colors of New Hampshire and Vermont, and in spring along the rocky, historic North Shore.

Everything was exhilarating. It was a wrench to face the end of the year and a return to honest work. I will never forget Harvard. Its greatness rests, of course, in its faculty, libraries and laboratories, but there is an atmosphere of tradition and devotion to scholarship about the place that appeals to the spirit as well as the intellect.

My one regret was that I did not get along too well with Louis Lyons, the venerated Nieman curator, ordinarily adored by newsmen. He seemed to regard me strangely from the first day, when I asked advice on finding housing and transportation. Perhaps he considered that beneath him, and told me I was on my own.

But it was a fine year, and I returned full of great expectations. The girls returned from having spent the year with their mother, a generous act on her part, and we bought a new, larger house on Blankenbaker Lane—a move upward. A strange thing happened while we were contemplating the move: Barry called me in and confided, enthusiastically, that Dave Beard was moving from his home in Glenview, just across from the Bingham home, and that his house would be for sale. I looked at him as though waiting for the punch line, and he continued that the price was very good, and he thought I could get the place for around $100,000. I saw that he was serious, and wondered how in the name of sanity he expected me to afford such a home on what he was paying me. I was making at the time about ten thousand a year. Did he not know how much I was making? Or did he have such a poor understanding of the facts of employee life that he didn't know that the price was, for me, absurd? I thanked him but said that I didn't think I could quite swing it just then. He asked if my wife's family was not willing to help, apparently unaware that I was not one of their favorite things.

Tom Wicker and I had become friends at Harvard, as had my wife and Tom's wife Neva, and we were pleased when Tom called from North Carolina and said he was coming to Louisville to talk to Barry about a job. Barry told him that there was no opening just then on the editorial staff, but that he could have a reporting job until there was one. Tom accepted, and he and Neva stayed with us while they looked for a house. But before they could get settled, Wally Carroll called from Nashville and offered an editorial post, and Tom very wisely took it. I hated to see him go; he was bright and fine company. But after he had been in Nashville only months, Carroll was hired by *The New York Times* for its Washington bureau, and asked Tom to join him. Tom was on his way.

That year, 1958, also saw the arrival of Hugh Haynie. Grover Page had been planning for some time to retire, and one day at conference Barry announced that he had hired a young cartoonist from North Carolina named Hugh Haynie and asked me to show him around and help him find a house. I showed him through neighborhoods I thought a young cartoonist could afford and was surprised when he seemed dissatisfied with all of them and settled on an impressive white house on a corner lot in Indian Hills. It appeared that he had family money from a fishing business in the Chesapeake Bay. He was a pleasant enough sort, but reserved and self-confident. He soon brought along a short, pretty, dark-haired quite pregnant wife named Lois, and they were at once well-liked, giving good parties.

Hugh quickly put his mark on the paper, becoming enormously popular almost overnight. His mail was heavy, and requests poured in from public figures and private individuals asking for originals of his cartoons. He had a distinctive style, bold, carefully crafted, and clever, and he buried in each cartoon the name of his wife, Lois. I thought that was gimmicky, not befitting the artist he was, but people loved it, loved to pore over the drawing until they found Lois' name. I wondered at the time what he would do should he and Lois part company, a conjecture which proved prophetic.

It soon became evident that Hugh operated on a higher plane than the rest of the staff. Several of us had asked from time to time for improvements to our offices, but were told, in brief, that it really wasn't necessary. I had long wanted some bookshelves, and watched enviously as workmen came, tore Hugh's office apart, paneled it and filled it with furniture to fit his cartoonist needs. The favorite son.

Hugh was not what you would call a team player; he did not eat lunch with the rest of us and was seldom at editorial conference, disappearing into his office in the morning and usually emerging late in the afternoon, when he showed Russell his cartoon for the day—for Russell's inspection, not approval.

Another event occurred in 1959, seemingly innocent, that was to cost me dearly. Wilson Wyatt, head of the law firm of Wyatt, Grafton and Sloss, a former mayor and chief counsel for the Bingham companies, decided to run for Governor. Urbane and well spoken, with a polished air and a rich, rolling voice, he had a sparkling record, both locally and with the Roosevelt administration in Washington, where he had been postwar housing expediter, and a founder of Americans for Democratic Action, a liberal group formed to give liberal Democrats an alternative to Henry Wallace's left-wing Progressive Party.

Barry asked me if I would mind helping Wilson with his campaign, doing some writing and so forth. This was not unusual. In prewar days, especially in the South, when a newspaper endorsed a candidate it often lent him a reporter or writer to help with speeches, policy papers and the like. Barry didn't tell me to help Wilson; rather he asked me if I would like to do so. I decided I would, (I often wondered what would have happened had I said that, no, I didn't care to) and the next evening Dick Harwood and I went to Wilson's home and wrote his platform. Just like that. I knew what he wanted and knew how to phrase it. No big deal.

Wilson was challenging Harry Lee Waterfield, Happy Chandler's lieutenant governor, whom we had once supported against Earle Clements but whom we opposed when he joined forces with Chandler. But Harry Lee was only part of the problem. No sooner had Wilson announced than Bert Combs, who had run against Chandler in 1955 and lost, announced that he was also in the race. Wilson was indignant at Bert's announcement. He had thought that he had Bert's assurance that he was not going to run, and Wilson was expecting his support. In Wilson's camp, we joined in the denunciation of Combs.

His announcement changed the picture radically; it was soon apparent that if both Wilson and Bert stayed in the race they would split the anti-Chandler vote and Harry Lee would win. It was a bad situation; Bert and Wilson shared a more liberal philosophy of government and had no solid grounds on which to oppose each other. Though they bad-mouthed each other good-naturedly, Democrats who supported Wilson were friends of those supporting Bert, and vice versa. Both, of course, were willing for the other to drop out of the race, or take second spot, and there seemed to be no acceptable compromise. Constant talks between supporters produced nothing. Meanwhile, Harry Lee was conducting a smooth and effective campaign, with the help (or at least the contribution) of Happy Chandler, who could not resist the temptation to get into a race. Happy was flaying Wilson as "Ankle Blankets," implying that Wilson was a city slicker who wore spats, and ridiculing Bert, again, as "the little judge." "I thought I beat him bad enough last time to teach him a lesson," Happy would say. "Guess we'll just have to do it again; he don't learn real fast."

Earle Clements saw what was happening and decided to take a hand. In a showdown meeting at the Standford Field motel, he produced poll results that showed that Wyatt was running a poor third, and that Harry Lee was winning. He convinced Wilson that he could not win, and persuaded him to run for lieutenant governor on a ticket with Bert, promising that the combined ticket would endorse the Wyatt platform and carry out his plans for the state. An agreement was reached and Earle called Bert, who was speaking at Mount Sterling. Bert raced back and, with Clements beaming from the wings, he and Wyatt made a joint announcement to the media.

At the time, it made little difference to me. I had been working with Wyatt, now I worked for the two of them, though most of my work was still with Wyatt, since Combs had Ed Prichard, the best in the business, working for him, writing his speeches. I had met Combs briefly when he was running against Happy in 1955, but was not very impressed. Combs was not your ideal candidate. A former circuit and appellate judge, he was quiet, slow-smiling, almost shy. When Happy Chandler entered a room, everyone was aware of it; within thirty seconds he had hugged, kissed, shaken hands and exchanged confidences with everyone in the place, laughing and shouting, calling people by name. Bert sidled into a room as though he was intruding. He was not a good political speaker, spoke with a definite ridge-runner, Eastern Kentucky accent and sawed the air with an earnest, awkward motion, in sharp contrast to Wyatt's rich, rolling voice and dignified bearing. Later, when I was writing speeches for him, Bert said, with a grin but seriously, "Keep it to twenty minutes. Nobody's going to listen to this voice of mine for longer than that."

But after following him for a while I saw that Bert had learned. He had gained self-confidence on the stump, become a better speaker, able to work a little humor into his talks, and a smoother politician. And eventually I saw what I and others had been slow to see, that beneath the reticent surface was a moral sincerity and a sharp intellect, a wide knowledge of history and the law, and more vision of the state's needs and future than I had ever encountered in a candidate. Together, he and Wyatt waged a hard campaign, won by a relatively small margin and were inaugurated in ceremonies that heard Happy warn that he would be back, an announcement the Combs crowd booed lustily. And Bert Combs became, in my opinion, the best governor Kentucky ever had.

Barry had been skeptical of Bert, but was soon won over, especially after Bert asked approval of a sales tax to support a bond issue with which to pay a bonus to state veterans, but then used the bulk of the money on a broad program that revolutionized state education. Indeed, in his first months in office he moved so fast in so many directions that Harwood characterized his first legislative session as "a quiet revolution." Included in the revolution was a plan to expand and modernize the state parks system, build the first four-lane highway into Eastern Kentucky, create the Kentucky Educational Television network and a system of community colleges. Wilson headed up a division devoted to economic development, a promotional post in which he was happy.

A few weeks after he took office Bert came to Barry and asked if he would free me to be Conservation Commissioner, knowing Barry's interest in the environment. Barry said he couldn't spare me for four years, and Combs then asked if I could serve on a board he was going to appoint to oversee the expansion of the parks. Barry consented, on the condition that board members not be paid, a provision that won me little thanks from the other board members, former highway commissioner Henry Ward, and Herndon Evans, former editor of the *Lexington Herald*. I think Herndon, a basically conservative man, looked somewhat askance at me, whom he probably remembered only as a boisterous urchin running around Pineville and later as a voice of the liberal *Courier-Journal*. But we joined in support of development of Pine Mountain State Park near Pineville and gradually got along well.

And that began one of the most interesting periods of my life. The legislature passed a $20,000,000 bond issue for the program (a lot of money in 1960), and Bert asked us simply to work as fast as we could, get the most for our money and keep free of politics or anything that could be criticized as political favoritism. I think we did that. As far as I know, there was never a squeak of scandal or charges of politics. We chose the best architects and contractors we could find, with no consideration to political party, and demanded only that the construction be carried out expeditiously. The park system today stands as evidence of our work, and I am proud I had a hand in it.

But by taking the state post, though it paid nothing and actually cost me money I could not afford, I incurred a lot of criticism within the *Courier* organization. In Barry's day, and in my early days, involvement in politics by journalists was not exceptional, and widely accepted. Snooks Crutcher, of Morehead, Orville Baylor of Paris or Gracean Pedley of Princeton were always ready to help Happy Chandler, as Tyler Munford was eager to work for Earle Clements. Barry had been active in both of Adlai Stevenson's campaigns, in which both Jim Pope, Jr. and I had worked. Mark Ethridge and Jim Pope came to loggerheads over the Senate race between Wilson Wyatt and Thruston Morton. But a new group was coming along to whom objectivity was a shibboleth and avoidance of conflict of interest an obsession.

And they were probably right. Objectivity is a rare talent, but I am not sure it is always a virtue. I think it was Walter Lippman who first demanded objectivity on the part of newsmen; before that reporters painted with a broader brush, and educator John Dewey held that reporters should tell the story behind the facts as well as the pertinent facts, a philosophy now in some disfavor.I doubt that the controversy surrounding it will ever be settled.

In writing speeches for Bert, I was violating the new rules, though I was also obeying my publisher. But in small ways the paper suffered, in that readers had one more reason to suspect that the it was guilty of a conflict of interest. Happy Chandler made sure no one overlooked the situation. Combs, he said, couldn't write or give a speech himself and had to rely on me. (Prich had returned to his law practice after the election.) "Pearce will write him a speech," Happy would say, "and Combs will stumble through it, and then Pearce will race back to Louisville and write an editorial about what a fine speech it was. You could say it's the shortest double-play in history: Pearce to Combs to Pearce." They don't make them like Happy any more.

On the other hand, even had I wanted to, Barry would not have permitted me to distort facts or our editorials because of my links to Combs. This became painfully clear during the episode that became known as "the truck deal." Bert had named Earle Clements highway commissioner. We and many others objected, fearing that Clements would let politics govern the Highway Department, at the time the largest and most important department of state government, but Combs really didn't have much choice. Earle had plucked him out of obscurity, had elbowed Wilson out of the race for first place, and had for all practical purposes furnished the margin of votes that made Bert governor. And Earle wanted the highway post.

Earle had contracted for a number of heavy-duty trucks—actually built for loads heavier than state highways would permit—from Thurston Cooke, a genial Louisville car dealer who had helped in the campaign, and was a close friend of Wilson's. They were used trucks, but they cost as much as new trucks of lower weight capacity would have cost, and there were loud criticisms, especially from the Frankfort bureau of the *Courier-Journal*, of the apparent political purchase. We demanded that Bert rescind the purchase. We also criticized his appointment of Earle, who, we had reason to suspect, wanted control of the politically influential Highway Department to build support for Lyndon Johnson at the approaching Democratic presidential nominating convention. I had to write those critical editorials. Bert knew it and understood that I had to make them as tough and effective as possible. Eventually he got rid of Earle. Though we had demanded it in the name of morality and clean living, I think that was a mistake, and that we had been wrong. It tore apart the liberal wing of the Democratic Party, and probably cost Bert re-election. But that was our official policy, and it was my job to enunciate it. Which brings up an interesting point: should an editorial writer write from conviction, or on order? It is a question that invites hypocrisy, not to mention a good deal of self-aggrandizement.

Shortly after WW II, a rascal (a very accomplished and professional rascal) was discovered writing editorials for the liberal *Collier's* magazine, and at the same time doing the same for one of our more conservative newspapers. Indignation flared among self-righteous editorial writers who swore loudly that they would never violate their own principles if ordered to do so by the boss. They would quit first. I have an idea that this was 90 percent crap. Editorial writers, especially those on good papers, cling to their word processors with claws of steel; as the old song goes, a good job nowadays is hard to find.

But, cynicism aside, it does pose problems. No man likes to see his paper take a position opposite his own beliefs. Barry had an unwritten law that no writer should undertake an editorial with whose position he did not agree, a good policy. Yet, when the manpower ox was in the ditch I have written editorials about which I was ambivalent, and done the best job I was capable of for two reasons; I felt that when Barry was absent, I should try to do as he would do. Further, I found later that when we disagreed, events would prove him right a majority of the time. And he had the cooler head, the better judgment.

I was reminded of this once when, during his second administration, Happy Chandler went to Chicago as Kentucky's favorite son, hoping for a presidential nomination. It was obvious from the beginning that he had no chance, but Happy believed, and very sincerely, that he was fated for great things, including the presidency, and he worked the convention like a Kentucky barbecue. The eastern press made great fun of him, referring to him as "old cornpone," with a smile like ham fat "with collard greens on the side," and we, like many Kentuckians, were unhappy about the episode. When the convention was ending, I wrote a short editorial saying, in effect, it's over, Happy, come on home. As George Burt said when I handed it in, it was brilliant but vicious, using ridicule like a stiletto. And totally unfair. The target of a personal attack by an editorial has no recourse; he does not even know for sure who his attacker was. Of all the editorials I ever wrote, it was one of the best done, and the one I most regretted having written. And when Barry returned a few days later, he told me in cold terms that he did not approve. We do not attack personalities, he said, we attack policies. He was right. I didn't do that again, though tempted.

Fortunately, I had to write few editorials about the Democratic race. The convention nominated not Johnson but young John F. Kennedy, who became the king of Camelot and the idol of the younger generation. I liked Kennedy; I met him once in Washington, when I was visiting Senator John Sherman Cooper, and was impressed with his looks and energy, but feared he was a handsome lightweight. I was glad at the time that he won and considered him decidedly superior to Richard Nixon. But I have since come to believe that Johnson would have made a better President, and was, in his turn, a better one, despite having to carry Kennedy's (and Eisenhower's) legacy of Vietnam. The Hippies hurled excrement and screamed "Hey, hey, LBJ, how many kids did you kill today?" But the fault could better have been placed on Kennedy's doorstep. From the beginning, Johnson saw the danger of our involvement in Vietnam and looked in vain for a way out.

But I was embroiled in state, not national, affairs. I was soon acting as something of a messenger, a go-between. Barry would call me into his office and say, in effect, "Do you plan to see Combs any time soon?" (as if he didn't know), and I would say yes, and he would say, "Why don't you suggest that he do...(so and so.)" I'd jump in my car, whip over to Frankfort, into the governor's office and say, "Barry mentioned to me that...so and so...and I thought you might like to know it." Bert would say, "Do you expect to be talking to Bingham any time soon?" (as if he didn't know,) and I'd say yes, I suppose, and he'd say, "Why don't you suggest to him...so and so?" Into the car, back to Louisville, into Barry's office. "Combs thinks maybe it would be a good idea to...so and so."

It was not a bad technique. Bert, sensitive to the influence of the *Courier-Journal* and the importance of its support of his programs, wanted to keep on Barry's good side and have a chance to explain his moves before criticism developed. Barry wanted to make his views plain to Bert without appearing to interfere. Indeed, I suspected that it was for this reason and not my great intellect or administrative ability that Bert wanted me in the Parks job, and why Barry was willing to have me there. In this way they both accomplished their goals and managed to keep aware of the other's plans without anyone becoming committed. The state, I am confident, benefited from it. I didn't, except that I gradually came to admire and respect Bert Combs above almost anyone, and managed, after he left office, to form with him a most valued friendship. And that was worth the beating I took because of it.

We don't have many deep, lasting friendships, and I treasure my memories of him. We had good times together in Florida, on St.

John Island, at his farm in Powell County. When he became a federal judge I used to fly with him, and he would let me read cases he was considering and ask me how I would decide them, knowing how much I liked Constitutional law and interpretation. And his advice was invaluable. When I was uncertain on some point of state law or politics, I could always drive up to Lexington for lunch or to his farm for the weekend and have the advantage of his knowledge and judgment. His mind was not as mercurial or his knowledge as wide-ranging as Ed Prichard's, but it was more judicious, and more compassionate. I miss them both, but Bert most of all.

9

The News Behind the News

Of the people who came to the papers while I was there, I suppose Norman Isaacs made the most instant impact. No matter where he went, he left prints, and when he came to the *Louisville Times* as managing editor he brought others with him who also left their marks, men such as Dick Harwood, who left to join the *Washington Post*, Bob Schulman, who became media critic for the *Times*, and Geoffrey Vincent, the short, smiling, bustling former assistant to Lester Markel, tough Sunday editor of *The New York Times*. Born in England, Geoff had had a widely varied career by the time he came to Louisville to head up the *Courier's* Sunday Department. He contributed a lot to the papers and in turn got a very shoddy deal.

Isaacs was a charger. I think he nurtured the image of a bright, tough, hard-bitten, hard-driving, capable newspaperman, which he was. No-nonsense Norman. He did not endear himself to many people, but those who liked him liked him very much and respected him for his ability, which he had in good measure. I did not like him, and, I think, with reason. He was another of the people on whom I did not make a good first impression. I don't know why. There apparently is, or was, something about my personality that rubbed some people wrong. Buddy Atkinson shared my view of Norman and was regarded much the same.

Shortly after Norman arrived, we were attending a party at Joe Creason's home. I mentioned to Norman that I would like to fly the company plane when it was not being used for photographic jobs. He seemed to find it incredible that I could fly; I had been going out to Bowman Field, usually in the mornings before work, and had renewed my private pilot's license. Norman dismissed this, saying rather brusquely that Billy Davis, our chief photographer, was our pilot. Later, I was in a group discussing I forget what, and added my bit of wisdom, upon which Norman whirled on me and said, "You don't know anything about this." "Probably not," I replied. "I was agreeing with you." Not a wise move. He turned away.

Norman certainly had a sound career. Born in England, he moved to Canada and then to Indiana with his parents, began work on the *Indianapolis Times*, where he rose to be managing editor, then quit to become chief editorial writer for the *Indianapolis News* before he resigned to become managing editor of the *St. Louis Star-Times*. When he came to Louisville, staffers who did not like him joked that they hoped he would not sink the *Louisville Times* as he had sunk the *Star-Times*, but the facts were different. He had run a good paper in St. Louis until the publisher, who knew more about drinking than publishing, sold the paper to the *St. Louis Post-Dispatch* without giving anyone notice. That left the staffers shocked and stranded. According to Geoffrey Vincent, who had gone from New York to join Isaacs in St. Louis, Norman got on the phone and sat at his desk, day and night, until he had found jobs for every single member of his staff. In the world of journalism—or in the business world generally, I suppose— you do not very often find loyalty from the top down like that.

The only problem that I could see with Norman was that he seemed to be eternally politicking, conniving. He made people around him uneasy, wondering what he was up to, what he might do to them. It was rumored that Norman was out to undercut Jim Pope as executive editor; when he became executive editor, it was said that he was trying to undercut Mark Ethridge and had persuaded Worth Bingham, when he was breaking in Worth to take over, that Mark drank too much. When Mark retired, in 1963, these rumors persisted, and may have been the source of gossip, repeated by authors writing about the Bingham family. As usual, the gossip was ridiculous. Barry said at the time that Mark had asked to retire two years earlier, but had been urged to stay on until Worth and Barry, Jr. could get their feet on the ground. In the summer of 1963, Harry Guggenheim, editor and publisher of *Newsday*, the nation's largest suburban daily, asked Mark to become editor. They had been friends for years, and both relished the idea of a new venture. But Mark had also been offered the post of director and lecturer in journalism at the University of North Carolina, and he asked Guggenheim and was granted the right to lecture there one day a week while running *Newsday*. And he remained a director of the Courier and Times Company. So much for gossip.

***

Norman attended editorial conference, which was significant. Jim Pope had seldom attended and then offered little unless asked, content to run the news organization of the two papers. Norman was not reticent about offering opinions. He differed with me on occasions when there was neither need nor justification (or so it seemed to me). Once while I was on vacation, he raised objection to an editorial I had written, and Russell published what amounted to a retraction, the first and only time that an editorial of mine prompted retraction in over 20 years of editorial writing. I had written a harmless short filler, quoting Newton Minow, Federal Communications Commissioner, to the effect that radio stations were turning opinion programs over to people of dubious qualification instead of airing their own opinion programs and taking responsibility for opinions expressed. Norman got a call from a station manager at Fort Knox taking issue with this, protesting that his station regularly aired editorials, and Norman stormed into conference denouncing the editorial as half-baked and demanding a retraction.

But there was no denying that he brought in good men, and he made the *Times* a serious rival of the *Courier-Journal*, to which it had long played second fiddle, at least in reputation. As a matter of fact, the *Times* had for years had a larger circulation than the *Courier*, and had produced more revenue. While the *Courier* was the flagship, and the focus of Bingham pride, the *Times* blanketed Louisville and the immediate shopping area, and was for that reason a better advertising medium than the *Courier*, much of whose circulation was out in the state, giving it more influence in statewide affairs and political circles.

But I got the feeling that Norman would like to see me go somewhere else, and I was wary around him, though we never clashed openly. Nevertheless, a couple of times when I got offers to go elsewhere, I was tempted. I was unsure of my position and saw no future in continuing in the editorial department. This feeling took firmer root one afternoon when Mark glanced at the editorial page proof and asked me to sit down. Mincing few words, he advised me to resign from the department and either get a job in the newsroom or go to another paper, since there was no evident future for me in editorial. This shook me, partly because I did not know whether he just wanted to get rid of me or because he was sincerely concerned.

I revered Mark Ethridge, though I felt that he was not overly fond of me; he intimated at a party one night that I was lucky to be where I was, not having paid my dues in the newsroom. And I felt that he had become somewhat disillusioned in his final years on the paper. In 1938, when he spoke to us at the University of Kentucky, he delighted us by declaring that good reporters and writers should be paid what they were worth, rather than being rewarded with promotions that usually made them sub-editors and removed them from reporting and writing where they could be of greatest service to readers. But in the early sixties, when reporters on the *Times* led an effort to organize the papers under the Newspaper Guild, Ethridge fought them bitterly. "If you want to deal with me at arm's length," he told the movement leaders, "so be it."

It was an unhappy time. It didn't affect us on the editorial staff much, since editorial writers were considered extensions of the publisher, paid to express his views, and directly dependent on him for pay levels, but we had friends on both sides of the fight. Joe Creason, I remember, was more or less the leader of the anti-Guild employees, earning the dislike of a lot of his fellows. The Guild effort sputtered out, but the fact that the newsroom people had felt that a union was necessary to protect them dimmed the image of generous, if paternalistic employers. I doubt if morale was ever quite as high afterward.

A few days after my conversation with Mark, I mentioned to Barry that it had been suggested that I might do better to get into news and asked him what he would advise. He seemed surprised, and said certainly not, that I would do better where I was. But I had a friend in the *Time-Life* organization who had asked me if I would like to come to New York. I thought carefully about it for some time, but decided not to. Then the Kennedy campaign came along. Jim Wine, a friend of mine from UK days with whom I had kept touch, joined the Kennedy organization, and managed the anti-anti-Catholic campaign. This put him in a sound position for some post when JFK took over, and he proposed to me that we form a public-relations firm with offices in Washington and Frankfort; he would handle the former, where the opportunity for political lobbying was obvious, and I would handle the Frankfort office. He said he had sufficient backing to finance the undertaking through its lean initial years.

This intrigued me. I felt in a rut that was getting deeper. I could see nothing rosy in the immediate future. And I heard constantly at home about the manner in which we had to live for want of money. Doing without had become a burden for me. We lived in a beautiful home, but I was constantly fielding complaints that others had what we didn't. Dinny and Betsy were getting older and would soon need lessons and advantages we couldn't afford. I was tired of having to scrimp. For years I had taken ten dollars each Monday morning to cover my expenses during the week, lunches, parking and, until I finally quit, cigarettes. I was constantly going over my limit, and still couldn't afford a beer after work.

So I wrote Barry a note, told him what I was considering, assured him that it was not because of job dissatisfaction, and promised to give sufficient notice if I decided to leave. He called me in and told me that he thought I would make a mistake to leave, that my future lay in journalism and that he could see no reason why it should not be bright. And he added, "As you know, we don't make commitments in these situations, but I want you to know that I have never had anyone in mind for editor but you." He also gave me a sizable raise, and I decided to stay, though I resented somewhat the fact that I got the much-needed raise only when I threatened to leave.

***

Jim Wine went on to become Ambassador to Luxembourg, and then came back to the State Department. Nice fellow. Shortly after college he had married Emmy Lou Turk, daughter of Centre President Charles Turk, and for a while practiced law in Pikeville. But after he left the State Department they bought a small farm in Virginia, not too far from Washington. Then Emmy Lou died and Jim, at loose ends, took a house in Danville, near Emmy's old home, and we visited frequently. Then, suddenly and without notice, he left, went back to Washington and died.

I settled into my rut at the *Courier*. But changes were being made that would change the nature of the paper. In 1962 Jim Pope retired as executive editor, quietly and without much explanation. Later there were the usual rumors about the causes of his leaving. One writer said that Ethridge had fired him because he objected when Norman hired a black woman, Charlayne Hunter, later Hunter-Gault of the McNeil-Lehrer News Hour. Jimmy Pope, Jr. denied this hotly. "That is absurd!" he said. "For God's sake! My father was executive editor of two major newspapers. Why would he concern himself with a girl summer intern? As far as Ethridge firing him, that's even worse. Mark and Dad were close friends, before and after they left the papers. Mark and Willie Snow used to visit my parents in Panama City (Florida) every year, and they visited the Ethridges in North Carolina.

"As for why Dad quit, the only thing I know is that he told me that he was sick of having Norman go over his head to Barry; he said he was eligible and ready for retirement, and that he didn't like the fact that Barry permitted Norman to go around him, didn't want to get into that kind of office politics."

But there were reasons for suspicion about Pope's attitude toward Hunter. I never heard anyone, in management or staff, comment on Hunter except to say that she was not lacking in self-esteem. I met her only casually, and formed no opinion.

Jim Pope, Sr. was an old-school Southerner, charming and courteous in private life, but cool toward racial integration, and opposed to what later became affirmative action, giving a person an advantage on the basis of race when it came to hiring. By today's standards he was undoubtedly racist, though by some extremist standards anyone who holds that Snow White and Frosty the Snowman were not black are blood brothers of Simon LeGree. George Gill, probably the most objective executive on the papers in my time, told a story to illustrate Pope's racism. Just after the North Carolina drugstore sit-ins by black students, some local students decided to try to break the color line in Louisville with a similar sit-in at a Fifth Street restaurant. It was an interesting story. The students made the mistake of indulging in rowdy conduct, unlike the decorous Carolina students, squirting mustard across the counter at waiters and so on. The cops came and threw them out. Gill went back to the office, wrote the story and handed it to the City Desk. Later he asked the desk man where the story was and was told there was no story.

"What do you mean?" asked Gill. "That's a helluva good story." The editor shook his head. "There's no story," he said. "Pope says there's no story, so there's no story."

At the same time, Pope was a stickler for style-book democracy. (Practically every newspaper follows a book outlining rules governing punctuation, spelling, word usage, sentence structure, verb tense, etc.) At the time, we had two prominent madams in town, keepers of houses of prostitution, Betty Moran and Anna Haynes. A story appeared in the paper naming Anna in the lead, or first paragraph, but referring to her later as "the Haynes woman." When Pope saw it, he charged from his office with fire in his eyes.

"We do not," he snapped, "refer to a female as "the woman." The style book says that she shall be called Miss or Mrs. and that's what we do. I don't care if she's the lowest whore in town, you will follow the style book!"

The males of the *Courier* had nurtured a friendly attitude toward ladies of the evening since the days when the paper occupied the building at Third and Liberty, and one of the town's better brothels occupied the opposite corner. The jolly fellows of the composing room would stand in the window and call good-natured proposals and promises to the soiled doves across the street, and they would reply in ribald fashion, expressing doubt of the boys' masculinity and equipment. All that came to a screeching halt when the Army moved into Fort Knox for World War II and demanded that the city clean up the houses, lest the boys should get a sample of what they were fighting for before they went off to die for it. This pleased the churches and uplift ladies, but curled lips elsewhere.

The madams were involved in another bit of difficulty with the City Desk, this one caused by an unfortunate oversight. Each year at Derby time the madams, I and others firmly believed, bribed or persuaded friendly cops to raid their houses just before Derby Day and take some of their girls down to the station, where they would be given fines and sent back to work. The story invariably appeared in the following day's editions, causing mild interest and some tongue-clucking among the more moral circles.

On this particular occasion, however, the reporter on the police beat didn't get the story in on time, or it was misplaced by the City Desk and the next day an irate Betty Moran stormed into the newsroom. "Herschenroeder!" (John Herschenroeder, veteran city editor) "You sonofabitch!" she screeched. "Where's the story about me and my girls getting arrested?" Hersch shrugged and said he was sorry, which did not placate Ms. Moran. "Sorry?" she squawked. "Everybody coming in for the Derby, how are they to know I'm still in business? I'll have to bribe every cabdriver in town!"

Hersch promised to make amends, and the next morning the *Courier* carried a full account, with names and, as Betty insisted, addresses clearly set forth for the edification of Derbytime fun-seekers and the prosperity of the ladies in question.

But to more serious matters. There was the matter of Worth Bingham, who had come back to the paper after working in Washington, Minneapolis and California, and who now took over as assistant to the publisher. I believe that was among the happiest days of Barry's life. Everyone, including Worth, expected Worth to become a great publisher. He was much in the pattern of Ben Bradlee, the famed managing editor of the *Washington Post*, arrogant, able, colorful, an absolute dynamo. Barry told Norman to take him under his wing and teach him the local ropes; Worth needed little encouragement. He rode delivery trucks, sold ads, solicited subscriptions, spent hours in the composing room, with reporters and on the copy desk. He was not overly aggressive in editorial conference, but spoke his mind and seemed to have a good bit of knowledge of affairs, national and global.

Barry, Jr., the younger brother, was also home, after Harvard, the Marines, and a brief career in television, having made some notable documentaries for NBC, and was taking control of WHAS, TV and radio. That seemed logical, though it was rumored that he was not happy about leaving New York, and liked work behind the camera more than behind a desk. He was far more reserved than Worth, but that was of no concern to us, since we seldom saw him.

I have often wondered whether Worth would have been another Bradlee. He seemed not to have Bradlee's knack for picking good people, and no publisher is going to be better than his trench soldiers. For reasons known only to God and himself, he chose a former press association man whom he had met at a convention of some sort, for managing editor, without giving him the advantage of a day out in the state or on the city desk. I suspect there was significance in this, and that it indicated that Worth put little store in state events as compared with national and international news, which may have accounted also for his lack of appreciation for my emphasis on state matters. In any event, the new man was a nice fellow, but totally lost and didn't last long.

Worth sprang Bruce Van Deusen on us without warning, just introducing him one morning at conference as our new editorial writer.

We soon heard rumors that Bruce was slated to be the next chief editorial writer, which caused no joy in our ranks. He was cold, aloof and uncommunicative. When we harness horses invited him to lunch with us, he gave us a terse "no thanks," nor did he ever consult with any of us about working routine or company policy. He seemed literate enough, though his editorials were rather pedestrian, and at conference tended to state his opinions as dicta from above. I remember one day when we were discussing government tobacco price supports. This was in the days before smoking became the prime evil, and we were always happy to hear good news for the burley belt. So we were somewhat taken aback when Bruce, in the middle of our rather desultory discussion, slammed his hand down on the table and demanded that we quit this dishonesty, face the fact that tobacco was harmful, and call for an end of government subsidy of a killer. Everyone, including Barry, looked at him, amazed. We reminded him that tobacco was our top cash crop, the vehicle on which farm boys traditionally rode to college. Bruce brushed this aside. Let's be honest, he insisted, and quit this subterfuge. He lasted only a few months before Worth called him in and told him he was sorry, but things hadn't worked out. We were somewhat saddened, somewhat relieved. Strangely, once he left the paper and bought the *Voice of St. Matthews*, he became quite friendly, invited several of us to his home, a handsome place in Anchorage. Nice guy, bright, well educated and obviously from a substantial family background. He eventually sold the *Voice*.

This was in the era of the flying managing editors. First there was John Day, a Fleming County boy who had graduated from UK, worked for the Lexington papers and worked his way up to Time-Life, with a stint in London before returning to Kentucky. But I think he missed England, and after five years he quit to go back and buy a newspaper there. Jim Pope had been named executive editor, but I don't think he was ever comfortable in the role. The executive editor of dual papers is over managing editors of both, but if the managing editors are doing their jobs there isn't much for him to do in the day-to-day news operation, which Pope knew and liked, unless he steps on the toes of the managing eds. Otherwise he is sort of a middleman between operations and top management.

Ben Reeves, one of the most likeable men ever to serve in the boss ranks, was made managing editor of the *Courier*, only to run into massive misfortune. It happened, of course, on Derby Day. With the grandstands crowded and the Run for the Roses only minutes away, a small fire broke out in the southeast corner of the stands. At first it seemed minor, and the people nearby, expecting someone to come and douse it, simply moved away and continued watching the track. But the fire soon spread and for a few minutes there was the horrible danger that it might get into the roof and spread throughout the old wooden stands, where perhaps 75,000 people were sitting or standing, most of them unaware of the potential danger. Mercifully, the fire was put out before the threat increased; indeed, some people in the other sections of the stands never knew there was a danger, but the firemen who doused the blaze knew that it might have become the worst fire tragedy in American history.

The next morning, however, the Sunday *Courier-Journal* hit the stands with the usual picture of the Derby finish plastered across page one. Pictures of the fire were buried on page eight. Pope and Ethridge, among others, asked, in tones of outrage, why the hell the fire wasn't on page one. Reeves, who had been on duty, said he didn't think it that important and, furthermore, he didn't want to risk giving Churchill Downs a black eye. He was like the Washington reporter who returned to the office and said there was no story from the White House, and that the press conference had been canceled, since the President had been taken to the hospital. Ben's explanation, and his concern for the Downs, did not impress his superiors and he was shortly assigned to the Washington bureau. It was not a bad job, but he had deciphered the handwriting on the wall and soon resigned to take a job as a congressional staffer with Congressman Carl Perkins, a good job he held for years.

Reeves was followed by the unlikely Bill Sexton, who was followed in turn by Mike Davies, another native of England, who had made an impression with his direction of the new *Scene Magazine*. And he was followed by George Gill who was followed by Carol Sutton, and so on. It would have been far better for everyone concerned had Gill been allowed to remain either managing editor of the *Courier*, or executive editor of both papers. George was tough and not the most diplomatic person in the world. He had a way of intimidating people even while agreeing with them. But he was totally able; he could perform any job in the room, totally dependable, and underneath was a fair and likeable guy. Some of the staffers objected when, as general manager, George became chairman of the local Chamber of Commerce, partly as an effort to show the business community that we were no bomb-throwers. That, too, was a demonstration of George's versatility.

But I am ahead of myself. Relations between Buddy Atkinson and Norman went from chilly to freezing. It was not a surprising development. They represented opposite sides of an old journalistic debate between hard-news reporters and interpretive or explanatory writers. Reporters believe it is the paper's duty, in the news columns at least, to record the facts of a case and let the reader use his own intellect to interpret the meaning of those facts. The writer feels that the reporter often cannot report the entire truth of a case because he knows but cannot prove the facts to the point of defendability in case they are challenged, and that a writer with the leeway of interpretation gives a better picture and is less likely to be sued for libel.

But Buddy was not only a writer but a humor columnist, the toughest job on any paper. No man—well, few men—can be funny consistently, and trying to be often drives them into depression or drink. Or both. Most columnists—such as Art Buchwald, or the late Lewis Grizzard, who I considered a cornball—have a formula, a shtick. Dave Barry is funny in a broad sense, and creative, and about once in a century we encounter someone like Russell Baker, whose humor is subtle and intellectual, and often more deadly for that reason, but he is more than a humor writer. And often the most polished writers cannot produce humor; they may be witty and clever in person, but they cannot process it through the typewriter. Bryan Wooley, probably the best writer I ever knew on the papers, got funny ideas, but they seldom produced laughs. The same with John Fetterman and sports writer Johnny Carrico. I remember once when Wooley wrote a piece submitted to the magazine entitled "The Enchilada that ate El Paso." The bizarre hyperbole made it a great idea, but Geoff Vincent turned it down, asking Wooley to rewrite it. Wooley was furious. He brought it in to me and demanded my judgment—actually my approval. I twisted and weaseled. It wasn't too good—not bad, but no more. I could occasionally write humor, as well as nostalgia, political and governmental criticism and straight reporting, and for that reason considered myself, as did one or two others, among the best and most valuable writers on the staff. I admit that is self-aggrandizing, but can you name anyone else who is going to write good things about me?

At any rate, Buddy and Norman proved to be water and oil, a low-key, funny Southern WASP, a high-strung northern Jew. And Buddy was beginning to look stretched a little too tightly. *Collier's* magazine, from which he had taken the difference between comfort and penury, had folded (as had my hallowed *Saturday Evening Post*), and he was pulling hard to keep the family wagon rolling, compiling columns into a fairly successful book and determining to write books. He was having trouble at home, too, which was not surprising; he and Anne were as unlike as two samples of the same genus can be, and his tension at the office didn't make him easier to live with. He started drinking again, furtively at first, publicly later.

The *Times* restaurant, across Armory Place from the Courier building, boasted two waitresses, Pat and Ruth, of considerable physical charm (did I put that nicely?). Pat was slender and red-haired, Ruth shorter and possessed of a noble bosom. When Buddy had a drink or beer too many, he would grope vaguely toward one of the girls, sometimes grabbing a button on her white uniform. They liked Buddy and did not take seriously his attacks, but now and then the barkeep would hear a squeak, see one of the girls jump back and come around the bar threatening to beat me up, why, I never figured out. Several times I intervened between Buddy and others who took affront, and each time became suddenly the object of their nonaffections. It was tormenting to see such a sweet, talented man forced to grasp at the only straw he knew. There was only one thing, it seemed, that steadied him and put him back on the glory road—Sanibel Island. When he was too far down we would get in the car and wheel down to Sanibel, where we would walk the beach, fish, look for shells and deplore journalism. Gradually he would ease off to one beer a day, though it was painful for him. I recall sitting one evening, watching a gorgeous sunset, and hearing him say, "Goddammit, why can't I just have a couple of drinks, a few beers like everybody else? That's all I ask. That's not too much, is it?" I could only reply that I was afraid so.

10

Don't Shoot Me, I'm a Messenger

It is hard to attach specific dates to events, but I am sure the big Kentucky River flood that almost wiped out downtown Hazard occurred in 1957. Billy Davis took a terrific aerial photo of the flood submerging the downtown section; it still hangs in many offices. My contribution was less dramatic. I whipped up to Hazard as soon as the waters receded and wrote about it. The town was a mess. But what I remember most clearly is Willie Dawahare, patriarch of that remarkable family, mayor of Hazard and owner of Dawahare's Department Store. In his office, Willie had just started describing the tragedy when he suddenly looked at me and asked: "What size are you?" I told him I was a 39 or 40. "Come out here," he said, leading the way to the front of the store. "I got some suits just about fit you; real bargains."

I said, "Willie, are you going to palm off some flood-soaked stuff on me?" He held up his hand. "Never got a drop on them. I got 'em up on shelves myself."

He sold me two suits at, as he said, bargain prices. Good suits, too. Lasted for years. I loved Willie. The Dawahares are a great family, and I feel I have ties to them. When the first Dawahare came into the mountains (I guess that would have been Willie's daddy, or grandfather) he stopped off in Norton to see his cousin, old Sol Cury, head of a Syrian family that had moved to Norton with the coal boom and established a good store, D. Cury's Department Store. The Curys were good people. Young D. and my brother Don were friends and hellions together. Anyhow, Sol Cury advised Dawahare to go across the mountain to Jenkins or Whitesburg, where business was starting to get good with the coal boom, and lent him some stock to get started with. Some years ago, Don told me that the last Cury had left Norton and that the store was shut down. You can see what happened to the Dawahares. They spread out everywhere—Lexington, Louisville, and all over Eastern Kentucky. They could sell you a snake and charge you for the bite.

Hazard was also the home of Kelly and Sturgill—Dick Kelly and Bill Sturgill. They were becoming very big in surface, or strip mining. Dick was a soft-spoken, courtly man from over in Tazewell, Virginia, home of my grandparents. Dick had a genius for developing mine machinery. He built a huge auger, for drilling into a seam of coal, that cut a seven-foot slice and was known as the Kelly Giant. Sturgill, bulky, muscular former all-state footballer who also played basketball at UK for Adolph Rupp, was a tough man, shrewd with contracts and figures and could drive a coal operation. They later broke up their partnership, but not before they became rich, chiefly on contracts with TVA. I never found out why they broke up, but regretted it, for I liked them both. I could understand why they did not like me, for we waged an editorial war against them, with me writing the editorials, charging them with rape of the land, pollution of mountain streams and failure to restore the hillsides they stripped. Still, when we won the Pulitzer Prize for our work on stripping, Sturgill called me demanding half of the prize, since, as he said, we couldn't have won it without him as villain. It is a credit to something that Bill and I have always gotten along despite philosophic differences. He has been a good friend.

***

On the other hand, I later became friends with L.D. Gorman, who was forever feuding with Sturgill, and with Bill Perkins, a United Mine Workers of America field man, who feuded with them both. If you let editorial policy make enemies of everyone you criticize, pretty soon you won't have a friend left since, before it is over, you will criticize just about everybody.

I heard about Perkins well before we met. "Any time you see a tipple burning or a bridge blown, look around and you'll see that blue Chrysler barreling across the hill," operators said. Bill was a union man, through and through. Born in the hills, he had gone into the mines at 15; within a few months they carried him out of the mine on a plank, his back broken, and put him down in the family kitchen, to get well or die. "Bastards didn't even come to see whether I lived," he said bitterly. But he got well and, after a stint in the CCC (Civilian Conservation Corps) went back into the mines, where a machine accident tore half his thigh off. Again, he recovered, but he was in a fight with his foreman and was blacklisted. It was then that he became a field man for the United Mine Workers, and a fearless one.

About five feet, eight, he weighed 230 pounds, all muscle, and did as he admitted, "anything John L. Lewis wanted." Bill and Tom Raney, out of the Pikeville office, led the famous drive to unionize the Clay and Leslie County mines. It almost ended in tragedy. For it was then that Bill ran up against Elmer Begley, Leslie County Judge and coal operator. Good-looking, flat-eyed and ruthless, Elmer had sworn they would never unionize his mines, and he did not mind using his authority as County Judge to back up his words. The UMW caravan wound from Hazard through Hyden and into Manchester, where they held a rally on the courthouse lawn, paying no attention when, occasionally, someone whanged a shot off the courthouse wall. But back in Leslie County, Elmer was waiting for them. He had deputized and armed more than a hundred men and placed them in the bushes on each side of the road, and when the union men drove back through on their return to Hazard, he arrested and jailed them in bunches.

I was talking one day in Hazard to banker and coal operator L.D. Gorman, who had inherited control of the bank, as well as his place in politics and coal, from his uncle, Dewey Daniels, for years the Republican boss of much of Eastern Kentucky. We got to talking about Bill Perkins, Elmer Begley and the union drive. L.D. said, "Oh, God, I remember that. Uncle Dewey was sitting here when a call came from Hyden, and he jumped about six feet straight up."

"He WHAT?" he hollered. "Listen, you get to him right now and tell him that if he does that, the party will be dead in Kentucky, and he'll spend the rest of is life in prison. Now, go tell him I said so!"

"What the call was about," L.D. explained, "was from this fellow in Hyden who said that Elmer had packed the county jail with union men and was planning to have somebody blow the jail up. Settle matters right then. Kill 'em all." Apparently, the message got through, and the jail wasn't blown, and the union men were released the next day.

Bill Perkins was one of them. But it didn't stop him. A few weeks later, he led another string of cars toward Manchester, this time from down in Barbourville, but some union critics were lying in the weeds along the road and shot up the cars, stitching eight shots down the side of Bill's car and creasing him across the back. It didn't stop him. He did some time in prison over in Richmond, not unusual for the time; the coalfields were riddled with violence, and union men almost invariably got the blame. He got out and was soon leading a strike, riding from one picket stop to another, eating Moon Pies and drinking coffee with pickets sitting around fires at rail crossings, jollying them along. One time I took a new labor reporter, who had come from Chicago to work on the *Times*, and Bill let us ride with him as he made his rounds, turning our hair white as he screamed around the narrow mountain roads in the blue Chrysler, turning around now and then and grinning to see the reporter's eyes bugging out.

"Doesn't it make you feel bad to see your men out on strike?" asked the reporter.

"Why, hell, yes," said Perkins. "See those houses up there?" he pointed to a row of miners' houses on a hillside. "I could fuck a woman in every one of them if these bastards would get back in the mine so I'd know where they were."

The reporter looked shocked at this version of union leadership. Bill grinned at the success of his put-on.

After he got out of prison, Bill called and asked me to help him get his son into Annapolis. The boy was a fine athlete, and a top student, and I promised to see what I could do, but before I could try the boy joined the Navy as an enlisted man. And time caught up with Bill. He ran his car off the road, broke his back again, and the doctor told him it was time to quit. He went down to Hazard, walked into the bank, and told his old antagonist L.D. Gorman he wanted to borrow some money.

"You know the building down the street that burned? I'd like to fix it up, start a restaurant downstairs, a bar upstairs."

"Well, sit down and let's talk," said L.D. "How much you think it will take?" Bill said about $80,000. L.D. turned and called to an assistant in the back. "Mr. Perkins is coming back, wants some money. Give him a check for it."

That was that.

"How come you let Bill have that money after fighting him all that time?" I asked L.D.

"Oh," he said. "That was nothing personal. I knew Bill's word was good; if he said he'd do it, he'd do it."

"Yeah," Bill affirmed later, "I always got along with L.D."

I went back to Hazard a year or so after that and, sure enough, there on Main Street was the B&G Grill (for Bill and Gertrude, his wife) with a good bar upstairs. Bill remembered me. We had a nice talk. I like Bill Perkins. He has never told me anything but the truth. And his career, from mule-cars in the narrow, gassy, wet mines, through the introduction of giant cutting and loading machines, to the strip coal operations of today, from the bitter union wars of the Depression, the days of John L. Lewis, to the cold-blooded operators and truckers of today's mines—Bill's career has been a mirror of the coal industry. Bill experienced it all.

***

Harwood and I went to see Elmer Begley. He just laughed at the story about blowing up the jail. We talked for hours, exchanging improbable stories. Face to face, Elmer was a likeable guy; he insisted that we come up and go fishing with him over on Greasy Creek. Prettiest water left in Kentucky, he promised. I never did go, but wish I had.

I had one other contact with Elmer. The mountain congressman retired, and there was a "buffalo stampede" of candidates for the job. I think there were about a dozen men running. Elmer was one. He called me one day and said, "Pearce, I'm running for Congress, and I need some things written, and you're the only one I know I can trust. I need a press release I can send out to papers, and a platform. Make it sound good." I sat down and wrote out a release, "Leslie County Judge Elmer Begley today announced his candidacy for Congress .....promising to run on a platform designed to "restore responsive representation to the mountains...." and so on, and listed the ten points of his platform. Elmer was, of course, to the right of Atilla the Hun, but I wrote him a platform that would have made Adlai Stevenson look conservative, cradle to grave welfare, conservation of natural resources, universal health coverage, etc. A few days later I picked up a Middlesboro paper and there was my release, word for word. I thought oh, my God, Elmer didn't read it. But the next day he called. He was delighted. Everybody printed it, he said. He insisted that I come fishing. Elmer didn't win, but he ran a close race, remarkable for such a liberal.

***

In 1962 my wife finally asked Mama to visit. I had hoped she could come the year before, when I was selected chairman of the Mountain Laurel Festival and was marshal of the parade down Kentucky Avenue and around the courthouse square. The festival is one of the prettiest events in the state. Each year every college and university in the state selects a queen to represent the school in the Festival, and they walk around looking pretty. There is a directors' dinner at the country club over at Middlesboro, and a parade, and big luncheon, and then the girls all parade around the cove, the natural amphitheater in the side of the mountain in Pine Mountain State Park (no swim suits or meat show at the Festival), one is chosen queen and is kissed by the governor and that night there is a dance. There are lots of parties and everyone has a good time. It is truly a beautiful occasion, with the mountain laurel all in bloom.

Mama and I went down to the festival. On the way down we stopped in Frankfort and had lunch with the Wyatts at the Lieutenant Governor's mansion. In Pineville, we sat in the reviewing stand for the parade and at the head table with Governor Bert Combs at the luncheon, and when the afternoon festivities began, we were sitting in the middle of the cove, but Bert came back and got Mama and led her down to sit beside him. Mama never forgot it. Neither did I. It was good to see her so happy, returning to the old home town with dignity.

***

The next year, 1963, Bert threw all his weight behind Edward T. "Ned" Breathitt for governor, to run against Happy Chandler. Happy was back in full force, plastering the state with posters heralding "ABC In 63." Everybody thought Bert was nuts, that Happy would eat Ned alive, head, feet and tail feathers. He didn't. Ned was good on television, and Happy was not. He was out of his element. His was the old flesh-pressing, Main Street parade, courthouse square speaking, personal style of campaigning. Ned looked young and fresh, and made Happy seem old, and rather out-of-date. Prich wrote speeches for Ned and stood in the back of the crowd hollering, "He's clean! He's clean!" Ned beat the odds and won going away.

In one sense, it was rather sad. Happy had a big victory party all set for election night in the cabin behind his home in Versailles, with a throng of the faithful around to help him celebrate. The evening started in good spirit, with returns showing a close race. Everyone waited for the old champion to start pulling away. But as the hours wore on, it was Ned who gained the lead, and slowly it grew, as an unbelieving quiet fell over the victory gathering, until Happy finally went back to the house. It was the end of a long, successful and colorful career. We had opposed Happy at every turn, and he naturally disliked me. I regretted that. It was easy to oppose Happy on issues, hard to dislike him personally.

In Louisville, the Breathitt crowd tore the house down. Bert sat back, looking happy and smug. A nut yesterday, a genius today. The editorial conference next morning was jubilant. We figured Ned would take the general election from Republican Louie Nunn, and he did. It wasn't the prettiest of races. Bert had issued an executive order outlawing segregation in public facilities and it had, naturally, aroused redneck ire. Nunn picked up on this and, instead of running against Ned, ran against Bert and his order. With the flag unfurled behind him, a Bible in one hand and a copy of Bert's executive order in the other, Louie promised that his first act in office would be the repeal of the evil order.

It didn't work. Ned won and kept his promise to protect the sales tax and the school improvements it had financed and to back a law forcing strip-miners to restore stripped land to its original contour, or as near as could be. That wasn't going to be easy. Coal is critically important to Kentucky, and the coal lobby is always strong. For another thing, Ned was obligated, to some extent, to Bill Sturgill, who naturally opposed any tightening of controls. Some time later Bill told me, bitterly, that he had backed Ned generously.

"He came through here, campaigning," Sturgill said, "and I told him I was going to be for him. I took him out to the airport and told him I was putting my plane at his disposal. And I put a little cash on the seat of the plane. Then he turned on me."

The new law, passed after a bitter fight, during which we flooded the legislature with a special edition of the *Magazine* titled "Our Ravaged Land." I edited most of it and wrote an introductory piece condemning strip-mining. It won us the Pulitzer, in which I shared. It didn't amount to much. It carried no money; I didn't even get a raise, just the right to put Pulitzer Prize winner after my name. Somehow, the Pulitzer never seemed a big deal to me. I'd rather win one Nieman Fellowship than fifty Pulitzers. The Prize is just a matter of personal taste on the part of some editors and publishers who make up the board. Several times I didn't think much of their judgment. Hugh Haynie never got the Pulitzer, and there were at least five years when a dozen of his cartoons were better than the winner. I was nominated several times for work that was better than that for which I got the award. But we got it, and the paper made a big thing of it. Publishers love to boast of the number of Pulitzers their papers have won.

***

I felt some relief, too, that I was no longer involved in politics, for Ned did not re-appoint the Parks Board. I did, however, get caught up in a strange situation as Ned's administration was winding down. It had been a good administration, and the state was in a far better condition than when he and Bert entered the ring. The trouble was that the leaders of the Democratic party couldn't decide on a candidate to succeed Ned. All of the top dogs wanted Bert to run again, and he probably could have won easily. But Bert just hunkered down and said no, by God, he wasn't going to run, and that was that.

So a big meeting of the "Kingmakers," so named by the press, was arranged by Bill May, highway contractor, big giver and close friend of Bert's, to meet on Spanish Key, down in the Bahamas, and thrash it out. Spanish Key was a small, luxurious island owned by Texas billionaire Clint Murchison, with whom May did a lot of highway business and who let May use it when the Murchisons were not there, which was most of the time. Bert asked Barry if he would attend, but Barry chose instead to send me. That was fine with me; the accommodations were magnificent, the food delicious. After a day's fishing, Willard, the butler, would meet us at the dock with rum drinks and cigars.

But it didn't amount to anything. We finally met on the lawn of the big house, and May said "Now, goddammit, Combs, you've gotta run, and that's all there is to it." "No it isn't," said Bert, "because I'm not going to run. I said I wasn't, and I'm not going to."

"Goddamm you," May hollered, "you weren't anything but a dirt-road, shirt-tail lawyer when the party picked you up, made you a judge, made you governor, made you head of the biggest law firm, and you say you don't owe it anything. I say you do."

"Well, I say I'm not going to run," said Bert, and it was plain that he had dug in his heels, so after batting the air for a while, we settled down to see whom we could run. Henry Ward wanted to run. He was a good man. The trouble was that no one thought he could win. He wasn't a good candidate, honest as Jesus, but with a knack for ruffling feathers. A man could go into Henry's office demanding a road, Henry would give it to him, and the man would come out mad. May asked me what Bingham thought, and I delivered the masterpiece for which I had traveled all that way: "Barry thinks that Bert ought to run. If he won't, he thinks Henry deserves a shot."

And in the end, that's what they decided. Back in Frankfort, Henry heard that the Kingmakers were in Florida (the press was wrong again), to choose a candidate. "I don't give a damn what the Kingmakers say," Henry snarled. "I'll run if I want to, and I want to."

***

But I was into another venture that skirted politics, though I was careful to tell Barry about it. Bert, Jack Matlick and I bought five acres of land on the beach at Sanibel, hoping to sell subdivided lots for enough profit to build our own vacation cottage there. (Two years later, Jack, who had served as conservation commissioner under Bert, presented Mary Bingham and me the Governor's Medallion for Public Service for work in conservation, on behalf of the governor.) The property we had bought was not a very good piece of land, with low spots all over it, and we had a bad and expensive task filling it enough to sell lots. Bert was busy restarting his law practice; he went into a partnership with John Tarrant, and they were joined by Wilson to form the state's largest firm, Wyatt, Tarrant and Combs. Jack Matlick had a bad heart, and after an attack, asked to get out, and Bert and I bought his share. That left me to develop the property, and I had no idea what I was doing.

***

We faced another campaign, this one for mayor and county judge. And here, I think, we made a serious mistake. Local Republicans, tired of being out of power, put up two bright, progressive young men, William Cowger for mayor, and Marlow Cook for county judge. The Democrats looked around, couldn't find a likely candidate, and finally agreed to back William Milburn, an old Southern reactionary and former principal of Male High School. He was not known for being liberal on the subject of race. Most of us on the editorial board would have preferred to back Cowger and Cook, but Barry wanted to maintain influence with Lyndon Johnson by electing a Democrat, and we went for Milburn. I went, at Barry's order, to a meeting in Wilson's office, at which we tried to modernize Milburn or find an alternative, but he was glued to the ground and not about to get out of the race. I got the feeling he was going to lose. He should have, and he did, and as a result the *Courier-Journal* had no influence on local government. Cowger and Cook went on to sound administrations and Marlow ascended to the U.S. Senate. Good men. Bad mistake.

The next year we became involved in the long fight to save the Red River Gorge. At the time, few people outside the area had even heard of the spectacular valley along the Red River in Powell and Menifee counties. I think Joe Creason was the first one to call our attention to it, launching an effort to prevent the Army Corps of Engineers from damming the river and flooding the magnificent cliffs and natural tunnels and bridges that won it the title of Grand Canyon of the East. I had skirted the Gorge, coming down from Frenchburg and through Nada Tunnel, but after Creason wrote about it, I went through the Gorge and joined the effort. Soon the paper was hammering away on the issue, as people visited the Gorge and saw what we had to lose. The place became famous, as a scenic gem and as a symbol of the conservationist effort. People—hikers, campers, canoeists, nature lovers, conservationists—swarmed over the place, until on weekends you couldn't find a place to park along the road and it began to seem that they might wear it out. The Sierra Club took up the fight. Supreme Court Justice William O. Douglas came down and led a much-publicized hike through the valley. That was another fight we won.

Prior to this, I had stuck my nose into a squabble on the University of Kentucky campus, where the student newspaper, *The Kernel*, was fighting off censorship by the trustees who objected to editorials by the brash young editor, David Hawpe. Brash he was, but bright as he could be, a good writer and fighting happily for campus press freedom. I also met Richard Wilson, another bright young guy, who was trying to decide whether to jump into journalism full-time. He decided to do it and became the best education reporter Kentucky has ever seen, as well as a hard-working, conscientious newsman, and one of the most likeable of men.

I wrote some editorials, shaming the trustees and defending the student crusaders. I made some friends. Both Hawpe and Wilson were to have long-term influences on my life and career. In 1965 Hawpe, fresh out of college, turned up in Louisville with the Associated Press Bureau, but admitted that what he wanted most was an editorial writing job on the *Courier*. There was no opening, but then George Burt showed me a letter from Nelson Poynter, publisher of the *St. Petersburg (Fl.) Times*, asking if he knew a bright young guy wanting to break into editorial writing. I thought immediately of Hawpe. He jumped at the chance, spent the next three years soaking up sunshine and experience, and in 1968 showed up again in Louisville, tired of Florida and still aiming at the *Courier*. I told Barry about him and introduced him the next day. Barry told him there was no editorial opening, but he would mention him to the state editor, who hired him and sent him to the Hazard bureau. That was fine with David. Though he had grown up in south Louisville, he had actually been born in Pike County, and it was a sort of return of the native. He liked the duty; I have never known anyone who went there who didn't.

***

But I have gotten ahead of myself again. I mustn't ignore 1966. First off, Cary Robertson had a mild stroke, and it became apparent that he would have to relinquish duties as Sunday editor for an easier post. Norman had been urging Geoff Vincent, whom he had known for years and who had worked for him in St. Louis, to come to Louisville, and in 1965 Norman and Lisle Baker, while in New York, took Geoff to dinner and insisted that he come down. The next day Barry added his voice to the urging, and Geoff, who was exhausted by his job on *The New York Times* and whose wife's death a short time before had left him shaken, agreed to come to Louisville as Sunday editor. Cary became book editor.

That was also the year when George Gill became managing editor of the *Courier-Journal*, which surprised no one. A product of Indiana University, George had started with the *Courier* in 1960 as a copy editor, then a reporter, covering civil rights, sit-ins, and space shots in Florida, and was soon assistant city editor, then city editor and in 1966 took over as managing editor. From the first, George made an impression—aggressive, confident, with a reputation for being tough but fair. Bob Clark, who had come from Owensboro to be a science and medical writer, spent time in the Washington bureau and won a Nieman Fellowship, was at the time managing editor of the *Times*.

The editorial department got two jolts in 1966. On February 2, a cold, snowy day, Russell Briney, editor of the *Courier* editorial page, was standing at Fifth and Broadway, on his way to the office, when he suddenly, without a sound, crumpled to the sidewalk, dead. It was a total shock, though Russell had become somewhat feeble, at times seeming uncertain. He did not like to go to the composing room in the afternoon to make up the editorial page unless I accompanied him, though he certainly didn't need me for the routine job, and I didn't need the experience. At the same time, he could get very snippy if I offered a suggestion he did not agree with.

I more or less took over his duties, since I and everyone else assumed I would be given the post, but a week later Worth called me into his office and told me that he had decided to appoint Molly editor. That was a surprise, but not as unpleasant as it might have been. I loved Molly and had to admit that she was not only as good a writer but probably had a wider range of knowledge and better judgment. Working with her was pleasant. She did not drive, and I drove her home each evening, and we had time to talk.

But we were at once shaken again, when Weldon James resigned with a blast at our editorial policy on Vietnam. That was strange, because we almost didn't have a Vietnam policy, straddling the fence with fierce ambivalence. I think a majority of the writers on both papers would have welcomed a stand in favor of getting out at any cost. Like Barry, I took a firm stand in the middle of the road, sympathizing with President Johnson, but wishing he could find a way out. Weldon, more of an Old Marine than we had realized, grew increasingly restive, daily advocating an all-out attack on North Vietnam in order to end the war before it tore the country further apart. Finally, in exasperation, he wrote Barry a letter of protest and resignation, condemning us, me specifically, for our wishy-washy foreign policy, and asking permission to write a final editorial notebook explaining his stand. Barry granted it, and Weldon wrote a rather sad column exclaiming "To hell with Ho-Chi Minh!" I think it was supposed to be reminiscent of Henry Watterson's "To hell with the Hapsburgs and Hohenzollerns!" It missed by a bit, but in a few days Weldon was back in uniform, and on his way to the Pacific. We hated to see him go.

***

The year saw other changes. Bryan Wooley, as fine a writer as ever served on the papers, joined the *Courier* staff, and I was selected for the National War College at Fort McNair, Washington, D.C. I think many journalists assume that military people are generally less than bright, either Colonel Blimps, or sadists. If so, a term at the War College would be a revelation. For me, it proved to be a fine experience. The curriculum was intense, we had stacks of reading every night, hot debate in class every day, and interesting lectures by national officials. Among the officers in attendance, especially our group leader and some Army officers from Fort Leavenworth, were some of the brightest and best-informed men I had ever met. I had to read my eyes out every night to keep up. I was so engaged in the program that our group leader called me over on the last day, commented that I seemed to like the work, and asked if I would like to come back the following year as a group leader. Believe me, that was a thrill. You may recall Leigh Hunt's lines in which he admits that fame and wealth have missed him, but asks that you add that "Jenny kissed me when we met, jumping from the chair she sat in. Time, you thief who love to get sweets into your list, put that in." And at times when I feel that I have fallen far short of what I should have achieved, I remember that I lectured at Columbia and taught at the War College.

But back home, tragedy struck. I was sitting in my office one morning following conference when I heard a sort of muffled, choking sound and feet running out in the lobby, and in a few seconds Thelma McGrath, Barry's secretary, came to my office and said, "John Ed, Worth has been killed! Mr. Bingham just left, going home to tell Mrs. Bingham. I just heard him holler, 'Oh, Worth! No! No!' and I went in and he was standing there, white as a sheet."

Joan, Worth's wife, had called Barry. She and Worth were driving down to the beach at Chatham, on Cape Cod, driving a hardtop, with the back windows down and a surfboard sticking out both sides when Worth drove too close to a car he was passing, and the surfboard hit the car on the right, and the left end of the board came around and hit him in the back of the neck, killing him instantly.

Another Bingham killed, another tragic death. We wondered how much the family could take. It was terrible for Barry, who had put so much love and hope into Worth, so much faith in his ability to take over and expand the empire. And it was unsettling for all of us on the paper. Everyone had had confidence in Worth, and it had been comforting to know that the matter of leadership was settled for the foreseeable future.

Mark Ethridge came back for the funeral and told Lisle Baker that he was willing to interrupt his other duties and come back temporarily if Barry wanted him. Barry declined the offer.

11

Dead Miners and a Blue Noodle

Considering that most people get, or say they get, their knowledge of world affairs from a few minutes a day of television, I wonder about our future. People can't be expected to make intelligent decisions on the basis of such skimpy information. Local newscasts, remarkably similar in format from one town to another, seldom look below the surface of stories, and devote an inordinate share of time to sports, weather and human interest or lost-dog heart tuggers. I suspect that communication schools today teach special tear-jerk classes, sadism for fun and ratings. Catch those tears! Get that sob! ("How did you feel, Mrs. Lachrimost, when you saw the truck run over your little boy?" "Is that your little baby, lying there, crushed to a bloody pulp by the fallen water tower, Ms. Blubber? Make you feel rotten?")

Network reporters are at a disadvantage in covering foreign stories in that they fly in, often with little background knowledge of the situation, report what they see and can show on camera, and fly out. Furthermore, stories from foreign bureaus of both networks and newspapers have declined sharply over the past fifteen years. People need to know the truth about affairs of the world, and not just governmental versions, if they are to vote and influence their representatives knowledgeably.

But there is no denying the power of television. Because it can get the news to people before newspapers can print and distribute it, it seemed for a while that it might run papers out of business. It is simply easier to watch than to read, and people who assume they are getting the news from TV see no reason to buy a newspaper to get it again. Television also robbed newspapers of much of their advertising, especially national advertising, forcing them to concentrate on their local marketing area, discouraging coverage of regional and national news. How many middle-size newspapers have overseas bureaus any longer? Thus, we are poorly informed unless we read metropolitan dailies or such magazines as *World Press Review*, *Foreign Affairs*, *The Economist*, *The Atlantic*, etc. Television offered, and offers, entertainment, not information.

I think we at the *Courier-Journal* were surprised by the impact of television because we overestimated the intelligence of the American public and underestimated the boredom of the average life, a boredom eased by having others in the living room. We had offered our readers the best selection of local, state, national and global news that we could muster each day, and assumed that we were meeting their wants, since they chose our paper. Then we found them turning to a raucous box that supplied a diet of trivia, ersatz humor, violence, sex and, increasingly, vulgarity. The lords of television discovered early on the profit to be made by selling things on the air. "It is our responsibility to use this technology to the greatest service to our customers," NBC boss Bill Paley reportedly told Ed Murrow, but the customers he had in mind were not viewers but advertisers. They demanded viewers, the more the better, and to reach the greatest number of viewers it was necessary to offer a menu that everyone from genius to moron could grasp. It is significant that they developed the sound track to make viewers believe that what they were hearing was funny and to become accustomed to laughing on cue, not at the material, thus effectively stifling genuine humor on TV. It may also be significant that grades of American students began their long drift downward in the fifties, hand in hand with the growth of television.

To counter this frightening competition, many newspapers chose to offer people the fare that drew them to TV. Others began printing versions of the checkout counter tabloid trash that seemed to appeal to so many women. They printed their pages in color, they flashed graphs and maps and charts like Ross Perot. They presented national and world news in capsule, leaving more space for recipes, decorating tips, advice, tabloid-style gossip, cat rescues, puzzles, contests, anything happening in neighborhoods that can be foisted off as feel-good or civic pride stories, and endless details on the lives and sexual habits of athletes, actors, entertainers and public figures. Voters became more knowledgeable of the sexual conduct of their public representatives than of their policies and official actions. In an effort to expand local circulation, editors published a disproportionate number of stories concerning black people and neighborhoods and innumerable shots of blacks, especially black children. These practices may have helped some papers to survive, though circulation in minority neighborhoods is still a problem. Could the lost papers have survived as purveyors only of news and information? Would our country be stronger, our people better informed had they done so?

The *Courier* faced another element of uncertainty. With the death of Worth Bingham, restroom rumors sprouted about the future leadership. There was talk, logically, that Barry, Jr. would take over, but we did not see this as imminent, since he knew next to nothing about news or newspapers, was reputed to prefer television, believed that it would soon drive newspapers out of business, and had consented to come back to the papers only to please his parents. It was rumored that he disliked reading in general, partly because he had been dyslectic as a child and never learned to read easily. (His mother insisted that this was not true and told me that Barry had been poorly taught to read at the old Ballard public school.) But we assumed that he would be allowed a considerable orientation, with Issacs or Gill showing him the ropes, and there was some surprise when Barry, Sr. announced that Jr. would be taking over at once as assistant publisher.

And one morning, without fanfare, Jr. turned up at editorial conference, somewhat uncomfortable, diffident. That was understandable. He was not by nature the brash, self-confident, shoot-from-the-hip man that Worth had been and no doubt felt the weight of being thrown among people years his senior in age and experience. Remembering my own disadvantage when the Navy shoved me aboard a ship without a day's training in shipboard life or technology, I sympathized with him. I still think much of the criticism aimed at him was unfair. He deserves great credit for giving up a career he loved in an environment he found fascinating to undertake an unappealing job for which he was not prepared. It is not fair to make a man a general who has never known the ranks, just as it may damage the soldier's morale to learn that the general does not believe in armed conflict.

Barry, Jr. was in a very difficult position; if he held back and appeared reluctant to make decisions, staffers put it down to weak leadership; if he thrust himself forward, he was criticized for acting in matters he knew nothing about. But he kept his poise and worked long hours at learning a job more intricate than appeared on the surface. When he developed Hodgkin's disease, an form of cancer, he handled himself with remarkable dignity—even humor—sending regular bulletins to the staff from the hospital, recounting matter-of-factly the nature and course of the disease and commenting on the paper. The staff, as well as the horror-stricken family, feared that his illness was but one more scene in the tragedy of the Binghams, and his missives were reassuring evidence that the new leader might not only survive, but that he had the emotional toughness and character to be a leader. He was pale and thin but resolute when he returned.

But from the start there were aspects of his personality that made us uneasy. We were discussing trends in journalism one morning, the growth of monopoly—Gannett, Knight-Ridder-Times-Mirror —among the journalistic chains, and the consolidation of so many information outlets in the hands of such corporations as General Electric, Disney and Westinghouse. We were jolted when Barry, Jr. shrugged and said that it really didn't matter, since we would probably not be printing information on paper in another ten years, but delivering the news electronically. He was wrong, of course; thirty years later the presses are still rolling, though time and technology are beginning to prove him more prescient than we realized. But our concern was not so much about the future as about the beliefs of the man who was going to shape the future of the papers—and of us.

Neither did he endear himself to the staff with his lurid accounts of hunting. Most of us had taken a turn in hunting during our youth, but had outgrown the joy of killing. The growing environmentalist movement had awakened awareness of the value and sanctity of life, and not just human life, and more and more hunting became identified with rednecks and blue-bellies. Our editorial policy had long been environmentalist and critical of laws designed to protect wildlife only so that it could be hunted and killed. And suddenly here was this young man recounting the thrill of killing an elephant, that magnificent and tragic survivor of time. The best shot, he explained, is to the knee; the elephant cannot support himself and move on three legs and so will fall and suffocate, allowing the shooter, properly attired in bush jacket, Australian hat and knee socks by Abercrombie and Fitch, to pose over the expiring beast. Barry also explained how it was best not to shoot a moose standing in the water, but to wait for it to emerge, so that dragging its body through the water, a boring task, could be avoided.

We recoiled at this, and I had little enough sense to suggest that it would be just as sporting, and much less demanding, to buy a cow, stake her out on the lawn, sit on the porch and blow her away. And, I added, the meat was better. This was a mistake. I saw Barry's face redden and reminded myself to keep my humor to myself. He did not take his white hunter role lightly. A few months later he was off to Africa on safari and returned with tales of how he saved a native village by shooting a crocodile that had been eating the citizens, especially young women (a discrimination of taste previously unsuspected of crocs, but proven by a necklace taken from the saurian's stomach). Behind his back, the news staff whooped, and one wag tacked to the bulletin board a fake dispatch from Kenya, praising the villagers for again managing to dupe a rich American with the "old necklace in the croc" ploy, luring him into hiring half the village to point out the crocodile, which had been imported for the occasion.

Barry was unperturbed. One day, after he had been out of the office for some time, he showed up with a Kaiser Wilhelm mustache, wide and turned up at the ends. No one could figure out why, but Molly speculated that it made him look older and set him apart and different from Worth.

I really had always liked Barry. We had made trips together through the strip-mine country, and he had seemed an agreeable young man, with a good sense of humor and eager to learn. But now I got the feeling that I had best go easy on the jokes. Barry, Sr. loved to joke, especially if the joke had a risqué touch, and did not mind a joke at his own expense. Jr. seemed more sensitive and thin skinned. And I gradually got the feeling that he did not like me. I couldn't figure out why. We didn't disagree on matters of policy that I could think of, and I couldn't imagine that my work was unsatisfactory. I had always been willing to carry more than my share of the load.

Once, before Worth died, Molly had gone to the hospital, leaving me with Bill Peeples and Bryan Wooley to put out the page. The job wasn't made easier when Peeples got sick, leaving just Wooley and me. I didn't mind much, because working with Wooley was pure joy. A lanky, bearded semi-bohemian from El Paso, Bryan looked frail but had once played football against the likes of Jack Pardee, of Dallas Cowboy fame. Bryan was great company, witty and with a wry sense of humor and a broad field of knowledge, and one of the finest editorial writers we ever had. He was not a fast writer, but when he wrote an editorial it was a thoughtful and persuasive piece of work. I was content to handle the hack work, doing whatever was necessary to fill the page, which sometimes took an unusual skill. One time, with deadline looming, we had an eight-inch hole in the page, so I sat down and whacked out a piece on some topic of foreign policy. Wooley proclaimed it the perfect editorial—it fit the space precisely, was literary and lofty in tone, and said absolutely nothing in such a puzzling manner that no one could take issue with it.

But even noble workmen make mistakes, and I made a fine one. Barry, Jr., after conference one morning, announced that he was going to write an editorial, and that afternoon handed me a single typed sheet. One look, and I sensed an elephant-size problem. It was amateurish. I took it to Wooley and asked what he thought I should do with it. He reminded me of Barry Sr.'s long-standing rule that no one's copy was immune from editing; further, he said, I was responsible for the content and reputation of the page. So I took the thing, tried to make it sound like what I thought he intended, and put it in the paper. I am not sure what I could have done otherwise. Perhaps the best thing would have been to put it into the page the way he wrote it, giving him a chance to see its flaws, but that, too, would have been risky; people tend to see their writing not as it is, but as they meant it to be. At any rate, the next day he was noticeably cool and when Molly returned he told her that in the future he wanted his editorials printed the way he wrote them. Why he did not voice his complaint to me, allowing us an exchange of views that might have cleared the air, is beyond me. But the fact that he didn't was another hint that he did not like dealing with me. And having responsibility without authority was an unfair burden.

But I had other worries. One day I went into Molly's office as Norman was coming out, and Molly looked at me and shook her head. "You'd better watch out for Norman," she said. "I don't know what he has against you, but he just warned me not to keep sticking up for you or it could get me in trouble." I wondered if his dislike accounted for Barry's attitude, or vice versa. In any event, I was hearing footsteps in the night and began writing letters to friends, hoping that some decent paper would have an opening. Several did, but not for a fifty-year old who had spent his career developing a specialty of Kentucky.

I got a weekend respite from this when Geoff asked me if I would like to do a profile for the *Magazine* of a professor at Alice Lloyd College, up in Knott County. I loved such assignments; they got me out of town and the pressures of home and office, let me meet new people and brought in some spare change. This was an unusual case. William Cohen was a professor of English literature and a poet whose holy cause in life was to stop the strip-mining of his beloved hills. For some unexplained reason, the professor had chosen to be known as The Blue Noodle; I have not to this day discovered why. He had a handsome blue blazer with a crest over the breast pocket, his award, he said, for having been named the Olympic Poet in the recent games in Mexico City. I was not prepared to challenge his claim, assuming it to have been won in fair rhyming combat, but I kept boring in, in my best hard-nosed reporter style, to find how an Olympic poet won the gold—by composing more or faster, reciting longer or louder, or by out-shouting his opponents? He regarded me with scorn and declared that I was the most linear man he had ever seen.

The professor, or Noodle, if you prefer, had arranged a caravan up a nearby mountain to an offending strip mine, with a view to blocking the road and halting operations. He assured me that we would have at least a dozen cars, crammed with protesters, which would make a fine story, but after we had waited almost an hour at a hamburger stand at the foot of the hill, he conceded that our three cars, mine, his full of grade-school children and a fat lady, and a pick-up truck carrying an elderly man and a small boy, probably constituted the assault forces of righteousness. I took one look at the road, which appeared to average about eighteen inches in mud and declined to put my car to the test, so we set out to attack Everest on foot. It took a while, slipping, dodging the deepest pools, and when we finally reached the criminal site we were somewhat let down to find the place deserted. It was Saturday, there was no one on hand to throw us out or have us arrested. The best we could do was to rip down the state mining permit tacked to the side of the tool house and begin our triumphal descent. Now and then the Noodle encouraged us to throw rocks and limbs into the deeper mudholes, until the elderly man suggested this might not be the best idea. "Fesser," he allowed, "putting them rocks in there's just going to give them trucks purchase." The Noodle agreed and we fought our way back down to the hamburger stand, where the kids wolfed burgers and chips and declared the day a great success.

The Noodle and I, though covered with more mud than glory, retired to his home, a beautiful log cabin on a steep hill overlooking Caney Creek and the college campus. There he slipped into a vividly-striped dressing gown, opened the bathroom door and introduced his wife, who was happily splashing and singing in the tub. While I was trying to weasel from him the nature of Olympic poesy, he motioned me to a huge bean-bag chair, from which I could not extricate myself, threw himself on the floor exclaiming, "I feel a poem! Oh, God, it's beautiful!" and began scribbling as though his blazer depended on it. I must say that it was a good poem, sensitive, graphic. I wish I could have kept it.

I finally escaped the bean bag by rolling over and over until free, shouted good-bye to our lady of the bath and drove down to Hazard, where David Hawpe and his wife, Linda, had invited me for dinner, following which a few friends would drop by to see the trained seal. It was my first chance to talk with Linda Hawpe, who turned out to be pretty and very bright. I paid for my drinks by recounting the day of the Noodle and the bean bag.

But then this photogenic young couple came in, all smiles and bouncy health like an orange juice ad, he a handsome young doctor just starting practice in Hazard, she a black-haired, blue-eyed beauty with a smile to melt railroad tracks. It was an era of informal entertaining, and she was in jeans and barefoot, and I remember saying to her wittily, "Young lady, you seem to have lost your shoes." She smiled. It was a memorable smile. The two of them were so wholesome, so pleased with their new careers, radiating love and confidence in the future that, watching them, thinking of my own crippled marriage, my fast-dissolving future at the *Courier*, I felt almost physically ill and was glad to say goodnight and drive up to La Citadelle, the mountaintop motel invariably called THE La Citadelle. I took a long drink of Johnnie Walker and sat on the side of the bed, wondering if I would ever find my way back to that happy, hopeful kind of life, wondering where along the way I had missed the turn, and why. Whiskey and self-pity make Jack repulsive. John, too.

***

It was only a matter of months before I was back at THE La, this time for a far grimmer purpose. There had been an explosion in the Finley mine on Hurricane Creek, over in Leslie County. Thirty-eight men had been killed and everyone from governor to county officials descended on the mine mouth, along with a flood of media people.

Congressman Carl Perkins came down from Washington, and rode down into the blasted mine on one of those hair-whitening man trips that force miners to lie flat. I don't now why any of us wanted to go down the grisly slope, back into that mine. There was little to see that made any sense to anyone outside the business. I did, however, discover one indisputable fact: I didn't want to do it again.

The site of a mine disaster isn't something you want to store away in memory's album, especially as night closes in and spotlights reveal the ugly, blackened drift mouth. Voices are hushed except for an occasional sob or moan as people, mostly women, try to comfort each other. Then there is a flurry of action as a car comes slipping out of the mine, plastic sheets or tarpaulins covering inert, horrifying lumps, and then screams and moans as the tarps are pulled back and the bodies recognized, while children bawl their confusion and fright and women collapse at the sight and significance of the still forms.

Some of us learned a lesson at the hearings that followed. Most of the testimony concerned the use of primacord, a rapid detonator that sparks the explosion loosening the coal from the seam, and we became so interested in this detail that we missed the most pertinent fact, the real cause of the tragedy, though it was laid clearly before us. The local coroner, a tall, solemn man who spoke in a low, steady voice, announced that from what he had found, he could say positively that the miners had died from suffocation. David Hawpe had come over from Hazard to cover the hearings, and he and I snickered at what seemed the incongruity of the hick coroner's testimony. What but suffocation could you expect when an explosion burns the oxygen from the air?

In our smart-alec way, we had missed the whole point. Why hadn't the miners put on their re-breathers, the safety canisters they are required to have with them in case of such emergencies? If they had done so, the majority of them, not in the immediate vicinity of the blast, could have put them on, breathed and found their way out of the mine. Without them, they had suffocated, choked to death, in a few minutes. The law specifically required the miners to carry re-breathers, required the mine operator to make sure they understood the law, and foremen to enforce it. Someone had failed to do his duty, and thirty-eight men had died.

It was a depressing trial of men guilty of failure, of a mistake that added up to a crime. Not bad men, not greedy men, but careless men, in an industry that cannot brook carelessness. I think we learned from the incident to listen more to routine words and not to be such smart alecs.

***

Then we got a jolt. Bert Combs indicated that he was ready to announce for another term as governor. We were elated, looking forward to four more years of progressive administration, when suddenly Wendell Ford, a smooth, hard-charging Chamber of Commerce type who had been Bert's administrative assistant and then served as lieutenant governor under Louie Nunn, announced that he, too, would run. The Combs people were furious at Wendell for turning on his mentor, but he was determined to run and did, and ran a good race, though taking the low road with a promise to cut the taxes that had been levied under Combs and Nunn, and on which hopes for school progress depended. Bert had handicaps and did not run a smooth race. Many Kentuckians did not understand, and Bert never adequately explained, why he would give up a prestigious seat on the Federal District Court for a Frankfort headache that paid far less, unless he planned to make it up some other way. His divorce from Mable, his boyhood sweetheart, and marriage to Helen Rechtin, a successful Louisville realtor, rankled mountain voters. Combs did not have a staff as energetic and enthusiastic as in his first races, he lacked the old fire, and his wife irritated his staff by intervening at strategy meetings. So Ford won.

I assumed that we would support Ford editorially rather than his opponent, Tom Emberton, but had no strong feelings on the matter. Ford came to lunch with the board and admitted that he would try to repeal part of the sales tax that Combs had fought and bled for, and that was education's mainstay. Barry asked me how I felt about the race, and I said quite honestly that I didn't care. This seemed to irritate him, since he thought a man should write from conviction, certainly a morally sound position. I wrote a series of lackluster editorials, gave them to Bob Barnard and left on a vacation on Sanibel. The editorials were edited almost to the point where I did not recognize them, and I was not surprised when I was accused of having made several mistakes in them.

I had explained to Barry, Sr. my involvement in the Sanibel development with Bert and Jack Matlick, and he expressed no objec-

150

tion until Bert decided to run again, when he asked that I either sell to Bert or buy out his interest, in order to avoid a conflict of interest should Bert win. Bert did not want to be bothered with the development while in office, so I bought him out. I had about $65,000 invested, with no prospect of immediate profit. Then Ed Konrad, handsome former Navy flier and an associate of my friend Priscilla Murphy told me that my tactics were wrong. The biggest reason you can't sell your lots, he told me, is that they are under-priced. People think there is something wrong with them. Increase the prices from $15,000 to $25,000 or $30,000. And when you sell a couple of lots boost the prices again. I followed his advice and within two years had sold all of the lots and made about $200,000.

But I am getting ahead of myself. The family and I had a good vacation on the island, as usual, and it gave me a chance to spend a little more time with my daughter Betsy. My wife had accused me of favoring Dinny and neglecting Betsy, and I determined to correct that. It was easy to love Dinny; she was pretty, sweet, smart and artistic. She had a love of children, and a knack for working with them. At one time during summer vacation, she had served at a local school for the autistic, certainly one of the most difficult areas of therapy, and had done so well that she was asked to come back and possibly help with an instructional manual. This was when she was about fourteen, and it was natural to admire her. But it was equally hard to ignore Betsy. She had an appealing self-confidence and a willingness to tackle almost anything. She seemed to pay only casual attention to her studies, but made good grades, methodically picking up a textbook, finishing the lesson, picking up the next, until she was through and ran out to play. She was more assertive than her sister, and I noticed that the kids galloping and screaming through the yard clearly regarded her as a leader. She began to be more pretty than cute and to show a determination that delighted me. Trying to learn to ride their bikes, the other children tended to fall, get up and give up. Not Betsy. I would give her a shove down the slope of the yard, she would wobble and fall, but bounce up immediately, declaring "I can do it. Don't worry. Let's try it again," and in two hours be rolling down the street.

The same thing occurred when she was in middle school and went out for cheerleader. Each afternoon we would see her out in the back yard, flailing her skinny limbs about, screeching out cheers. She tried out. She failed. "I was so proud of her, down in front of all those people," said Dinny. "I could never do that. I almost cried when she got cut." But Betsy simply retired to the back yard, again tortured her joints, and the next year made it. On Sanibel, she insisted on going out with me in the sailing dinghy that I had borrowed from Ed Konrad, and asked me to teach her to cast. She did rather well. I stood behind her, watching, and as she drew back her cast she snagged daddy neatly in the scalp. For a second she could not understand the tension on her line or the strange noises daddy was making. Daddy wasn't hurt nearly as badly as Betsy. The next day we rented a boat and went fishing on Tarpon Bay, where she hooked a big redfish, played him well, and reeled him in with disbelief and pride.

Being the father of daughters, especially nice, smart daughters, is the most abject slavery a man can know. Better to take up golf. Or dogs. Or, to paraphrase O.O. McIntyre, do not give your heart to a daughter to tear. Unless you are only slightly younger than God, you won't remember O.O. "Odd" McIntyre who in the years after World War I was a famous New York columnist and critic. His column lent the impression that he was a bon vivant, a boulevardier who lived in a sumptuous Fifth Avenue apartment with his books and his dog. As dogs will, his died, or so he said, and he wrote a eulogy to the mutt that brought from dog-lovers a flood of tears that washed from coast to coast. "Don't," he wrote, "give your heart to a dog to tear," and you could almost see him, tears on his noble face, placing a single rose on old Rover's grave. Overnight he became not only a man of the world but a man of heart, a hero twice told. There was only a slight smudge on this heart-wrenched: Odd didn't have a dog. He hated dogs. Made the whole thing up. Even the line about a dog tearing your heart was not his. He stole it from Rudyard Kipling. No one in the column business bothered to expose him, lest their own plagiarism be exposed some day. Indeed, it is doubtful that a handful of them had read Kipling.

I have now revealed to you a secret of the trade. Stealing one man's words is plagiarism; stealing the words of a dozen is research. Success, according to the bores who deal in such stuff, is ten percent inspiration, ninety percent perspiration. And the ten percent need not necessarily be yours.

One thing in my wobbly life went well, though. The time came for me to report to Fort McNair, this time as instructor, or group leader of the military-foreign study seminar. Again, it was a fascinating time, and it was capped with my being given my commander's stripes, qualifying me for the gold scrambled eggs on my cap. It was a moment of some nostalgia. I recalled that, during our first days as cadets at Lambert Field, Chug McCormick and I were strolling toward the hangar when we accosted a commander, resplendent in his dress whites, three stripes on his shoulder boards and gold braid on his cap. "I'd like to have one of those," I mentioned. "Why don't you just ask him to give you his?" asked Chug. "I'll wait," I said. I waited twenty-five years. I wished that Chug could have been there to see me in my golden glow.

But every silver lining has a cloud, every peach a pit. My wife's sister announced her engagement to a young man from Cincinnati. He seemed top grade, and everyone was happy. The wedding was to be held in the family garden, always a nice touch. The girls got new dresses. I shined my shoes. And then a surprise.

"Mother wants me to come and bring the girls," my wife confided, "but she asked that you not come. I hope you don't mind." I asked if this meant she intended to go without me, and she said she was sorry, but it was the only way she would get to see her only sister married. Not until they trooped off to the joyous nuptials did I think she would actually do it. I couldn't blame her entirely. It was not her fault that I was uninvited. But I thought she should have put up a protest on my behalf, and while they were gone I wondered how to explain my absence to friends ("I had a hideous case of diarrhea," "I was in jail for debt," "My brother, the elephant man, was in town, drunk.") Most of all, I wondered what the girls would think, how I could explain why I was an embarrassment in public. Actually, no one ever mentioned my absence. The girls said it had been lovely. My wife shrugged it off. I should have, too, but I didn't. Pride.

But again, the blind hog found an acorn. Ever since Weldon James had resigned to go back into uniform I had been itching to get to Vietnam, just to see what was really going on. It had become almost impossible to formulate a consistent editorial policy on the war. Everyone wanted to get out, including, I am sure, Lyndon Johnson, but no one knew how to go about it. Just get out, the peaceniks demanded, and they were basically right. But there were the usual devilish details. What would happen to the South Vietnamese who were our allies and the ARVN, the often confused, often lackadaisical, often resigned Army of the Republic of Vietnam? What of the village chiefs, who had sided with us? What of the peasants who wanted only to be left alone? We had seen how the ARVN couldn't stand up to the Viet

Cong or the NVA, the North Vietnamese Army. If we left, they would be slaughtered. On the other hand, were the conservative right in swearing that if Vietnam fell, the domino theory would shortly topple Cambodia, the rest of Southeast Asia, even Australia. So it went.

Then I got a letter from Commander Rod Kent, in the Navy Office of Information, asking if I would accept extended training duty to go to Vietnam, worm around, learn why the media were treating the military like an enemy and make a report. He could get me brigadier general's orders, with covering letters instructing all commands to give me any assistance. I had enough rank to move easily within the military, enough status to mingle with the media people. I jumped at the chance. Barry had turned down my request to be sent to Saigon, though the news side sent photographer Bill Strode and would later send reporter Joel Brinkley and photographer Jay Mather to Cambodia, where they won another Pulitzer.

Barry was funny about money. He did not consider it a subject for gentlemen to discuss. He was more than generous when I went to Harvard on a Nieman Fellowship, but he could become indignant over a piddling expense account. I forget the date when Dick Harwood and I went to a Southern Governors Conference at the Maple Grove Inn, near Asheville, North Carolina. I do remember that George Wallace had just lost a race for governor of Alabama to John Patterson. "He out-niggered me," said Wallace, previously considered a racial moderate. "He won't out-nigger me again." And he didn't.

There was a good crowd of journalists on hand, including a madman who kept calling the Asheville chief of police to learn where the whores hung out. The chief did not take kindly to the query or to the charge that he displayed a low level of hospitality. But there was little of importance happening, so Harwood and I drove down to Lake Lure, rented a boat and rode around the lake. And suddenly we rounded a bend and there, in a quiet bay, was Chimney Rock Camp for Boys. I was startled, then saddened, for time had not dealt kindly with that scene of my most idyllic summer. The dock was rotted and falling in, the diving tower gone. The shutters on the windows of the boat house flapped on broken hinges. I considered for a moment going ashore to see if good old Cabin Five was still standing, the mess hall and tennis courts. But I decided to let them remain in memory the way they had been that summer when I and my world were young.

That night Dick and I gave a small party for the press corps, nothing fancy, some sandwiches, a samovar of coffee, a few bottles of whiskey, some set-ups. When we got back to the office, I turned in an expense account for $75 for the party. Barry was mad as hell. He said that such entertainment was not our policy (it was when he and Mark traveled.) But I decided then and there not to put entertainment on an expense account again.

I was sorry that, while we were at Lake Lure, we had not driven down to Rutherfordton. Our family had been so happy there, happier than we would ever be again. But I swore that the next time I drove to Florida I would go by and see the old home place. And I did. I think I took the wrong exit from the road leading from I-26 and came in on the north side of town and found myself suddenly on North Main Street. I topped a gentle rise and there on the left, without warning, was the house, our house, as pretty as I remembered it, set on its slight rise, the surrounding pines standing as they had then. And for a flick of time it was as though my boyhood, wrapped in innocent happiness, was spread before me, just out of reach.

12

Vietnam

Being back in uniform felt surprisingly good, especially with the silver leaves on my collar and the scrambled eggs on my hat. Better than the last time, though it occurred to me that I would gladly exchange places with the lowly cadet of 1942. I have an idea that more men volunteer to recapture, however fleetingly, that feeling of being young, back in the company of men and away from the day-to-day tyranny of home and office, than from patriotism.

I have never understood patriotism very much, anyhow, love of country, love of the flag and so on. I don't know that I love this country, especially. There are parts of it I love; take me back to San Francisco, let me die in the Huntington Hotel, after dinner at Masas. I can stand some time in Mendicino, North Captiva. I do love what this country is supposed to stand for; I'm not sure that I love a lot of what it seems to stand for today—punitive drug laws, the death penalty, hatred of differences, Christian intolerance, greed among the rich, contempt for the poor and working people, a Congress that is truly a parliament of whores, our public offices from president to county judge for sale, gun fanatics, puritans anti-everything from abortion to jock itch. No, I'm not crazy about that side of the U.S. There are aspects of Costa Rica I find more admirable. Everyone votes. I've never heard of a bought election. And 97 percent of the people can read. What's wrong with this rich capitalist nation that we can't afford enough good schools to teach our people to read? What's wrong with us when we itch to spend five times as much per year on a prisoner as we spend on a collegian? Why are we the only advanced nation that refuses to take care of its sick? We're based on good principles, but we have our ideals skewed.

The same with the flag. It's a piece of cloth, nothing else. It's what it stands for that counts, it's the ideals behind it that deserve reverence. I've got no use for old farts who weep when the flag goes by, then turn and kick a coked-up addict or ostracize a homosexual.

Anyhow, back to the chase. I went to Washington to get security clearance and catch a plane for San Francisco. Washington is not a bad place to kill a couple of days except that I had to sit by the phone for two days, ready to fly on an hour's notice. When I finally got the word, I called home, the departing hero saying good-bye, don't worry about me, and expecting fond words from wife and kiddies (the Donna Reed bit, smiling through her tears, lips trembling, "Take care of yourself, darling. We'll pray for you." "Good-bye, Daddy, we love you," maybe a little sniffle, while in the background the band plays "I'll be seeing you").

It didn't work out that way. My wife was furious. The sump pump in the basement was stopped up and she had no idea what to do about it. I suggested that she call a plumber and recited again my "I'm off to the wars" speech, but she was having none of it. "Go on," she snapped. "Go kiting off to Vietnam and leave me here with this mess. Just like you." I got a cab to Langley and caught a flight to San Francisco, wondering if perhaps I could write my story and sell it as one of those "Can this marriage be saved?" epics.

***

I spent two days at the Navy station on Treasure Island in San Francisco Bay, free to go into town, one of my favorite places on earth, but chose to sleep, read, jog around, and enjoy the view up the bay toward the bridge, recalling good times there. I got a good flight to Pearl Harbor, where I was briefed and given a dozen shots—plague, cholera, dengue, yellow fever, you name it. The corpsman told me I could stretch the shots out over two or three days if I preferred, but I chose to get them over with. "You may be a little sicky poo this afternoon," he said. (Sicky poo? What had happened to my Navy?)

For some reason, I felt deeply at home in the Makalapa BOQ (Bachelor Officers Quarters) and found myself wishing, though not very sincerely, that I could get back into the Navy, not a likelihood considering my gray hair with face to match. But then a pleasant thing happened. Who do you think was serving as public affairs officer to Admiral Krulak at Navy-Marine headquarters? None other than Major Weldon James. Margaret called and asked me to dinner, and we sat on the verandah of their home on Makalapa Heights, overlooking Pearl Harbor and the lights of Oahu beyond, a dramatic sight. And sitting there, sipping a glass of scotch and enjoying the soft breeze off the Pacific, it occurred to me that there was a measure of irony in the scene: I, the semi-dove, was heading out for the battle zone, while Weldon, the hawk, lolled in this Pacific paradise.

The next day Margaret let me have her car, and I drove through Honolulu and through the Puka in the Pali, pausing for a few minutes to gaze at the massive green cliffs plunging down toward Kaneohe and the blue Pacific. There is always something romantic, reminiscent of the old Havaiki in the soaring, windy cliffs of this lovely offspring of the ocean, looking much as it must have before we came. I had lunch at a cafe out over the water at Kaneohe, drove up the north shore and dived for shells for a few minutes, then returned through the pineapple fields of mid-island to Makalapa as the lights came on in the ships in harbor. It was an idyllic day, and it was a jar to be rousted out next morning and tossed aboard a transport for Saigon. I have an idea that most wars would be pleasantly memorable if it weren't for the fighting. It was a long, uneventful flight, the Ton Son Nhut airport a swirling, bawling mob, hot and dirty.

I will bore you only briefly, I hope, with my war stories, partly because they didn't add up to much, partly because once old retreads get started it is hard for them to stop. Writing his own war story is about the only chance the average slob gets to read about himself as hero.

What I found in Vietnam saddened me and made me fear for my country, but I am glad I went and want to return some day. The war seemed to make some sense at a distance, but was insane up close. I still can't understand how we let ourselves get suckered into that mess.

I checked into Navy headquarters at the Rex Hotel, drew fatigues, helmet, flak jacket, boondockers and a .38 that looked ridiculous in view of all the Viet Cong running around with their AK 47s. Right off, I began running into old buddies from WWII, the jgs and lieutenants of 1945 now commanders and captains. A sharp-looking commander in whites came up to me and asked if I was John Ed Pearce.

I admitted it. From Louisville? Yes. Well. He was Harry Towns, former sports writer for the *Louisville Times*, who had found civilian life less than expected and gone back into uniform. He had seen on the sheet that I was coming and offered to show me around. There was a lot to see. Saigon had once been known as the Pearl of the Orient, and it was easy to see why. Despite the damage and sandbags, streets crammed with refugees and military, it retained a lot of its beauty and charm, with its French architecture and tree-lined streets, not to mention the beautiful, dark-eyed girls riding their motor-bikes in their graceful dais, with their long, dark hair waving in the breeze.

After finding temporary quarters, I went over to the Caravelle Hotel, looked on the register and found that, as expected, my old friend Dick Harwood was in residence. His eyes seemed likely to leave his face when he saw me, in uniform and all, and I had to explain that the Navy offered me my only chance to get to the war. We went up to the Continental Palace, had a couple of drinks and then went to a floating restaurant down on the Saigon River and ate a lot of mediocre food. I don't care for sweet-and-sour. After dark we went up to the roof of the Majestic Hotel and watched the evening edition of the war. Literally. Down the Saigon River toward Vung Tau, planes were bombing and rocketing some enemy ground forces, and the ground forces were rocketing in retort. It was rather bizarre when you remembered that those were our boys shooting at their boys and vice versa. Tracers lighted lanes through the black sky, and bombs went rump, rump, while I reported on things back in Louisville, which sounded even worse in the telling. Dick had assumed that I would be editor by this time, and I could not explain my slide down the slope of fate.

***

It soon became evident that this was a weird war. For one thing, the brass lived awfully well in Saigon, and there seemed to be an awful lot of brass about, playing tennis, swimming, eating off linen with waiters smiling around, going out to the races, enjoying steaks and French-style cooking, stopping by clubs where little golden-skinned, sloe-eyed doves came fluttering out of the dark, ready for fun. No tents for these boys, and all the time they were racking up field time that would count toward promotion. This impression was misleading, of course. Such officers represented only a small fraction of the commissioned ranks, but to the media they seemed to symbolize a war gone wrong.

The roof of the Rex Hotel was a scene out of fantasyland—an expanse of tables, with long lines of food, two bars, and a flaming pit where you ordered your steak, cooked to order. Pretty girls flitted about, and friends, there are no prettier girls than in Southeast Asia, and the singer with a rock band moaned that he wanted to go home. Why, I don't know. The Viet Cong had a rude habit of riding past the Rex on their little motor bikes and heaving plastique bombs against the sandbags. Why they didn't catapult a few up on the roof is beyond me. They could have killed half the local officer corps. And it was not just the officers who were enduring this crucible. The streets and bars crawled with grunts, and others lounged or slept under the trees. Now and then a gaggle of hard-eyed children would surround a soldier or U.S. civilian and try to rob him, climbing all over him and rifling his pockets when he used his hands to beat them off. I was told that the best thing to do was to kick them, and hard enough to hurt, which would cool off the others. A great war.

One problem with this nutty war, at once evident, was the inability to tell friend from foe. Vietnamese look like Vietnamese, and trying to tell Viet Cong from South Vietnamese was like walking down a street in New York and trying to tell Republicans from Democrats, and any one of them capable of killing you at any moment, or driving by and heaving a plastique into the doorway. Allies, enemies, security, victory—such words had shifting meanings.

Case in point: one day Harwood asked if I would like to inspect a pacified village, a native hamlet taken from the VC, rebuilt with school, town hall, stores, bridges, and homes and turned back to the natives, part of the U.S. aid program. A young fellow named Miles from the State Department on loan to USAID had offered to show us around, and we met him at the airfield where he had gotten a chopper. Since this pacified village was only three miles down what appeared to be a good road, I asked why we didn't take a Jeep. Miles hemmed and hawed but finally admitted that this might not be 100 percent safe, since the VC had a habit of hiding along the road and killing unsuspecting folk. We took the chopper.

The village was a showpiece, all right, all new concrete block buildings, painted white and red, an attractive village square with a flag pole (but no flag.) The village chief was polite and smiling and

Four-year-old John Ed Pearce, Jr.

Uncle Frank let me and my sisters Rose and Katherine pose on his new car around 1922.

Second grade at Pineville, Kentucky. That's me on the far right.

My skinny self; around 1940.

Norton, Virginia, 1935.

A camping trip, 1935.

(Above) Navy aviation cadet, 1942.

(Right) Not flying, but at war.

On the deck of the USS Forrestall off the coast of Vietnam, summer 1967.

To the left on a riverine boat on the Mekong River, South Vietnam, 1967.

With President Harry Truman and Wilson Wyatt, 1950.

With Bert Combs at a banquet for Harry Caudill, 1986.

At the Mountain Laurel Festival, Pineville, Kentucky in 1965. My sister Katherine is at right.

Betsy, Alida, Susie, Marnie, and Dinny with me in 1980.

With friend and Sulgrave Press publisher John Moremen at the SPJ dinner, 1986.

Same dinner, with Courier-Journal publisher Barry Bingham.

*With Sara and Bert
Combs at their wedding.*

*Off to a party with Mary
Lawrence Young.*

*Heavy talk around the
kitchen table with Lois
Mateus, David
Musselman, Steve
Wilson, and just-elected
governor of Kentucky
John Y. Brown, Jr.*

showed us around, but it was obvious that something was making him nervous. Harwood, too, noticed, and said that the place was too tense for his tastes, and in a few minutes Miles came over, said he had been talking to some of the people and had learned that the local Cong had been there the night before, rounded everyone up, read them a pep talk and warned them not to fly the South Vietnam flag anymore. But they also expressed high satisfaction with the restoration job the Americans had done and told the people to keep things in good shape until they got back to take over. The villagers said the VC were out there in the bush now, probably watching. I got the impression that they were watching us all of the time, hating us, waiting for the word to attack. Some pacified village. We were just doing the Cong's reconstruction work. I was greatly relieved when the chopper returned and took us back to Saigon.

We asked Miles, the AID man, why MACV (the U.S. command in Saigon) called these villages pacified, when in reality they were at best militarily ambivalent, ours by day, the Viet Cong's by night. He looked depressed by the question and asked if we were going to quote him. We assured him we were not, and he launched into a description of a worrisome situation. With Washington throwing more and more men and money into the war, President Johnson and Congress, especially Johnson, wanted to know why we weren't doing better. The pressure on the president was terrific, and politically dangerous. Protesters were marching, kids were rioting on campuses and at the Pentagon, and press and politicians were beginning to say we should win or get out.

The people on the ground, Miles said, were honest in their reports, admitting slow progress. But Washington, under pressure, was putting pressure on the command in Saigon, and Saigon was passing it on, so when a cautious report reached district headquarters, the tendency was to interpret the report to make it look as good as possible. The same thing happened in Saigon, and by the time the report passed through the Pentagon to the White House, it was rosy. No one had lied, but everyone had put the best spin possible on the truth. Small wonder, then, that the president wondered why all the rosy reports didn't add up to more progress, more victories.

An instructive day. I began to understand why the media so often refused to believe military reports. A couple of times I had attended the afternoon press briefings derisively called the Five O'Clock

Follies, at which some poor Army or Navy officer got up, read figures and reports that had been handed him, and then braced for questions from the hostile media. I also began to see why the military resented and distrusted the media; when briefing officers had claimed advances or victories, the press people had demanded proof, such as enemy killed or captured, to back up the claims. In response, the military began reporting body counts, most of which the media did not believe, and the military, by the very nature of a guerrilla jungle war, could not prove conclusively. Senior officers especially, accustomed to the friendly press they had known in previous wars, blamed much of the situation on reporters who did not know what they were seeing and did not believe what they were told. A sour situation.

***

Another time I rode a riverine boat out of Can Tho, down in the Delta on the Basac, a branch of the Mekong, which wanders all over. A big, muddy river. Our boat was of green plastic, about twenty feet long and loaded with guns of every type, commanded by a muscular black boatswain's mate and three seamen. That boat would fly, but you could take a .45 and put a bullet through it sideways. By nine o'clock the temperature was nuzzling 100, and after being aboard for five minutes we were soaked, dipped our helmets in the sweet Mekong and poured it over our heads. The crewmen laughed; they were used to it. In my flak jacket, boondockers and helmet I wondered what I was supposed to do in case we were sunk. We weren't.

It was, in my opinion, a nasty couple of days. We passed a free-fire island, so called because no one was supposed to be on it, and we were free to blast it with everything aboard to discourage the locals from hiding anyone there. We blew hell out of that place, but as we passed, out of the jungle fringing the river came this aged mama-san, poling a sampan loaded with bananas. She gave us what for, bothering an honest woman at her garden chores.

The next day we had an incident that disturbed me. Any time we encountered a native boat, we stopped and shook it down, making sure it carried no money, which would have indicated it carried a VC tax collector. These fellows, usually VC officers, traveled the region, collecting taxes from the villages and turning the money in to their headquarters in Saigon. We stopped one boat, ordered the crew aft and tore it apart, taking up floor boards, tearing down overhead, dumping produce. Finally a sailor found what he called a "pack of P's," a bundle of piastres, the local currency. Guns were pointed and the oldest man aboard the boat was ordered aboard ours. He was a handsome man, tall for a Vietnamese, prominent facial bones, graying hair. He sat down on the fantail, looking around in a casual, interested way, picking up deck tackle, inspecting it, smiling at me as if in mutual admiration for the workmanship. He seemed to have no fear of what awaited him, but sat, serene, dignified as we pulled into a small landing, and followed the boatswain when he motioned to him. In a minute the boatswain came back and we cast off. He had traded some K rations for papayas and a long, slender melon, and one of the sailors opened some rations and heated them on the manifold. I asked the boatswain's mate what was going to happen to the tax man. He shrugged.

"They'll kill him," he said dispassionately. "When we get a collector, we turn him and his money over to the nearest chief. He is supposed to turn him over to Can Tho or Saigon for questioning. This one's got too much money. The chief will kill him, keep the money, say nothing to nobody."

I noticed in the crowd of children who came down to gawk at us, several with fair skin and blue eyes. "French dudes been here before us," said a sailor. Everyone laughed. Traces of love.

Just after sunset, we saw rockets in the sky upriver, and turned toward them. A smaller boat had a young girl, maybe 12-13, who had been hit in a fire fight in her village. Half of her face was blown off, and she was blood all over. As gently as possible, we took her aboard, called Can Tho and they had medics ready when we reached the dock.

"Who hit her?" I asked. "Probably us," said the Boats. "Can't tell."

Twelve hours on the Basac with the temperature never below 100 can tire a body. I went into the head. A drunk jg was vomiting. Two others were laughing about a fight between Marines and SEALS in the enlisted bar. The SEALs, specially trained Navy men, operated from choppers, in rubber boats, by scuba, sneaking ashore to destroy or assassinate. Tough boys. A Marine had been cut. Someone would draw a court martial. I went back to the hotel, drank a lot of water, slept about a year.

***

Harwood took me to a party in the apartment of Lee Lescaze, chief of the *Washington Post* bureau. A lot of good people were there, including many whose by-lines I had seen. I had on khakis, since I had no clean civvies. The conversation turned to flights in and out of various airports. I mentioned that we had had a smooth flight in, and R.W. "Johnny" Apple, well-known reporter for *The New York Times* looked at me and sneered. "Yeah, I guess it's nice when you've got those pretty little things on your collar, not like us peasants."

"What's wrong with my tabs?" I asked, puzzled by his hostility but not wanting to make a scene of it.

"Oh, they're cute," he said, but Harwood stepped in.

"Lay off, Johnny," he said, "he's one of us. He's been in the news business longer than any of us."

"He's not one of mine," said Apple. "Not as long as he's in that monkey suit."

Others calmed him down, and the party went on, but I remembered what Rod Kent had said about our being the enemy. It was disappointing to hear a man from the respected *Times* talk that way. I concluded that we could not expect objective reporting out of Mr. Apple. I think it was Joe Alsop who said condescendingly to a young reporter that he never spoke with anyone less than a colonel; the reporter replied that he never spoke to anyone as high as a colonel. They were both wrong, of course. Such bias is not only pointless but can shut you off from avenues of information. But the exchange was illustrative of generation differences about the war. I didn't blame reporters for being disgusted with the brutalities of the war, but the brutalities were the direct result of orders that reflected strategy. Men were told to clear a village of Viet Cong, but who was VC and who a harmless kid? They took fire from hooches, and burned the hooches often killing old women and children. My Lai, I was assured, was no isolated incident. The trouble was that once men got used to killing and found it convenient, it seemed routine. They were just young Americans, lost in chaos, longing only for home, but to the media they often became symbolic of a hated military that perpetuated the war.

***

I got a hop north to DaNang, where I was told to report to a man named Dick Blaisdell. I found my way to this large office and was standing there waiting for information when someone called "Attention!" Everyone jumped to his feet and braced and I, good former cadet, followed suit. I kept looking out of the corner of my eye to see who had come in until it dawned on me that it was I. I had not gotten used to my silver leaves. I snapped "Carry on!" in sharp tones. Commander.

Blaisdell got me a weird room in a building called the White Elephant. A cozy spot. Even the furniture sweated, and the air trembled. Diagonally across the street the world's noisiest generator pumped out power for the Navy compound. Our building was directly in the flight path of planes approaching the DaNang airfield, a mile away, and on the roof of the building across the street was the loudest rock and roll band ever permitted. I knew I could never sleep in that sound chamber, but shucked my fatigues and boots and lay down. I awoke eight hours later, to find an elderly mama-san looking at me in a kindly fashion. My clothes, however, were nowhere in sight, and I did not know how to ask for them. Pulling on my underwear shorts (anything for modesty) I made dressing motions; she smiled and nodded, and a moment later produced my wardrobe, spotless, creased, the boots glistening.

That was the beginning of a lovely romance. I became accustomed to the fact that my love cared little for privacy, especially mine. Whether I was in the shower or on the potty, in she would waltz, mopping and jabbering away. I tried to find out how I could repay her for my crisp laundry, and after a lot of motions and giggles, she got a piece of paper and wrote on it Whitman. Then I remembered that in the bar on the roof they sold tins of Whitman's chocolates, though not to the Vietnamese help. I went up, bought a tin and gave it to her. She shuffled into the hallway, cawing like a crow, and within seconds, my cozy room was mobbed by about five maids, all chewing and smiling at me. From then on my clothes could not hit the floor before happy hands grabbed and started the one-hour laundry. And every time I woke up, two or three of my ladies would have ironing boards on the floor, pressing and chattering. I was either a hero or one of the girls. All it took was a little chocolate. Every time I came back from a trip, there they were, grinning, cackling and salivating. We became buddies. I had pictures of my girls in a folder that I kept by my bed, and when the maids found out they were mine, their admiration grew. Sons were fine, they said as best they could, but daughters were better. They would not be drafted and killed.

Down in Blaisdell's office, an enlisted man was waiting for me one day, probably to put me in the brig for slipping Whitman to the maids. "Commander Pearce?" We went through the saluting routine. "Admiral Vanover of the Amphibious Fleet requests your presence aboard the flagship for lunch, sir!" Naturally, I thought a mistake had been made, but he insisted, and I followed him down to the dock where the Admiral's barge lay, shining like a new dime, and off we went to this mammoth ship. I clambered up the gangway and saluted none other than Captain Bull Durham, an old Louisville boy who once headed the Naval ROTC unit at the University of Louisville. He was chief of staff to Admiral Vanover, who was none other than Jack Vanover, from Madisonville. He shook my hand, and gave me a big grin. "God, John Ed," he said, "I've heard about you as long as I can remember, some good, some bad. Come on aboard."

We had a fine lunch, and I had my picture taken with the two of them before returning to real life. I was gradually learning that rank had its good points, sure enough. Being an ensign was just a small cut above pot walloper; being a commander at least sounded good. I remembered telling Mama that I had a good chance of making captain, but she was not impressed. You ought to stay commander, she said, it sounds so much better. Strange thing: I was down at the Marine press tent that evening when I heard a press man and a Marine talking about an amphibious strike being planned to go north and hook around Nha Trang, and the next morning I asked Blaisdell if he could get me aboard. "What!?" he screamed. "Where'd you hear that?" I told him. "Oh, Jesus Christ," he said. "That's too secret for me to talk about. Let me outa here!"

He returned presently and asked me a lot of questions to which I had no answers. "Good thing you mentioned it," he said. "Gave us time to call it off. If we'd gone ahead, every Charlie in I Corps would have been out there to welcome us. Wonder how in hell that got out? Man, security over here is something."

So I missed my big chance. Just as well. The next day I got a chance to go out on the *Forrestal*, that big, beautiful aircraft carrier (there is something dramatic, exciting about a carrier), and I accepted. I got a room with a member of ship's company who was not overjoyed to have me crowd in, but the captain offered to let me fly on a recon flight over the North Vietnam coast. It would have been a pleasant flight had the terrain below not been unfriendly, and the next day I caught a flight back to DaNang. I was having lunch at the officers' mess when someone asked what I had been doing, and I replied that I had just come from the *Forrestal*. This bit of information caused a furor, and I learned that, about an hour after I left, the ship had been racked by a serious fire. A latch holding a rocket to the wing of a fighter plane had given way, the rocket had fallen to the deck and activated, roaring up the flight deck and causing fires and explosions among everything in its path. Only some fine damage control had saved the ship. That night I admitted to the Lord that I owed him one.

Blaisdell gave me a Jeep and driver to look around the area, and we drove out to Marble Mountain, manned by Marines and supposedly a hairy place. One thing I noticed, though: it was a well policed base, and the Marines, though sometimes sporting a layer of the good earth, were sharp and disciplined, in contrast to a lot of grunts I ran into out in the greenery. Among the Army troops I traveled with, discipline seemed casual. Enlisted men and officers seemed to feel and show little respect for each other, and when enlisted men would talk they hinted that they had little confidence in their officers to lead. After the war I learned that the mountain, only a few miles away, was honeycombed with caves, all well stocked and supplied, from where the VC watched the base and the traffic on the north-south road. On the way back to DaNang a sergeant driving a six-wheeler almost ran us off the dusty road until we pulled over and let him barrel past. I asked my driver what the hurry was and he said that people got nervous driving that stretch of road, which was good ambush country. I suggested we put pedal to metal.

***

DaNang was a strange place. By some happenstance I fell in with an enlisted sailor who was involved in a Navy local-support project, restoring historic Khmer statuary in a small park not far from the river. Centuries before, the Khmers had swept out of the west, what is now Cambodia and Burma, and overrun much of present Vietnam, building an attractive and fairly progressive civilization until the Vietnamese came down from their sanctuary in South China and took back the land. Among the peculiar statuary left by the Khmer were dozens embodying phallic symbols; it was rather startling to see a ten-foot penis, cleaned up and white, with kiddies or animals playing around its base. The sculptors had had their minds on other things, too, though. Out in the bush, only a few miles to the west of the peter park, were the remains of what must have been a handsome palace, remnants of animal carvings still distinguishable, and on the long marble lintel that must have topped the palace gate or entry were the words that, my guide said, asked of the passerby "Look upon my work which we have loved, and be kind."

I could have dug in DaNang but time was fleeting, and Blaisdell got me a puddle-jumper to Pleiku. I had no special reason to go there, but I had read that it was the center of the highlands and home to several tribes of Montagnards. Barry, Sr. was interested in the fate of the Montagnards, who were treated badly by the Vietnamese, and wanted me to see if I could find anything about them. I found that they were considered primitive by the Vietnamese and often referred to as "the niggers of Vietnam." Since not all of the Mont tribes dealt in metal money, it was hard for Saigon to collect taxes from them and usually just rounded them up and put them to work on the roads. One dispiriting story told of an Army major at Pleiku who had a Montagnard friend who had performed heroic service for the Americans as a scout. To reward him, the Major took him to Saigon for a holiday. The MPs stopped them and would not let the Montagnard pass the check point.

Pleiku itself was not a bad looking spot, a substantial base alongside an airstrip in a long valley flanked by heavily-forested mountains, and a town with a lively marketplace. It frequently drew the attention of the VC, which used nearby trails to shuttle supplies and guns from north to south, and was often the center of activity. Some was taking place when we landed, and we went through the usual routine of hearing the sergeant advise us to make haste, an unnecessary bit of urging as we ran across the strip and dived into the slit trench, as the plane went its way.

In DaNang I met Lieutenant Commander Clark Gamel, a new operations officer assigned to Saigon and on his initial inspection tour. A great guy, with a sense of humor that took everything in stride. As he went about his business in Pleiku, I had the good luck to meet an Army major called Doc, though he wore no medical insignia. Over dinner I told him of my interest in the Montagnards, and as luck would have it, it turned out that Doc was not a doc at all, but an aviation operations officer who had made a hobby of local history and culture wherever he was assigned and had taken on the Monts as a sort of humanitarian project. He said he was going to visit a tribe not far up in the hills the next day, to help them celebrate a feast day, and would be glad to have me come along.

We got a Jeep, driven by a second lieutenant who gave me a gruesome but pleased description of the Mike forces, Montagnards employed by the Army to clear the way for landing zones. "We pick out a site, drop a company of Mike forces, and they kill everything within a mile radius."

"What if there are Vietnamese, Montagnards, cattle, people within the kill site?" I asked him. He smiled.

"Everything," he said. "Down to birds and snakes. If it moves, kill it. When our boys drop in there, they don't want anything in their way."

After about an hour of bumping over dirt paths, we came to this nondescript village of perhaps two dozen houses, all built on bamboo stilts, with split bamboo floors and thatched roofs. The chief came out and saluted the Doc and everyone crowded around, exchanging pleasantries with Doc and smiling at me. Nice-looking, red-tan people, tending toward short and stocky, with thick black hair. The younger women, who simpered and giggled to see us, were rather pretty and had fine breasts.

Before a proper feast there must, of course, be cocktails, and the chief had concocted his own special brand. He half-filled a huge crock with fermented rice over which he placed a few layers of banana leaves, and then filled the crock with water. The water seeped down through the fermented rice, forming a high-proof wine at the bottom. He then took a thin, hollow bamboo stem and stuck it down to the bottom of the crock, and it was ready for the taste test. Curiously, it was not the chief, but the chief's mother, who got first pull—and that is what it was, as the drinker sucked the wine up through the straw. Along the side of the straw small marks were painted, and a small float was attached to the straw that fell as the level of the wine fell. Descent from one mark to the next was called a level, and each celebrant was expected to down a level. After the chief's mother sucked up a level, the chief followed, then the chief's wife, and finally the guest or guests of honor, in this case the Doc and I. I stepped up and sucked down a level, smiling broadly and smacking my lips, as Doc had warned me to do. Otherwise the hosts would feel affronted and possibly ask us to leave. Rapidly.

As the levels fell, spirits rose, and one by one we were called back to partake of more liquid hospitality. Again, I showed my manhood and gagged it down without gagging it up. Everyone applauded. The chief smiled on me. Everyone took another pull. I did my best for international relations. I think I would have died then and there had the girls not brought out the canapés—banana leaves filled with a thick, slimy green paste dotted with little seeds that did not help the medicine go down. That night I said a special prayer of thanks to God for letting me keep that mixture down.

Next came the entree—water buffalo that had been roasting over an open fire (like chestnuts) for a few days. The chief, full now of rice delight, stepped forward and sliced off a piece of haunch that could have fed a platoon and handed it to a villager who was smiling woozily, at which everyone cheered. It seems that it was his buffalo, and he had gained a good measure of dignity and honor by donating it to the feast. That, I gathered, was tradition. The rich man of the village was not the man who owned the most buffalo, but the man who sacrificed the most. Well, the man said it is better to give.

After everyone had settled down, the Doc began his rounds, looking down throats, into ears, eyes, noses and any other orifices, asking of digestion, inspecting sores and cuts. He had a potion for everything and soon had a waiting room full of patients. There was only one small drawback to his practice: to show the patients that his medicine was good, he had to down a sample of it first, and I watched in amazement as he gulped, rubbed and poured all sorts of stuff on and into himself, after which the villagers happily and trustingly took theirs. Strange occasion. Here we were, an aviation specialist who knew nothing of medicine except what the base doctor prescribed after he described symptoms, treating a tribe of animists who worshipped the god of the stream, the god of the forest and the god of the wind, who would not plow more than an inch deep for fear of hurting the earth god, and would abandon a good field if a snake crawled through it. And yet they listened happily to rock music from a U.S. military station, on transistor radios they got from working at the base, whose huge radar mats and electronic wizardry lay ominously at the foot of their mountain.

I really didn't feel much like dinner that night.

***

Gamel was ready to move on next day and we caught a flight east to Nha Trang. I am going back there some day, if I live long enough, and build hotels on that beach and watch the waves and the millions roll in. Nha Trang has one of the most beautiful beaches I have ever seen, but it was so littered by concertina wire that it was hard to get to. I got a driver to drive me a mile or so down the beach, where I had heard they sold pretty triton shells. An old guy offered to take me out snorkeling and we had a fine time. The water was clear and cool over sandy bottom around the small islands that dotted the long crescent bay. I didn't find many shells, but enjoyed a beautiful afternoon, and was back in the Army compound before I found out that I had been wandering around VC country. The Lord takes care of fools. He does not take care of fool's swimming trunks; I hung mine out to dry behind the compound and never saw them again. I trust the thief has by this time found that there was a fatal curse on them.

Gamel and I got a hop to Phu Bai, where the Navy, in its exalted wisdom, had scraped the landscape so bare that every little breeze whipped up just a little more red dust to add to the ten inches already overlaying everything. I was given a cot in a large tent and was about to lie down when a Marine captain stalked up and said I had his bunk. I protested, honestly, that the sergeant had assigned it to me. The Marine disputed that and we stood nose to nose; I was confident that he was not about to risk trouble hitting a three-striper. The sergeant was called, apologized, and gave me the opposite bunk. The Marine and I patched up the interservice rivalry. I told him that he looked like my brother, who was also a Marine, and he said that was funny because he was sure we had met before. It turned out he had just come from recruiting duty in the federal building in Louisville, where he often attended our Reserve meetings. A friend is born. My stay in Phu Bai was unexceptional except for a good movie that night, something about a duck, with Tuesday Weld, that was interrupted by some incoming artillery, prompting our lads to respond in kind and delaying the movie.

The next day we took off for Dong Ha in a C-130 loaded with Marines and, up front, an Air Force colonel who had been assigned to General Westmoreland's staff and was inspecting facilities in I-Corps. Big blowhard. Hero. Oughta get this mess over with. Bomb the gooks. Win the hearts, yeah. Grab 'em by the balls and their hearts will follow. Oh, har, har.

We got to Dong Ha which, to the naked eye, was not the Riviera. The co-pilot screamed that Charlie (VC) was shelling the place, and we'd have to circle a while. The heroic colonel took one look and declared that there was no use in his landing, since it was obviously too windy for choppers to fly an inspection of the area. We sneered. The pilot shrugged. When we did land, the pilot kept the engines going, dropped the rear ramp and a sergeant screamed "Run, goddamit, run!" and we grabbed our bags, sprinted across the runway, and dived into the slit trench alongside. The Marines, looking bored, strolled over. No more fireworks came in, and we reported to the sergeant who grinned at us, told us to keep our head out of our ass, charming phrase, and pick out a hole in case of shelling. A while later he came back and ushered us in to see the Marine general, who was not happy to see us.

"What're you doing here?" he bellowed. "Couple goddam tourists! We're trying to fight a war, got no time for tourists." Gamel explained that he was on assignment, and I squeaked that I was out of Detachment Charlie in Saigon. "Goddam tourists," he repeated. "See that?" he pointed to a hole in a green metal locker big enough to accommodate a basketball. "The NVA paid us a call this morning. Get out of here as soon as you can. Sergeant tell you anything you need to know."

I don't think the sun ever shines in Dong Ha, nor does grass grow. Each morning, the triple barbed-wire gates swung open and Marine trucks rolled in, filled with native workers, who came in by day and left each evening. "Hey, Charlie," the Marines would holler at them, "that you shooting at us last night?" The native workers stared stonily. It was generally believed that the workers came in and, in the course of the day's work, paced off distances from the fence to key points and delivered the data back to the gunners waiting in the bush.

Happily, we were not shelled that night, and the next morning the general sent for us. He said he was sorry to have been so abrupt, that his nerves got thin sometimes, and would we like to take a tour of inspection with him. We would.

We flew over Ghio Linh, a denuded hill ringed with artillery, Camp Carroll, another gun base near the Laotian border, and the Rock Pile, which was what the name says, a vertical rock with a platform on top from which Marines watched for Charlie. Then we got to Khe Sahn, a tough-looking piece of real estate at the foot of two considerable hills from which the North Vietnamese had tried for months to shell the Marines into retreat. For a while they had cut the road from the South, and Khe Sahn had to depend on air support, and the sides of the air strip looked like an air junk yard. The Marines looked tired, but in good spirits. Why they had to hold that godforsaken place I have never understood. It served no purpose, didn't block the Ho Chi Minh Trail, which ran well to the west along the Laotian border. But Lyndon Johnson had a thing about Khe Sanh, asked about it every morning. The chiefs of staff had a hard time convincing him that the place was a waste of men and money. Not long after we visited it, the North Vietnamese launched a full-scale attack on it that failed, after which they paid it no attention, apparently wanting it for morale as much as military purposes. It was rumored around that it would be abandoned any day. After the NVA attack failed, John Carroll, correspondent with the *Baltimore Sun* and one of the best reporters on the scene, noticed that the heavy stuff, tanks and artillery as well as men, was heading south and wired his home office that we were getting out. This enraged MACV in Saigon, though it was common knowledge on both sides of the line, and Carroll got his accreditation suspended. It proved an inconvenience for a time.

Funny thing: twenty-five years later, Knight-Ridder sent John to Lexington, Ky., to revitalize the newly-acquired *Herald-Leader*. He did an outstanding job, created real competition for the *Courier-Journal*, and took away much of its circulation in Eastern Kentucky. By that time I had retired from the *Courier*, but was still writing a Sunday column for it, and John poked a hornet's nest when he persuaded me to write a column for him, too. David Hawpe, then editor of the *Courier*, was furious, would hardly speak to me, and the *Courier* finally dropped my column. Then, having led me into the cauldron, John quit the *Herald-Leader* to become executive editor of the *Baltimore Sun* papers. I miss him. He is a fine newsman.

With a non-reluctant farewell to scenic Dong Ha, we caught a ride up to Cua Viet, a Navy tank farm just south of the DMZ. It was a curious hybrid of a base; on one side of the compound, white prefabs housed the small Navy offices, while a few yards away the South Vietnamese soldiers who were supposed to defend the base lived in makeshift hoochs, and sat around cooking fires in the open. I was surprised to see women pursuing their chores, cooking and sweeping, while the men sat by with their rifles.

Gamel and I sought out the commanding officer and asked if we could beg a shower and a meal and were told that both were in short supply, and the shower was out of the question, though we could take a dip in the ocean nearby or go down to the Cua Viet River. We accepted a sandwich and sat talking, and I discovered that the CO was Norm Albertson, from Roanoke, Virginia. When I revealed that I was from Norton, we started playing do you know, and do you remember the time, and he relented to allow us a shower, if we would keep it to soap and rinse.

It seemed to me that the place was a target, with the fuel tanks so close to the DMZ and the guns of the North Vietnamese, but Albertson said that his main concern was the South Vietnamese troops assigned to protect the place. It was not just that they were poorly trained and disciplined, but they insisted on having their wives with them, and quitting each day at four and going home. Not only that, but the senior ARVN officer had stated flatly that he was taking no orders from any damned Americans.

We thanked our host for the welcome shower, hitch-hiked aboard a truck down to the river and caught a Navy landing craft going to DaNang. It was a strange but not unpleasant cruise. There was a good breeze after the hot day and we sat on deck smoking and, again, watching the war, as our planes dived on the enemy, tracers and rockets making a colorful pattern, while the enemy returned the fire.

In DaNang I found my old quarters taken, reported to the office and found that a wire had been relayed from Saigon requesting my presence at home. I said good-bye to Gamel, caught a flight to Saigon, and soon was on my way. Our plane had been hit by lightning near the Philippines, which made us a day late landing at Edwards Air Force Base, where I caught a bus to San Francisco.

There was more than the usual dreamlike quality about the change in environment. I wrote a long perspective piece on the media-military clash, but no one on the paper wanted to publish it. It was a good report. What it said, briefly, was that much of the media in Vietnam were openly hostile to and suspicious of the military, thought the military chiefs wanted the war to continue, looked on it as a means of getting field time for promotion, and lied to the media. The military thought the media wanted to see the U.S. get out at any cost, even if it meant great human loss, did not know enough to report the fighting accurately, and distorted what they were told. There was some truth on both sides.

My wife had planned a welcome-home party for me, which I considered a good omen, but when my wire arrived saying I would be late, she decided it was too late to postpone the festivities and proceeded with the party. It was, she said later, the best party we ever had.

13

Failure is a Lonely Thing

John Fetterman won the Pulitzer Prize in 1968 with one of the finest, if not *the* finest, pieces of writing I have ever read in a newspaper or magazine. I can reread it today and still be affected by its sensitivity, impressed by its craftsmanship. Every word is what and where it should be, and the picture they draw, the story they tell, is true and honest, touching the heart not by flowery language but by a straightforward account of an event central to the human experience. It is the story of the funeral of Little Duck Gibson, a young boy from the mountains of Eastern Kentucky who was killed in Vietnam and has been brought home for burial, amid the scenes and people among whom he grew, laid to rest with the tears and memories and feelings of pride that attend the soldier's farewell.

The Pulitzer was cause for great pride and boasting by the management of the *Courier*. Champagne was opened in the newsroom and the news was splashed next morning on the front page. Beyond that, the prize was an occasion for joy among the staff, for John was truly loved, and his success was almost a shared thing. As his prize-winning story, and his book *Stinking Creek*, showed, he had compassion without condescension for people tripped by fate and stranded on the back roads of life, and the love felt for him was an echo of the love he felt for others. Strangely, he received two nominations for the Pulitzer, one by Geoff Vincent, the Sunday editor, another by Gene Graham, an old friend from Murray, Ky., then teaching at Southern Illinois University. John joked to Buddy Atkinson that it took him two nominations to get it.

***

It was not an equally big year for me. Once more, I managed to offend Barry, Jr. The Democratic presidential nominating convention was to be held in Chicago, and the storm clouds gathered even before the delegates. It was the year of the Hippies, protests against our involvement in Vietnam were at their peak, and the protest leaders were determined to make their opposition felt if it tore the Democrats in two. Lyndon Johnson had taken himself out of consideration for the nomination and thrown his support behind Hubert Humphrey, a good and peace-loving man who was thrashing on the horns of an historic dilemma: he could not repudiate Johnson or his policies without antagonizing a majority of the Democratic rank-and-file. Further, it would be dubious political strategy; over 60 percent of Americans either favored our intervention in Vietnam or were neutral. On the other hand, support of Johnson's refusal to get out of Vietnam would galvanize the Hippies, the peaceniks, and much of the liberal-intellectual community, including supporters of Eugene McCarthy. What Humphrey needed was a peaceful gathering, and that he could not get. His efforts were further frustrated by the tyrannical demagoguery of Chicago's mayor Frank Daley, who hated the noisy youth and all they stood for, and promised to keep them under control. The resulting battles made history and wounded the Democrats. Curiously, a large minority of youthful warriors went on to vote for Richard Nixon, who only prolonged the agony of Vietnam.

Naturally, I wanted to go to Chicago, and when Barry would not send me, I took a few days off and went at my own expense. Rooms were impossible to get, of course, but Jim Tunnell, a *Courier* reporter, said I could have a pillow and six feet of floor in his room. Bill May, who was always an important figure in the Democratic camp, was flying up and asked me to fly with him. Hugh and Lois Haynie and Joan Bingham, Worth's widow, were also going on Bill's plane. We met at Bowman field, but when May's plane came in, Hugh took me to one side and told me that something had come up that made it impossible for him to go and asked me if I would keep an eye on Lois and see that she got out some. He said he would reimburse me for any expenses, but I assured him that that wouldn't be necessary; I liked Lois and would be glad to have someone to go out with.

As we approached Chicago, May called me up forward and

said he wanted me to do him a favor. He had a suite at the Allerton Hotel, he said, where most of the Democratic delegates were staying, but he would not be always be there; so he wanted me to stay there and, if anyone called, to say, honestly, that Mr. May was not there at the moment, but would return the call when he came in.

The convention was, as you may recall, a madhouse. I remember at least once standing by my hotel room window and watching the cops and kids belaboring each other. I was sorry when I had to return home early. So I was taken aback when Molly, after discussing my experience, fixed me with a disapproving eye and said that I had succeeded in outraging Barry, Jr. again. The story had gotten back to him that I had spent my time in Chicago sleeping with Lois Haynie, while poor Hugh sweated over a hot drawing board at home. I didn't know whether to throw up my hands or just throw up. Why, I asked her, couldn't someone have accused me to my face? Or asked Lois? Or Hugh? I told Molly about my airport agreement with Hugh and added that I had taken Lois out twice, but never alone. Once I took her to dinner with May and a friend, another time to a Kentucky reception and dinner with a couple of hundred others. Molly said that Barry's main concern was that Hugh would find out and perhaps try to kill me, in which case the paper stood to lose either an editorial writer or its star cartoonist. I was touched.

But the incident was typical of our relations. I asked John Richards, whom Barry had directed to check up on my outside activities, why the man didn't come to me. That's just his way, said John. He doesn't like confrontation. Worse than his father.

***

But it made no difference. In 1971, Bob Barnard, night managing editor, was named to the *Courier* editorial staff, and Molly said he would likely be named to succeed her as editor. I wasn't too surprised. He was a very meticulous man and had been marking typographical errors on early editions of the editorial page and sending them down to Barry, Jr., an intimation, I suppose, that he could do better, and Barry seemed to agree; he had his brother's knack of impulsive selection. When Molly retired, Barnard was named editor. One of his first actions as editor was to circulate a memo saying that he expected us to put shoulder to the wheel, adding that "management will be kept aware of performance." Sonofabitch, I thought. If management was not aware of my performance after 22 years of doing everything but cleaning the ashtrays, management was denser than I thought, and I remembered the times when I was left to produce the editorial page alone or with Bryan Wooley.

Not long afterward, Barry, Sr., called me to his office, said that he was sorry that things hadn't worked out between Jr. and me, and that he would have to ask me to accept a transfer to the Sunday department, where Geoff Vincent was eager to have me writing full time for the *Magazine*. I told him flatly that I thought I deserved an explanation, and from Barry, Jr., adding that this was a far cry from the semi-commitment to make me editor. He said, yes, he was sorry things hadn't worked out. And that was that. The next day David Hawpe came in and said he had been told to take over my office. David said he was sorry, and I think he was, though he now had the editorial job he had always wanted. I moved what few things I had up to the Sunday department on the fifth floor, including a ratty old armchair that Adele Brandeis had given me when she retired, and an old Royal typewriter that I had swapped to a fellow-officer in Panama for a small record player. Barnard, the new editor, came up and told me to return them, that I could not take department property. I kept them, but felt that he had gone far out of his way to rub my nose in it.

My transfer to Sunday was humiliating. Everyone knew that I was in disgrace. It was rumored that Barry, Jr. had insisted that he didn't want me on the paper at all, and that only his father's intercession had saved me. I think that was right. I was now at the bottom of the slippery slope. Geoff was jovial and helpful, assuring me that we would do great things, but I saw nothing for me, great or small. I was given a desk in a corner of a large room where small offices were planned but not yet built, and left to contemplate the future. No one came in to speak. Buddy had quit the paper, Harwood had gone to the *Washington Post*.

Failure is a lonely thing. As in the Lonesome Valley of folksong, can't nobody go there with you. Lamenting it only serves to confess it and call attention to it. Fortunately, I suppose, few people outside the building appreciated what had happened; few people knew the difference between a magazine writer and an editorial writer, and aside from my family no one cared. My wife was sympathetic and supportive, though I knew that she was both disappointed and embarrassed. It made no difference to the girls, to whom I was simply a writer for the paper. But later, when I went to Sanibel, Ed Konrad asked how I was feeling and what I was doing. I told him I felt fine and was doing the same old thing, writing for the paper. He said he had heard that I had had a mental breakdown and quit my job.

Buddy had some harsh things to say about the paper, the Binghams and the management in general. His departure had also been bitter. I saw it coming. After *Collier's* magazine folded, he had trouble finding another regular publisher. I knew that he and Anne were not getting along, to put it diplomatically. And he was drinking. At first he confided that he was drinking "a little, but only vodka, since no one could smell it." Where he got that idea I will never know. He was still writing well, but he looked bad. All of his friends, and he had many, worried. As Buddy had often complained, Isaacs did not care for him, and now the disapproval grew more noticeable. When Buddy got sick and had to be away from the office for a few days, I went up to his office and cleaned out his desk of vodka bottles before someone less sympathetic did it. There were, as I recall, sixteen of them.

Buddy said that Isaacs wanted him to travel around the state and write his humorous articles about random Kentuckians. "Wants me to be a goddam laughing Creason," he snarled. I don't know what the truth of that was. I know it didn't work. It was just a matter of time until Buddy quit. He went to work for an advertising agency, where he was considered quite successful. He was enormously talented. Shortly, he and Anne were divorced, and he was torn between bitterness and longing for his children. He was a very loving father.

***

I cannot for the life of me remember what made me decide to leave home, end our marriage. I vaguely remember sitting by the window in my office and thinking "My God, life has to be more than this." I knew my wife was unhappy; so was I, with work as well as marriage. I had aimed high, fallen low, and didn't even know why. I felt a strong irony and small comfort when, at a dinner in Frankfort several weeks later, Ed Prichard referred to me as "the state's best editorial writer since Henry Watterson, and probably better than Watterson." Sadly, it hadn't done me any good. And no one had named an expressway for me.

I was lonelier and lower than I had ever imagined. I was fifty years old, and I could not envision spending whatever years I had left feeling so adrift. Aside from the children, I had nothing to show for the years. Susie was in college in Connecticut, but then called and said that she was pregnant and married to a boy named Douglas Barnes. I went to see them and was satisfied that she had made a good choice, even if she had made an unwise move. Marnie was at Transylvania and I saw her infrequently. I got along wonderfully with Dinny and Betsy, and I grew fonder of Alida, our youngest, with each day. But there was no getting around the fact that my wife seemed not to care for me, though she finally insisted that we consult a marriage counselor. We did, but the outcome was not helpful, and a therapist that we finally consulted reported that we were an incompatible couple, aggressive woman, a fairly passive man who did not know how to fight back, and had lost his will to do so. I think that was fairly close to it.

No divorce is one-handed, and I know that I was at least partly to blame for the bitter arguments that seemed to flare without warning or apparent cause. But to this day I cannot say what it was that I did or said, or left undone, that so irritated my wife. The marriage counselor asked us to say what it was about the other that we found irritating. He asked my wife to respond first and she talked for fifty straight minutes, at the end of which time I felt as though I had been found in a dumpster. And thrown back in. At the next session, he asked me what I objected to in her, and I said, as truthfully as I could, that I objected to the fact that she objected to everything I did, as she had revealed in our initial session. I may have been unfair to her; she was reared by a hard father, and probably considered me weak, namby-pamby for my failure to discipline the girls more forcibly. Furthermore, in retrospect, I feel that, like her mother, she tended to disapprove of ideas that were not hers. Such traits tend to be inherited.

I felt that the greater part of my life had slipped by, and that I faced a future without much levity or hope. And once the girls were gone, what would I have? I sure to God did not want to spend my downhill years with a woman who had so little use for me. At any rate, one day I put my typewriter, most of my clothes and a few books into our VW bug and left. That's it. Drove off. How did I feel? I tried not to think of the girls. Otherwise, I thought, I felt like Martin Luther King, "Free at last." I knew that deserting the girls was going to leave king-size guilt and misery, and I was right. Divorce scars the children, and I am never free of the knowledge that it hurt mine. But there has never been a day when I regretted leaving, or wished I could go back. I was determined, no matter how selfish it might be, that I was not going to be miserable for the rest of my life.

I went to Sanibel, naturally. I needed to, for I had taken the money I had made from the beachfront development and bought forty acres of the most beautiful land on earth on the northeast side of the island, fronting Dinkin's Bayou, a quiet lagoon that emptied on the pass separating Sanibel and Captiva. I had formed a friendly acquaintance with Garvice Kincaid, the Lexington financier, while writing a magazine profile of him, and when on a trip to Lexington asked him for advice. He gave me plenty, including an introduction to a bank in Miami that agreed to lend me a quarter of a million dollars to develop the forty acres into building lots. The loan manager at the bank told me that I had a property that should make me comfortable from then on.

***

It was on my way to Sanibel that I drove through Rutherfordton, where we had lived before the Depression fell on us. I parked across the street from the house that had been home, looking, remembering and rolling, as I did too often, in self-pity. Or self-flagellation. Or both. Backward, turn backward, and all that. The Nanney's big white house next door had burned; the blackened foundation still stood. Life had been so rich and exciting when the houses were new and we were young. I had expected great things to come my way as a natural process, my just desserts. Lord, I thought, how I had failed.

The place looked even prettier than it had that day in 1929, when we got out of the car and gazed at the glistening, white stucco house, with its red tile roof and porch, and its sunroom to one side. In the rear was a two-story, two-car garage, with servants' quarters above and two storage rooms behind. A low brick wall bordered a garden that had gone to weeds but showed the traces of loving care.

The house must have been fairly new at the time; it smelled new. The floors and light fixtures, sconces and dining room chandelier gleamed. All the closets, even the laundry chute, were of cedar and the rich smell permeated the house. From the upstairs room that would be mine a window looked across the flower garden to thick woods beyond. A vacant lot filled with tall pines separated our house from the house toward town. Our house, I could see, was better than nearly all the houses around.

Then we drove downtown, past the big limestone courthouse, past Jiggs' Chocolate Shop, Belk's Department Store and the Keeter Hardware to where the office of the *Rutherford Sun* stood on a high corner. The *Sun* was far grander than any paper we had had before, the office light and airy. A mousy woman sat at the desk near the door, Miss Louise. There was a lot of help around.

I had no idea what had happened, but I knew that, overnight, a great change had taken place. A child senses social status by attitudes and tone of voices, and when I went to Baptist (again) Sunday School in the big red-brick building on Main Street near the center of town, I could sense that I was well regarded, and it gave me a confidence I had not known. And a nice thing happened. As we walked out into the sunlight through the side door of the basement, the prettiest girl in North Carolina looked at me and smiled, and as she passed me she took the small parasol she was carrying and poked me with it, grinning. And I had my first girl friend. Her name was Vivian Keeter. She had black hair, cut in bangs, and brown eyes, with a red sash around the waist of her white dress. I could hardly breathe, my world was suddenly so full. I had no firm idea what I was to do with a girlfriend, but I had one. She had a twin, Lillian, who was the girlfriend of Powell Nanney, who lived next door. Everything fell into place.

Rutherfordton was a quiet, pretty town, comfortably Southern and largely middle-class, with a few wealthy mill-owning families that sent their children off to school. There were a few old families that had never recovered from the Civil War but were still respected, for while money was an accepted gauge of status, it was little more important than breeding and manners and "knowing how to act." There was a handsome Episcopal church at the foot of North Main Street (the son of the minister was a fat boy whom I did not like; we had a couple of fights), but the moral precepts of the more numerous Baptists and Methodists were generally accepted, if not observed. We knew what was right and not right, and how far we could wander into the regions of not-right without courting trouble.

Life was as secure as it was provincial in Rutherfordton. We literally did not lock our doors. I never heard of a car being stolen. There were the usual Saturday night troubles among the black people. After a week's hard work, they were expected to let off steam and did, getting drunk, getting into fights, now and then cutting or shooting each other. It was fairly standard procedure for the police to arrest them, throw them into jail until Monday morning, when their bosses would arrive at the jail, pay their minimal fines and take them to work, docking their pay for the amount of their fines.

***

There was about our neighborhood the good smell of pine woods and muscadines, juicier and more flavorful than any domestic grape, and the sight in the fall of golden persimmons. Oak leaves were crisp and heavy underfoot after frosts, and squirrels chipped along the limbs and rabbits scurried along the fence rows. There were lots of birds. Unfortunately, there were also lots of hawks. I raised pigeons, and had some beauties, one big red, a white with head plumage, others soft gray with blue markings, but a hawk found their cote over the garage and, one by one, killed them, as I raged through the woods with my .410, to no avail.

In the summer we would hitchhike to Woodland Park and go swimming. The water was cool and refreshing, there were sometimes girls there, and we usually had a nickel for a frozen Forever Yours. Through the paper, we had passes to the movie house in Spindale and went often in the summer; it was there that I first saw John Wayne, in *The Big Trail*. Now and then we would hitchhike, or get Daddy to let one of his printers drive us up to Lake Lure, where we would camp, build a fire and fish. Once Forrest Eskridge and I caught a half-dozen big, fat catfish, and the next morning sold them for a dollar to some men who came by.

Another time we camped near a dance pavilion called Hillside Gardens, which was built out over the lake, with tall trees thrusting up through the dance floor and colored lights running around the circling railing. Rich people who had summer homes around the lake or were staying at the fancy hotels, Rocky Broad Inn or Lake Lure Inn, came to dance. Moonlight filtered through the trees, and the band played "Heartaches," as the girls in their long dresses and the men in their white jackets circled the floor, or stood by the railing, smoking and laughing. I still recall the song, played slowly, and not to the fast rumba rhythm that later became popular. "My loving you meant only heartaches. You may be happy with someone new, but my heart aches for you." Listening, I was thrilled with the knowledge that some day soon

I would drive up to Hillside Gardens in a sporty car and dance with Vivian Keeter to soft music, or stand by the railing, smoking, making clever talk.

Why try to describe or explain the lithesome joy of the youthful spirit unfolding to life, the euphoria that lifts and bears along as on a magic wind a boy's formless longings, his dreams and hopes and yearning. My world, like that of every young boy beginning to feel adult life and manhood approaching, was not free of hurt or the fear of falling short of great expectations. But the world was good. Our house and town were fine. Sidelong looks and soft-voice words of girls held the excitement of future promise.

***

Then, in the second summer of my life in Rutherfordton came an experience that carved itself into mind and memory like initials carved deep into a young tree, to weather growth and the years. I went to Chimney Rock Camp for Boys, on Lake Lure. I had heard of it, heard that rich boys went there. But Daddy made a deal with the camp management to print the camp paper, and in payment I would go to camp free.

It is easier to recall a thrilling dream than to describe that summer at Chimney Rock, the cabins among tall trees along the hillside above the lake, where I would wake in the night and sit in wonder as the moon shattered into diamonds against the mirror of the lake, and the breeze stole softly through the trees. Even today I can smell Lifebuoy soap and see the outline of the shower building, the stables, the tennis court, the gym where we played basketball. One time we traveled to Camp Sequoia to play their basketball team. I can't remember whether we won or lost, but I remember that we spent the night, and the next morning plunged, with the Sequoia boys, into the coldest water this side of ice. We inched along the narrow path to the overlook at Chimney Rock and rode in trucks to Hendersonville and beyond to the top of Sugar Loaf (where today an expensive housing complex stands) built campfires and watched the mists rise in the valleys around us. We took canoe trips to the far end of the lake, and on one occasion crossed the lake in our white ducks to a dance given by Lake Lure Camp for Girls. "Get out there and dance," our counselor said to me. "Don't worry," I said, "I'm going to." I wasn't about to admit that I couldn't dance and had come only to see the pretty girls, so pretty that finally I ventured to ask one to dance and stumbled around as best I could. She didn't seem to mind.

But it was the boathouse and waterfront that I remember best. After qualifying tests, we were issued badges that permitted us to take a canoe out on the lake. With a red badge, you had to stay within the bay, but if you could show the guard on duty a white badge, you could go out on the lake as far as you wished. One day I found a white badge in the canoe I had checked out, showed it to the guard and spent the afternoon cruising my kingdom, poking into coves, going ashore to climb a large overhanging rock and watch small fish in the clear green water, riding the waves spread out behind power boats.

I got into a fight with a boy named Pieck from Cincinnati, about what I forget, and for weeks we would tear into it when we met, until one day I bumped into him, alone, on the dock, and immediately drew back, as did he, as we both realized the silliness of our conduct and grinned. We became good friends and partners in the canoe jousting, in which one boy would paddle while the other stood in the bow with a padded pole and tried to knock the bow man of other canoes into the water. Pieck and I won every match we were in.

But camp ended, Mama and Daddy came to get me, and I returned to reality a little sad, but very full of myself and the new knowledge I had picked up among the boys, many of them Yankees. Some-one asked me if there were niggers among the Yankees.

***

Strangely, considering the furor that has since swept the country in the intervening years, I cannot recall that race was an issue in our lives then. Blacks were simply not a part of my life; we usually referred to them as colored people and regarded them, if at all, with neither affection nor dislike. "Don't call them niggers," Mama told us, "tacky people do that, and they don't like it." That was all right with me; we didn't call them at all. With the exception of a few black women who worked by day for some of the neighborhood families, trudging home in the evening, and colored men who did menial jobs downtown, they did not intrude into our world, and we did not venture into theirs. It was apartheid with an overlay of Southern gentility. There was a saying among the colored people that Southerners loved them as individuals but hated them as a race, whereas Northerners loved them as a race but hated them as individuals. There was something to that.

We had heard that up north the colored people went to school with white people, but we didn't think that was true. At the same time, I recall only one report of violence against blacks, and that aroused disapproval as though the perpetrators had broken the unwritten law on which civility between the races was based. One morning as we were waiting to catch a ride to school, some boys were talking about something that happened the night before; Nig Hardin and Bill Lipscomb, along with some other boys, most of them on the football team, had driven through Milltown, hollering at colored people. They called this colored boy over to the car, and when he leaned down to see what they wanted, one of them grabbed him around the neck, and the driver gunned the engine, dragging him along, with him begging them to let him go. Finally Nig said, "Hell, if he wants you to let him go, let him go." They turned him loose, and he tumbled along the road, head over heels as they drove off, not even waiting to see how badly he was hurt.

The incident was discussed in guarded tones. Some of the kids thought it was funny, but I remember Ross Hill, son of the elementary school principal and a good friend, said that he thought they should be punished. "Hell," he said, "niggers are people, too. How'd you like it if a bunch of niggers grabbed you that way?" If anyone disagreed with him they were ashamed to say so.

***

Summer neared its end, and Powell Nanney suggested that we ask our girls to go to the county fair. He said his daddy would drive us, and his mother called Mrs. Keeter and vouched for our character, and Saturday morning we went by and picked up Vivian and Lillian. Big-time stuff, boy. We were only thirteen, but we had dates, and with the cutest girls in Rutherford County.

It was a glorious day, full of the sounds and smells of a county fair, the whirring music of the ferris wheel and merry-go-round, and the thrill of sitting close in the stands to watch the donkey races, and riding shows. We bought the girls hot dogs and pop, feeling quite grown up. But the afternoon whizzed by, dusk descended, and the sky exploded into a magnificent display of fireworks. Then it was over, and we went to find Mr. Nanney for the ride home, excited, tired.

On the way home, Vivian leaned her head against my shoulder and smiled at me, and with a pounding heart I made a wild stab at putting my mouth against hers. She smiled, not seeming to mind, and snuggled closer. I did it again, and this time let my lips linger against hers in a fair approximation of a kiss. Then we reached the Keeter home and walked the girls to their door, happy but wishing the night never had to end. I said good night, and Vivian, my girl friend, the girl I had kissed in the back seat of a car, squeezed my hand. When Mr. Nanney let me out, I wanted not to go home, but to spread my arms to the night, and run and sing beneath the moon. Since that night, I have never made fun of puppy love.

* * *

But as the school year began, and we kids planned for the year ahead, I got a strange feeling of something going wrong, something I could not place or name, an uneasy feeling of time winding down too fast. There was worried talk around town about hard times. I had heard talk about a depression, but it had no meaning for me. When grown people talked with worried looks about how the mills were laying off men and shook their heads, I didn't attribute it to the vague, shapeless depression that people were talking about and that took up so much space in the *Charlotte Observer*. Even when we heard that the bank had closed, it didn't make an impact on the daily lives of us at school. What did a bank do when it closed? Why did people care? Why couldn't they just open it again?

Then one day while we were in school—we heard about it that afternoon when we got home—a crowd of men, mostly farmers, gathered in front of the bank and demanded their money. Mr. Taylor, the bank president and one of the big men in town, came out and tried to talk to them. He said the bank was broke, that it couldn't collect on its loans, and that it was having to foreclose on loans and things trying to get money to pay depositors. This didn't satisfy the men, and one fat-face farmer walked up and spit in Mr. Taylor's face! Mr.Taylor! Then I felt, we all felt, that something was going wrong.

Nothing had changed for us, but one day I saw Mama standing at the back door, looking across the garden toward the woods. She had a sad, hurt look on her face, and when I said hi she just looked at me, shook her head and turned back into the house.

Then a bad thing happened. I got hurt. We were playing football, and I was running with the ball when I got tackled near the edge of the field. They had cut a row of hedges along the side of the field and there were stubs of it left, less than a half-inch long but long enough to slice into my leg like a butcher knife. I felt a sharp stabbing pain, and when I looked down I squealed like a cut hog. A gash cut across the muscle running from my knee to my foot, and a six-inch cut ran along my thigh. My shoes were filling with blood. Powell ran to get his daddy, and Frank Smallwood went to get Mama. They wrapped a cloth around my leg and took me to the hospital, where the doctor gave me a shot and sewed up my leg.

"You're lucky," he said. "A little deeper and you wouldn't be able to use that foot. Stay off that leg as much as you can for a while. Come back to see me in a week or so." And I was carried home, the fallen warrior, and stayed propped up in bed for a week.But then the real blow fell, and no one, even I, paid much attention to my leg. Daddy had lost the papers. We were broke. We were going to have to move.

For a while, I couldn't believe, couldn't grasp the reality of the tragedy that was to rob us of our lovely home and the life I found so rich and good. I learned, without quite understanding it, that Daddy had over-extended his capital. He had borrowed on the *Sun* to start a paper in Spindale, borrowed on that to start one in Tryon, and was just starting one in Spartanburg when the Depression washed over us, and mills closed and stores that had advertised went broke, too. One by one, Daddy had lost the papers, letting one go to save the next. I couldn't understand why he couldn't open the *Sun*. It was his, wasn't it? What business did the bank have with it? But it was for nothing. We had nothing. We were broke. And one morning a moving truck came to get the furniture, and we got in the car and headed up North Main Street. A few friends came to wave to us; I was glad Vivian hadn't come. I didn't want her to see me that way.

It was a long, sad drive to Norton, and as evening closed in, we crossed the railroad tracks, drove up a slight hill and turned down Virginia Avenue to where our house, big, ugly, tacky looking, sat on a grubby bit of yard. A layer of smoke and mist lay over the valley. I felt as though a massive black gate had clanged shut behind me, closing off the scent of pine woods, the days of sunshine, the world I had known.

14

A Salute to the Magazine

One thing that both newspapers and television lack is readable commentary on local affairs. National Public Radio has Daniel Schorr, and TV used to have John Chancellor and Eric Sevareid, but by and large television dumps the news on the living room floor and lets you figure out for yourself what it implies. Schorr gives you insight, but the story is nearly always of national or international import. And few newspaper columnists make any effort to get beneath the surface of small-town happenings.

That is where the *Courier-Journal* had an advantage over papers with smaller staffs and less sophisticated technology. The *Magazine* was peculiarly equipped to present readers with stories of their home towns. Joe Creason began with a series of articles on Kentucky towns, and there was one thing you had to say about Joe; he liked people, liked people to like him, and wrote about people with understanding. A small-town product himself (he was from Benton, in far-western Marshall County), he had an appreciation for the qualities and handicaps of small-town living. And in his descriptions of towns, he made no effort to be critical. In the unusual event that he did, the criticism was mild and humorous.

At Geoffrey Vincent's suggestion, I confined my series to counties. I'm glad I did. A lot of Kentuckians are fond and proud of their counties. Ask a Kentuckian where he is from and he will often give you the name of his county rather than his home town. Counties are an integral part of Kentucky history and government. Until the advent of television, county political organizations could not be overlooked by a candidate. Until the Judicial Reform Act, the county judge was both chief executive and chief judicial officer of the county. The county school superintendent often held so much political power that no governor or political hopeful would cross him, and reformers, state or federal, ran up against state laws that protected local officials from clean-up efforts. And a lot of counties are unusual, with colorful histories and people. While I was writing for the *Courier Magazine* I wrote profiles of thirty-five Kentucky counties and regret only that I did not have time or opportunity to write more, although I was beginning to find a marked similarity in their histories and character. I loved doing the county profiles, and with few exceptions, the readers liked them, too, partly because most Kentuckians do not see much of their state and are impressed with the variety and history of other counties, and because counties seldom make the big daily papers except when there is a scandal or crime to report.

I met a host of people, found that I liked nearly all of them and learned again how much people were alike; everyone is, in a sense, from Norton. And people who had not cared for me because I was a faceless editorial writer saw that I did not have horns and eat babies. I resented being booted off the editorial page without explanation or excuse, but as it turned out it was probably the best thing that ever happened to me. The blind hog syndrome.

Speaking of people, I was out one time working on a profile, when someone suggested that I talk to a young lawyer, and I found that the lawyer was the young doctor's wife that I had met at David Hawpe's house when I was chronicling the saga of the Blue Noodle. She was even more attractive in business clothes than she had been in jeans, and I would have liked to expand the interview but found her cautious and evasive, giving me little information. Several months later, Hawpe said that she (I will refer to her only as M, since I know she would not like to be identified and discussed publicly) was working in Frankfort as an attorney for the state and was divorced from the doctor husband. David said she was feeling low and suggested that when in Frankfort I might ask her out for dinner. "If I were single, I'd sure ask her out," he said, a totally innocent statement that got taken out of context and disported, to my long-range hurt.

I did ask her out. She accepted (without enthusiasm, I might add), and on a bitter, snowy December night, we had dinner. It was not a very good dinner, and I was apparently not a very good dinner companion. I trotted out my famed charm, did everything but tap-dance on the table, to no avail. Neither of us suggested that we try it again. Too bad. The blind hog does not find an acorn every time. But I was seeing a woman in Louisville fairly often and paid it no mind. Almost exactly a year later, I was returning to Louisville from Lexington and had to stop in the office building where M was working and dropped by to say hello. Her secretary said she had two men in her office, but took my card and came back to say she would like to see me and asked me to wait. Again, it was not my infallible charm; she came out in a minute and said, "Oh, thank you. You gave me an excuse. Those were the two biggest bores in Kentucky. Come on in."

We talked for a few minutes, I prepared to leave and she surprised me by asking if I would like to stop by her place for a drink on the way home. I would. I did. We had a drink and talked. She was fixing dinner and asked me if I would like to stay. I would. We talked some more. It grew late. When she began to nod, I finally left. It is a wonder that I didn't go to sleep and kill myself on the way home.

But I felt, I knew, that something extremely important had happened. And I was right. I would like to avoid becoming too personal and know that you are not biting your nails to hear the intimate details of my love life, but for the next twenty-two years M was the greatest influence in my life. You pay for what life gives you, of course, and I paid for her. The price was higher than I might have preferred to pay, but I must add that she brought me the most enveloping happiness that I had known. I wish the relationship could have continued, but I was much older than she, and in time that proved a handicap too great.

***

Enough True Confessions. My daughter Susie had married a young man named Doug Barnes, I had visited them in Weston, a Boston suburb, and was greatly pleased with her choice. Doug was a nice-looking, bright young man who already had a fine job with a national accounting firm, and told me, in all sincerity, that he had it planned so that he would be worth a million dollars by the time he was forty and retire when he was forty-five. I felt comfortable with Susie and her new daughter, Betsy, in his care, and it was a great shock when Doug was killed driving home one night from helping friends move into a new apartment. I was not too surprised at how fundamentally Susie was upset, but was distressed when, only a year later, she married a young man who had been a friend of Doug's and in their wedding. I visited them in their attractive salt-box house in Newburyport, Mass., but was not impressed with George, the new husband, figured that Susie had taken him on the rebound, and did not predict a long and happy marriage. I am sorry to say I was right.

***

And at the office, another bad thing happened. Geoff Vincent, who was my friend and, I suppose, protector, became involved in an argument with Bob Clark, *Times* managing editor, over the creation of the Sunday CJ&T, the *Courier-Journal & Times,* which combined and carried the names of both papers for the Sunday edition, whereas previously the *Times* had had no part in the Sunday publication. Norman Isaacs, executive editor, sided with Geoff, and the CJ&T took rough form, but Clark remained opposed and uncooperative, though the new combination provided a service for *Times* readers of having their own Sunday paper rather than having to read only the *Courier.* The basic trouble, I think, was that Clark did not want the Sunday department to take over the entire Sunday operation—news, sports, editorial, special sections and *Magazine*—perhaps because he saw it as an empire-building operation on Geoff's part. Which it was not. Actually, it was one reason Geoff had been brought to Louisville.

Resistance to change was typical, I think, of the paper at that time. The *Courier* was becoming less innovative and imaginative. Perhaps there was a temptation to rest on its many laurels. We missed chances to give the paper a broader mission, a more metropolitan flavor.

While this stew was bubbling, I stumbled, fat, dumb and happy, into a fortunate development. Jimmy Pope often complained about the lack of good one-page features that could fill a hole in the *Magazine.* One reason we needed such filler was that John Fetterman had died in 1975 at the age of 55. He died of a heart attack, as had Joe Creason a year earlier at almost the same age. John had had some heart problems before, but no one thought they were critical, and his death was shocking for the staff. Though the attack was the final cause of death, I always suspected that the Pulitzer Prize killed John, and Geoff Vincent agreed with me. Ever since he won the thing, John thought that every story had to be another Pulitzer, and every story can't be, no matter how beautifully written. He tore himself in two trying and felt disap-

193

pointment when his writing was not the equal of the prize-winner.

So I ground out short bits of commentary to plug the holes. Several of these seemed to hit a nerve among our readers. People liked them, and Jimmy encouraged me to write more. I didn't mind. It was easy. Several of the pieces were routinely nostalgic, comments about porches, sidewalks, things we used to do, music we used to dance to. To the surprise of everyone, me included, these brought me a lot of mail that I didn't have time to answer. The world, I suspect, changes more rapidly than we like, especially after we pass fifty, and there is a natural longing within those of us who are older for the happier times and more leisurely pace of our youth. Without fully realizing it, I was meeting a need, a need few editors, most of them being younger, recognized.

I wrote the columns in addition to my regular work. Then one day in the summer of 1976 Geoff and the managing editor called me in and asked me if I would like to do a regular column. They would put my name, maybe a head shot, at the top of the column, give it big play. I said sure. Actually, I didn't care one way or another. Writing the column was often fun. Rich Nugent, my friend and photographer with whom I had worked on so many profiles and county articles, took a head shot of me in my office, probably the best ever taken of me, and it ran at the top of the column. From then on, people used that head shot whenever my name appeared on anything. It made me semi-famous, and office smart alecs referred to Nugent and me as Rich and Famous. Working with Rich, who had a great sense of humor and a keen intellect, was a joy.

I didn't mind writing the column, but I did not like giving up the county series. I had become intrigued with it. I felt I had begun the series, and the counties were mine. At the same time, I was glad to be free of the conflicts that sometimes occurred between me and photographers on county stories. It was a disturbing clash that involved paper policy. I would usually spend anywhere from a week to ten days in a county, after learning what I could about it from our library and the Filson Club. Sometimes a photographer would go with me, more often he would join me later. We would confer, I would tell him what I had learned about the place, and what I thought would best illustrate the story I would write. Usually we would drive around the county, the county seat and other towns, familiarizing him with it. And usually we agreed on photo coverage. I made no effort to dictate what a photographer should shoot, but liked to point out things I was going to write about or thought would be appropriate subjects.

Some photographers were very sensitive about this, and did not want any writer telling them what to do, but I seldom had trouble with them. Photographers maintained, and rightly, that they knew, better than a writer, what made a good picture. They also held that it was their function to show the reader their version of the story. I agreed with that to an extent, but I also believed, and still do, that the photographs should have illustrated the story, or at least shown scenes typical of the county and not just give the reader a view of some photogenic objects.

Both have a point. Rich paid almost no attention whatever to my suggestions and shot what he wanted, but we thought alike and only once did we wind up at loggerheads; he insisted on shooting some run-down shacks in Harlan County (photographers, as artists, love the scabs of life, dilapidated houses, miserable old people, pitiful babies) I considered the shots stereotypical and unfair unless shots of other, finer homes were used for balance. David Hawpe, who was then managing editor, agreed with me, and we left out the shacks.

I had real trouble with only two counties. One was strictly my fault. I was trying to write about Clay County. I never did get a handle on that county, partly because I was not feeling well, and on two occasions almost went to sleep during interviews, one very important. As a result, I got names mixed up, confusing one Sizemore with another, one Massengale with others. Terrible. I almost got sued.

The other incident concerned Calloway County, which saddened me because it is a county and a county seat town—Murray—for which I have a special fondness, and where I had friends. I was writing what I thought was going to be a good article and was joined by an attractive young woman photographer whom I knew could do a good job. We had dinner, and I told her what I had in mind, and showed her around Murray and environs. After I turned in my story we had what was known in the Sunday department as the color meeting, at which the *Magazine* editor, the Sunday editor, and the writers and photographers involved with stories to be illustrated in color met, viewed the color shots and decided on which ones would be used.

We met, I saw the shots the woman had taken and objected to them, politely at first, but then vehemently, saying that they were not typical of the county, did not illustrate the article I had written, and were bound to antagonize the people of Calloway County. She stuck to her guns and was backed up by the managing editor, who pointed out that it was Barry Jr.'s policy that the photography department was autonomous, and that photographers were independent of writers and had the right to choose their own shots. I have often thought that Barry would have preferred to have only pictures with a few short cutlines, as few words as possible. I was indignant as hell and sick about it. I was sicker when, a few days after publication, I received three hundred letters from Murray expressing outrage, most of them containing copies of a full-page ad that had run in the Murray paper giving me unshirted hell about the article, which they condemned as insulting. Actually, as I had predicted, it was not my copy but the photographs to which they objected. The photographer had taken some lovely shots of falling down barns and ratty roadsides, but had ignored Murray State University, the most important entity in the county, Murray's scenic park and courthouse. And while the photographer's name was published with the story, I knew that it would be my name, as writer, that readers would notice. And blame. I told the Sunday editor that unless I could have a say in the photography I would prefer not to write any more county articles. I didn't write many, chiefly because I was writing the column, and didn't have to put up with photo artistry any more.

That was the major sour note in my years of writing those county articles or the Sunday column. The column's popularity was made sweeter by the complimentary notes that I received almost regularly from Barry, Sr. and Mary Bingham. I certainly appreciated them, though I sometimes wondered whether Barry's generous notes were not an attempt to make up for the commitment not kept. Mary's notes, on the other hand, were but part of her lovely treatment of me. Both times when I was in the hospital, Mary came and sat with me, delighting me with her witty conversation. When I was bundled off in disgrace, she asked me for coffee and tried to console me. She was so gracious. I loved her. Needless to say, in all the years I worked for the *Courier*, and all the prizes I won, not once did I ever get so much as a nod in the hallway or a routine note from Barry, Jr. A charmer. Eventually, I was given a dinner by the Society of Professional Journalists, nee Sigma Delta Chi, and Barry, Sr., in his terribly kind remarks, declared that I was the best writer he had ever hired, and the best writer, in fact, ever to serve on the *Courier*. I almost felt sorry for Barry, Jr., who smiled through the whole thing. It was decent of him to attend. He didn't have to.

***

Barry, Sr. then launched one of the weirdest moves I ever knew of on the paper. Calling Barry, Jr., Isaacs, Gill, Clark and Geoff to a meeting in his office, he proposed, with a confidential smile, that they "play a little game." In the game, Geoff, Gill and Clark would each choose a job—*Courier* managing editor, *Times* managing editor or Sunday editor. Each could have the job he wanted, as long as it was agreeable to the others, the only provision being that the final arrangement be approved by Barry, Jr. Barry suggested that Gill take the Sunday editorship, Clark become editor of the *Times* and Geoff become managing editor of the *Courier*, but emphasized that it was only a suggestion, and that he wanted the three of them to meet and talk it out among them. The idea met with unanimous coolness. Gill did not want to be Sunday editor, Geoff did not want to be *Courier* managing editor, though Isaacs urged him to do so, saying that it would probably lead to the executive editor job. Clark indicated that he would be satisfied with anything but Sunday. In the end, Clark moved to the *Courier*, Gill became managing editor of the *Times* and later general manager of the company. Geoff stayed with Sunday. This apparently suited Barry Jr., and the whole thing seemed much ado about very little.

Geoff was funny to work for. He would get a hot idea, call us into conference and lay out a plan for developing the story. Then, when the story was completed, he would call us in and ask "Why are we doing this?" Geoff was a great believer in pleasing the reader. He loved polls and surveys showing what the reader wanted. He would go to great lengths to call together a scientifically-selected focus group and ask their opinions on things we did or didn't do. He would ask what members of the group wanted to see in the magazine. Well, hell, they knew what they liked or disliked when they saw it, but before that they really had only the foggiest notion. "We'd like to see more short pieces," they would say. Aha! Geoff's face would light up. Then he would give them samples of stories and articles that had run in recent months and ask them to choose their favorites. And what did they select? Without fail, they chose the longest damned stories that we had run, often my county articles. When people in audiences to which I was speaking (another fraud I perpetrated in my frantic grab for money) asked me how I tried to please readers, I answered, honestly, that I tried to find a subject that interested me, and then do the best job on it I could. That worked pretty well. People also asked me to what age level I wrote. That griped me, as if I would write down to an audience. I replied that I wrote the best I could and had yet to find an audience that could not understand it.

Norman's wife, Dorothy, who had written for the *Courier* under the name of Dorothy Ritz, developed cancer. Norman became extremely depressed and worried and started drinking rather heavily, though I never heard anyone complain about its effect on his work. But, surprisingly, he and Barry, Jr. began to disagree, on fundamentals and on details. I found this amazing, considering Norman's broad experience and Junior's lack of it, but he seemed to have a sort of Bismarck complex, a lust for dropping the pilot. I remember running into Norman one day as he came from Jr.'s office, shaking his head and saying "That boy's crazy," and wondered if that, along with Dorothy's illness, did not have something to do with his drinking. It was not long before he resigned and became director of the Graduate School of Journalism at Columbia University. I feel that his departure hurt us.

Bob Clark became executive editor, and Geoff's job was in peril. He carried on as though nothing was happening, but he knew his days were numbered; he had received a long letter from Clark, detailing what he, Clark, considered plans and promises that Geoff had not kept, goals he had not met, orders he had not followed, concluding that these things indicated insufficient ability for the job. Clark abolished the CJ&T. The combined paper was part of the plan for a Sunday department that Geoff had been brought to Louisville to establish, and he felt rather bitter when neither Barry nor Barry, Jr. supported him. He resigned and went to work for Cummings Engines in Columbus, Indiana. Everyone in the Sunday department hated to see him go. We lost a fine man, and I felt somewhat naked before mine enemies.

And with some reason. When Clark took over, he and Barry, Jr. notified Bill Strode, the *Courier's* prize winning photographer, and me that our plan to do commercial writing and photography in our spare time constituted a conflict of interest. Then new charges were brought against Strode, concerning his claim to film he had shot while on jobs for the paper but with his own film and camera after he had finished shooting for the paper. It was a sensitive decision, though a supportive management would surely have handled it better. Not only did management threaten to sue to keep film he called his own, but told me to have nothing to do with him, lest it harm my future (ha!) and reputation. Bill resigned. Another good one gone.

I began to wonder how much quality we could lose and remain a quality paper. The willingness of the Binghams to take as little as two or three percent on investment and plow profits back into quality had long been a major reason for the paper's excellence, and I think that the excellence began to fade when, partly because the Bingham women wanted more money, the family took more out and put less back in, partly because we lost too many good people. Incidentally, in the first year after the Gannett Corp. took over ownership of the paper, it showed a 26 percent return, or so Mary Bingham told me, in some bitterness, just before she died. You cannot milk a cow or a company that hard without hurting it.

***

During my years on the Magazine I added to my Pulitzer and Nieman awards the Headliner Award, the Meeman Conservation Award, two awards from the American Bar Association, the Professional Journalists Society award for Journalist of the Year, the Governor's Medallion for public service, a citation from the National War College, the Freedom Foundation Award, the Genesis Award and selection to the University of Kentucky Journalism Hall of Fame. I offer this list not just to beat my chest, but to explain why I felt that management was personally rather than professionally antagonistic. As an example, when I won the Headliner Award, I was asked to come to Atlantic City for the presentation, as had John Fetterman and Lana Ellis (our fashion editor) when they won the same prize. Barry, Jr. sent word that it would not be necessary for me to spend money for the trip, since they would send me the medallion that went with the award. Which they did. It seemed to me that this was getting pretty cheap.

Paul Neely, whose family owned the major newspaper in Oklahoma City, took over as Sunday editor. Paul was a good editor, and one of the few people who I knew would not only handle my copy professionally, but would probably improve it. He liked my work, and I felt that as long as he was in office and Jimmy Pope remained *Magazine* editor, my job would change but little. Then Bob Clark fell into disagreement with Barry, Jr.(are we playing musical chairs?) and was forced to resign, and Paul Janensch, an aggressive and often abrasive young man who had had an unusual career on the paper, succeeded him. That may have led to the ultimate disaster.

Janensch began as a reporter, moved quickly to editor rank, went to San Diego as manager of *Pollution Abstracts*, a new publication in which Barry, Jr. had invested, resigned to become managing editor of the *Philadelphia Times*, returned to Louisville in 1976 to become managing editor of the *Louisville Times* and then of the *Courier* before being plucked by Barry, Jr. to be executive editor. I always got along well with Paul, and he treated me kindly; one of the nicest things ever written about me in the *Courier* was a column Paul wrote about me and John Herschnroeder. But he had a run-in with the well-liked reporter, Bill Billiter, over the minor matter of a mislaid tape recorder, and other reporters resented his high-handed attitude toward an able, principled man. Bill shortly resigned and went to Los Angeles.

Mike Davies, who had been the first editor of *Scene*, a *Times* Saturday supplement, took over as *Courier* managing editor. I never thought too highly of the *Scene*, a lightweight, jazzy thing heavy on movies, places to eat and rock music, but it carried a lot of advertising.

Speaking of tape recorders, I had a funny experience with one in 1973. I traipsed off to Butcher Hollow, up in Eastern Kentucky, to write about the home of singer Loretta Lynn, and later when she came to Louisville in concert I went down to interview her in her special bus, parked outside Louisville Gardens. She welcomed me as though I were kin, and we had the most delightful interview I had ever conducted. I know little about country music, but I do know that Loretta Lynn is one of the most charming, naturally friendly ladies I have ever known. I was sorry when she had to leave to do her show, ending the interview.

I rushed back to the office, turned on my tape recorder and—nothing. Absolutely nothing. The batteries were dead. There was absolutely nothing on the tape. I drenched myself with sweat. Remember! I prayed. Oh, Lord, let me remember! However, I composed the whole thing from memory and the few notes I had taken, and while the profile was not as good as it could have been had I had the tape, it was sufficient. Those things happen. I also missed a chance to interview Naomi Judd, the famous country-music singer. She wrote me a generous letter that I misplaced and could not therefore answer. She is also very pretty. Remarkable family.

***

That was also the year of the Brookside strike hearings. About 180 miners had gone out on strike against Duke Power Company's mines in Harlan County. There had been some violence on the picket line, though most of it was apparently on the part of women pickets, who stood at the company gates and "switched" workers, and even a couple of state troopers, their switches being steel rods about four feet long. Dainty creatures. Some tacks were placed on the road, some rocks thrown through windshields, and one man was shot, though he was shot at a party where there was the usual drinking and probably had little or nothing to do with the strike. But Harlan County had a reputation for violence, not unwarranted, and pretty soon here came a congressional team to hold a hearing, accompanied by a pushy young PR man from the United Mine Workers. And a gaggle of media people, including the usual pushy and ill-mannered TV reporters and cameramen. There must be a course in communications school where they teach cameramen to be objectionable. Media people did their best to make the strike similar to and the equal of the strikes that tore Harlan in the thirties. Ridiculous. This strike resembled those as an April shower resembles Hurricane Andrew.

And the hearings were a farce as far an investigation went. One by one, miners, their wives, neighbors and local lawmen trooped to the microphone to tell of the horrors of working for Duke, the chief complaints being that the Brookside mine was wet, and that there was insufficient ventilation. The complaints were real, and the strike was probably justified. But no one from management was called, no foremen to give the company's side, no state troopers to tell of their efforts to keep the two sides separated and peaceful (one trooper, brought in from the Pikeville post, had bruises on his sides and thighs as blue as the sky as a result of the lady pickets' switches). The only lawman called was the sheriff of Harlan County, who promised the strikers that he was on their side. This was astonishing in a county where sheriffs have historically acted as enforcers for coal operators, but served to weaken the complaints of oppression and danger.

A friend of mine, Logan Patterson, whom I had known as a boy in Pineville, was attorney for mine manager Norman Yarborough, an embattled, seemingly confused man who had worked his way up from an ordinary miner to a position in which he had to defend an outside owner, Duke, that was almost universally unpopular. I went over to the office and talked with Logan, persuading him to hold a press conference to present his case, and when I returned to the hearings I was surrounded by strikers who accused me of being a friend of Yarborough's. I could honestly deny that, but had to talk fast to escape with a whole hide. That night I chided the congressmen for holding a dog-and-pony show rather than a real probe, and the next day the union PR man called the *Courier* office and protested that I was lobbying for the operator. I could understand his irritation, for he was accustomed to friendly media. Most of the media people, especially the ABC television crews, seemed to be there to present the miners' side of the story and snarl at anything else. So much for objectivity.

***

The Navy kicked me out. Wrote me a letter saying good-bye, you've been in 30 years. When you get old enough, we'll give you a pension. I replied that I didn't want to retire, that I was in a non-pay unit, costing the Navy nothing, and was a good PR man for the blue and gold. It was futile. I had been put out to pasture. And what did I have for all my years of service and devotion, except dozens of friends and acquaintances around the world and exciting experiences in England, the Mediterranean, San Francisco, San Diego, Norfolk, Hong Kong, Taiwan, Japan, Hawaii, Saipan, Guam, Okinawa—in brief, I joined the Navy and saw the world, and served aboard some of the most dramatic, powerful ships in history. I wish I could do it all again; I would do better.

My private life hovered around the insane. While I was sending every possible penny to my wife, so that she and the children would not be deprived by dint of my leaving, I couldn't afford suitable quarters of my own, but found a room and bath in the home of Dr. Wynant Dean and his wife Molly, one of the brightest and most courageous women I have ever known. The rent was next to nothing, and in the morning I would straggle downstairs and Queenie, the cook and major domo, would give me toast and coffee. Molly, crippled and confined to her bed by polio, was an indomitable woman, fiercely intellectual, an insatiable reader and a delightful conversationalist. She fought her illness to the end.

I was living there when the big tornado of 1974 hit, though I was lucky enough to miss the storm itself. I had gone to see M and was on the interstate when the tornado came in just behind me. I didn't even know about it until M told me what she had heard on TV. I rushed back to Louisville, but found that the girls were safe, though the tornado had hit houses less than a block away. At the Deans' house, two huge trees were down, but Molly was propped up in bed, waving her pipe about with the one arm she could use, and laughing about the experience.

When Molly died, I moved to Anchorage, where I rented an apartment from Dorothy Pinney, aunt of my friend John Moremen. I loved Anchorage and Aunt Dorothy, but my children declared it was not fitting for me to be bouncing about like a charity case and found me a condo on Cherokee Parkway.

At the *Courier*, the promotion department sages decided we should publish a book on the historic tornado, and Bob Deitz, promotion director, asked me if I would like to write it. I told him that I would write anything if the price was right, and we settled on an agreement that would give me (as I recall) a dime for every book sold. Mary Lawrence Young, the tall, strikingly pretty daughter of my old friend Lawrence Irwin, handled research, and we turned the thing out in a couple of weeks. It proved hugely successful, and the company sold more than 50,000 copies. At a dime a copy, I should have gotten five thousand dollars, but when Deitz saw how it was selling, he crawfished on our verbal agreement and paid me five hundred. Do people get promoted to management positions because they are cheap, or do they become cheap once in management? Cheap is contagious.

But that was small potatoes compared with my losing battle with the new government of Sanibel. I had just finished development of my forty acres when the people on Sanibel voted to incorporate, and the county refused to approve my plat and give me building permits so that I could sell lots, that duty now being in the hands of the new Sanibel town government. I asked the town council for approval, and for building permits for forty houses on the forty acres, but was told that I would have to wait until the council passed rules governing subdivisions and set up a regulatory committee. That took about nine months, at the end of which I was told I would have to widen my roads to the width and depth of main roads, though I had only forty lots, and increase the size of my water mains. At considerable expense, I did so, and went back for building permits, but was told I would have to wait until a geological survey was completed. Another year, at the end of which I was told I would have to install sewers instead of the septic tanks permitted in nearby housing. I had to wait for the next council meeting to file a protest, pointing out that sewers did not extend to my part of the island, and I would have no place for the effluent. I was told to develop a package sewer plant, went to Johnson Engineering in Fort Myers, who had developed my subdivision plan, and ordered blueprints for a package sewer plant. After another six months, I presented my plan, but was told there would be no place for the effluent from the package plant, and that I would therefore have to go with septic tanks, as I had originally proposed. Three years had passed. I was paying interest on a quarter-million dollar bank loan, plus the mounting expenses incurred in redesigning and reconstructing according to the council's orders. Finally I ran out of money. I was broke. A man came over from the Miami bank and tried to reason with council members, but got nowhere. The bank had no alternative but to foreclose on the subdivision. They got their lawyers, finally got building permits, knocked down the price of lots, and sold nearly all of them within a year.

That was a remarkably bitter pill. I sympathized with the council and what it was trying to do, enforcing strict development regulations and trying to preserve the island's ecology. But I had a good and beautiful subdivision and blueprinted plans for making it a horticultural showpiece. I had followed every direction and instruction. And I had never been given a reason, with which I might at least have argued, for the refusal to grant building permits. The mayor at the time, who would give me neither help nor reason for his council's actions, has since been elected to Congress, proving that God isn't always watching. I have spoken to God about this. He owes me one. I still feel that I was treated unethically and probably illegally. But I had learned, at least, to stick to my own business.

My own business was weird. The weekly column had become the most popular feature in the paper. There was talk of syndicating it. You wouldn't believe the mail, which I still didn't have time to answer. I was not accustomed to being liked, but found it agreeable. I think the management was hoping I would become another Joe Creason, but I was simply a different kind of writer. Joe had dropped dead in

1974 while playing tennis; he was only 55, grief swept the entire state, and hundreds tried to attend the funeral. The paper found no one to replace him or approximate his appeal. Byron Crawford later wrote a column similar to Joe's, honest and compassionate, and probably better written, but no one has ever equaled Joe's popularity, possibly because of his personality, which was a constant reminder of the good that can reside in men.

15

Not Always Sweet Home

My phone rang the other day and a man asked, "Is this John Ed Pearce?" I said yes. "Are you by any chance from Norton, Virginia?" Again I admitted it. "You may not remember me," said the man, "but my name is Harry Pack. My family ran a small hotel just down the street from where your daddy ran the newspaper. I live in California now, but come through here every now and then, and always see your name in the paper, and just wondered."

I remembered Harry Pack, all right; tall, blonde, wore double-breasted blue suits. Robert Osborne said that Harry had told a bunch of them about the horrors of clap: it would eat holes in your peter and when you peed it would come out in a spray, as from a watering can. The description was so disturbing that I did not think eagerly of sex for fifteen minutes.

But neither hotels nor sex were on my mind during those first days after we moved back to Norton, when I sat in my room and watched the students going into and out of the high school down the street. My room was the one comfort of life, a curious, eight-sided tower stuck on the slant of the roof, reached by a short flight of stairs and a trap-door opening upward. But I was concerned about my wound, which seemed to be festering. When I took the bandage off it smelled, and the stitches hung loose in the pus. I got scissors and cut the stitches, pressed the pus out, swabbed the wound with alcohol, and wound a bandage around it. In a few days, the pus was gone, the wound seemed to be healing, and in a week I was walking normally.

I had chosen an awkward time to start growing out of my clothes. Daddy took me to D. Cury's, where we bought gray pants, a blue sweater and, against my protests, a pair of yellow shoes, which were horrible but on sale. The next Monday, when I entered high school, I could feel eyes boring into my wretched head. The cutest girls in the class, who sat near each other in the next row, looked at me, then at each other and snickered. By lunchtime I was wishing for an early death. Later, Virginia Tate, one of the cute girls, told me that it was the yellow shoes that sent them into gales of humiliating snickers. Those shoes lasted forever.

Professor Burton, the crane-like, pop-eyed principal, ruled that Virginia schools were superior to those of North Carolina and put me back to the freshman year, which made my initial months easier. School was not unpleasant. With the side window of my room open, I could hear the first bell, leap from bed, struggle into my clothes, throw water on my face, and be in class by the final bell.

My teachers were agreeable. Miss McColgan was fat and good-natured and taught English. Miss Coffey, Latin, and Miss Cundiff, French, were young and very pretty. Miss Burks, math, walked with a limp and tended to straddle the corner of her desk, raising remarks. Miss Anderson, an elderly lady, taught history, though she could not bring herself to admit that the South had lost. Joe Hasty had been on the track team at VPI and also taught history, and so on. One more I should mention. Miss Lennie Blankenship was about six feet tall, and skinny as a miner on the dole. She had one eye that was slightly off center, and it was sometimes hard to tell whether she was looking at you. Mean boys in our class tried to make her life miserable, talking, throwing things when her back was turned, farting and then looking accusingly at one of the more bashful girls. But Miss Blankenship was a good English teacher, with a heart as well as an ear for English poetry, and a talent for showing how literature reflected society and history.

I assumed, without reason, that I would go on to college, like most of the children of good families, while the poor kids dropped out, or graduated, and went to work. My sister Rose had gone to college when we lived in Pineville. Grandpa Leslie helped her financially, with the understanding that she would get a teacher's degree and go home and "help out" if needed. She hated it. "I just wanted to get back to Pineville and my friends," she told me later. "And by the time I graduated we had moved back to Norton. Every time I think of Norton, I think of cold and dirt."

Katherine started college, but quit and married Ted Beverly and began a long, happy marriage. Ours was a good-natured family, and Katherine was the sweetest human being ever born, could laugh at anything, and made the best of bad situations. After she and Ted moved to Charlotte, we would all reunion at her house, eating too much, kidding Mama about her indignation at our drinking, all talking at once. I never heard Katherine say anything evil of anyone except for Jesse Helms. "I just want to live long enough to see that man defeated," she said. She didn't make it.

***

I was lucky in that I fell in with a good crowd. Social distinctions are very important in small towns. I sensed fairly soon that I was considered a nice boy, but not one that the mothers of nice girls wanted for their daughters. Life had changed.

For one thing, it became clear that if I wanted anything, I would have to work for it; there was no one to ask for money, no Uncle Doc to help with college. One rainy day not long after we returned to Norton, Mama, Daddy and I drove to Pennington Gap, where Uncle Doc lay sick in a boarding house where his nurse, whom he had married a few months earlier, had put him. He hardly recognized any of us. Mama was tight-lipped when we left. Uncle Doc had pneumonia, she said, and should be in the hospital in Norton, but his wife would not permit it. Mama said later that his wife wanted Uncle Doc to die so that she could get his estate. I don't imagine she got much, unless she could collect the thousands of debts owed to him by people who couldn't or wouldn't pay. Grandma got the little house in Pennington Gap but sold it and moved to Norton and lived in a dingy apartment in a ratty building we owned. Her eyesight was failing, and she was getting frightened and cross. On another cold, rainy day we buried Uncle Doc.

One afternoon shortly after we moved, I hiked up the mountain toward High Knob with two of my new friends, Ed Osler, whose father was receiver for Blackwood Coal Company, and Jimmy Foust, the son of Dr. G.T. Foust, two of the boys approved by mothers of nice girls. We got as far as Chestnut Flats, where the giant chestnut trees, killed by the blight of the twenties, stood white and leafless or lay scattered like tossed giant joss sticks. We could see the Knob up ahead of us, but it was late and we had to get home, but I made a promise to myself that I would hike to the top of the Knob at the first chance. Even then, it drew me.

I had known Jimmy when we were little pre-schoolers, before we moved to Pineville. I had gone to Chimney Rock Camp with Ed Osler, but had never met him until I entered high school, when I walked up and introduced myself as Pearce from Cabin Five. He seemed a little surprised when he came home with me; we did not live as he had expected a boy from Chimney Rock Camp to live, but he was charming to Mama, who loved him. Ed was already six feet tall and handsome. We became lifelong friends, though he was something of a model young man and I was not.

One of the worst things about a depression is the unrelenting monotony and dullness of always wanting and needing things and not being able to get them. Times were very hard. The former town mayor was on WPA, the government work program. There were reports that Dr. Bentley, Beekie Bentley's daddy and doctor for a coal company, would write heart attack on a baby's death certificate to avoid writing that the child had actually died of malnutrition. Almost every day someone would come to the back door asking for food. "I'll do any kind of work, sir, for just anything to eat," they would say. Some were nice-looking men whose clothes, like them, had seen better days. They would drop off the freight trains in the rail yards and sift out through the town, hoping to get enough food to carry them to the next town, the next chance for work.

Our diet was poor, and I have often thought that our health probably suffered because of it. We ate pinto beans, and that hard-time specialty, bean soup, with boiled potatoes and biscuits. It wasn't that Mama couldn't cook; she just didn't have much to cook. When we had Sunday company we tried always to have fried chicken; it's funny to think of how that one-time feast is now common. We would manage some sort of dessert, but we paid for it the rest of the week. One way we paid was with oatmeal. With canned milk. To this day I don't like oatmeal. We tried to raise a garden, but none of us knew how. It yielded some small tomatoes, onions and corn.

The coal situation was about as troublesome as food. We had an antique furnace in the basement, with a single register in the first-floor hallway that we huddled around in the morning, trying to get dressed without embarrassment. But the furnace ate coal, and coal cost $2 a ton. A lot of families sent their kids out with sacks to pick up

coal along the railroad tracks. The kids would throw rocks at the brake-
men on the coal cars, the men would throw coal back, helping to fill
the sacks. We never got to that point, but I thought about it, and several times I went through the alley, picking up discarded pieces of
wood for kindling. I put newspapers under my mattress, and sometimes slept in my clothes to stay warm enough to sleep, but getting up
in that cold house was, as Rose said later, a hateful memory.

One reason I liked spending the night at Ed Osler's was the
warm bed, another the big breakfast that Mrs. Osler fixed. I tried to eat
everything in sight without seeming to. We would have orange juice,
eggs and bacon, toast and jelly, things scarce or unknown at home. I
would find excuses to go back through the dining room and scoop up
anything left. Youth will find a way.

Still, we had good times. The girls in our crowd would have
parties and we would make fudge or taffy, we would go on hikes and
picnics, or to the movies where for a dime we could sit in the balcony
and kiss. Or play hide and seek for the same purpose. Later we would
pile into cars and drive up to the Copper Kettle to dance. The Kettle
was run by Charlie Absher, who kept the place orderly so that mothers
of the nice girls would let their daughters go there. In winter, when it
snowed hard, the town fathers would rope off Oak Street, which in
any case was too steep for cars in slippery weather, and let us use it for
sledding. We would get logs or old tires for a fire, and take a running-
go and belly-bust down the long hill. Girls usually went down sitting,
but sometimes they would jump on top of us as we zoomed past. It was
good to feel a real girl on top of you. Afterward we would go to
someone's house, possibly make fudge or popcorn, and dance.

***

I worked, not because I wanted to. I began modestly, cutting
grass, hauling trash, chopping kindling, but soon graduated to major
jobs. Bill Davis and I tore down Mrs. Wray's coal shed, while the
Wray girls, Jean and Din, made fun of us and brought us lemonade.
Junior Baker and I cut down a huge elm tree in the McDonald's side
yard and sawed it up for firewood. I got a job carrying water for a road
crew working toward High Knob, and I recall one hot day laying a
rock walk for Mrs. Trevathan, over on Park Avenue (more commonly
called Main Street).When I finished, trembling with fatigue, Mrs.

Trevathan handed me two dollars and told me to go home and go to bed. I did, but three hours later I was up, into my blue suit and two-tone shoes, off to the dance. It cost fifty cents stag, a dollar with a date. At intermission, if we had dates we would go to the Liberty Cafe, where for a quarter we could get a grilled cheese and coke.

They were good dances. We usually got bands that had played Knoxville or Roanoke and came to Norton on an open date, but now and then we would get someone like Jimmy Lunsford or Claude Hopkins, in which case the ticket went up to a dollar, date or stag. I was by this time a dancing fool because of one afternoon at Jean Wray's house when she, Libby Roberts and Virginia Tate got out the old Victrola. "Now, come on," Virginia snapped. "Put your arm around me—now don't act silly! Put your left foot—left foot, dummy—forward, now your right." I wonder if I would ever have learned had the girls not put their foot down.

The music was pretty good, too. The songs were simple, but you could hum and whistle, even sing them. "The Very Thought of You," "Stardust," "Sophisticated Lady," "Clouds." There were a lot of winter songs: "Walking in a Winter Wonderland," "June in January," "Let it Snow." And cigarette songs: "Two Cigarettes in the Dark." "Smoke Rings" and Fred-and-Ginger specials: "Cheek to Cheek," "The Way You Look Tonight."

On summer nights we'd go down to the Norton Bakery and buy a couple of loaves of Jitney Bread, so-named because it cost a nickel, eat it hot, and sit on the McDonald's long steps and sing: "Stars Fell on Alabama," "Smoke Gets in Your Eyes," "My Silent Love." We'd sit and wait for the moon to rise over the mountain beyond the railroad yards, turning the valley into silver, brushing away its ugliness. My heart would swell.

***

One summer I applied for the glamour job of soda jerk at the Norton Pharmacy. Doc Brown said Sonny Johnson, a college man, was going to be his fountain man, but he would let me hop curb, better than no job. I had a white mess jacket and stood out front, trotting to each car that parked by the curb, taking the order, then rushing inside to get the order from Sonny and rush back, carrying cokes and what-all on a tray that fit on the car window. The next summer I got the soda-jerk job, a good job. On nights when there was a game or a dance, we would be swamped, and I would throw out cokes, chocolate milks, milkshakes, Nabs and cigarettes like a madman. The mornings were slow and pleasant. The women from the offices would come in, drink coffee and smoke. And there was this pathetic character, our town dope fiend, who always wore the same blue suit and worn felt hat. He was the son of a good family, but had fallen among the thistles of life. He would come in, walking unsteadily and looking neither right nor left back to where Doc Brown filled prescriptions. Lightning, the colored boy, would shake his head. "Gotta get fixed up," he'd say, and in a few minutes the fellow would come out, smiling, nodding to everyone. It seemed a humane way to handle a painful problem. We don't have that much sense today. Or as much compassion. We are meaner today when we are rich than we were poor.

***

But in the winter of my sophomore year, Mama and Kat called me into the kitchen and said I was going to have to go to work. Daddy had tried selling insurance, but hadn't done too well at it. He had inherited a little bit from Uncle Doc and traded his ancient Chevrolet for a new Ford V8, but had tried to become a loan shark and had lost badly. Bruce Crawford, publisher of *Crawford's Weekly*, told Daddy he would give me a job running job presses, casting cuts, melting lead, helping with the press that printed the paper. I could come to work at noon and work till eight or thereabouts. That meant that I would have to go to school part time and drop behind my class like a poor kid. I was sickened, but the next day I went down and told Prof Burton that I was going to go to school half-time for a while. He called me a quitter, predicted that I would eventually drop out altogether. I was furious.

The job at the paper was terrible. I liked Bruce and his wife Kate and admired Bruce for having the guts to stand up for the miners in a strongly pro-operator town. But he had two printers whom I despised, and who returned the favor. The work was hot and dirty, and on press night, after we had stamped out the papers to be mailed, I had to carry the mail sacks across the street and down the block to the Post Office. By that time I was sweaty and ink-dirty and dreaded going out where one of the girls might see me. But the job lasted until fall, when

Mama told me I could quit. Rose had come home, and Daddy seemed to have gotten hold of some money. Funny, but those nasty press nights at the *Weekly* came into good use later. But they cost me a half year of school.

School could be ridiculous. One morning it was announced that all boys would report to the auditorium, where Prof Burton told us to sit down and listen to Dr. Bedenhaus, an authority. The Doc was a large man in a black suit, wearing rimless glasses and a chain across the front of his vest. He got right down to cases. He had been a boy, he said, and knew a boy's feelings. "We know," he warned, "what you do at night when you are in bed and your hands creep beneath the covers." (Oh, God! Who told?) "We know the urges of a growing body. We have borne the burden of the tyrant flesh, and it is during these important years that you must face the urge to experiment with that part that is the secret of your manhood, that lets you achieve fatherhood." ("Not if I pull it out in time," said Robert Osborne. He could talk without moving his mouth, driving the teachers crazy.) "There is within each of you," boomed the Doctor, his voice rising, his finger pointing toward heaven, as if to seek help in his soul-saving mission, "the urge to yield to THE SECRET SIN!

"You can always tell a boy who has fallen victim to (hold on, here we go) THE SECRET SIN!" bellowed the Doc. "His face will erupt with PIMPLES and PUSTULES!" (Half the boys were just into pimples, and sweat formed on their blushing faces.) And not just complexion was ruined. Next eyesight would fail, and soon the poor, hand-happy victim would become a mindless wreck, shuffling down the back alleys of life.

"I have known fine boys," thundered the Doc. "captains of the football team, presidents of their class until they fell victim to," up-pointing finger, quivering jowls, "THE SECRET SIN!" ("Thou shalt not cuff thy wee member," said Robert. We dissolved. "You better cut that out," said Fred Horne, known as Horny, of course.)

Well, to hear the Doc tell it, dogs wouldn't lift a leg on a boy who dabbled in (one more time) THE SECRET SIN!. "No decent girl will want to be seen with him, and decent boys will shun his company." ("I don't want anything to do with you, Horny," said Robert.) We put our hands to our mouths, feigning coughing to cover our giggles.

Outside, there was a great show of original humor. "Thank God I never got that habit," said Buddy Conner. "I may slap it around two or three times a day, but I never got the habit." We all agreed that Buddy was a monument to self control.

It was about this time that I had my first brush with Demon Rum or, to be more precise, Demon moonshine whiskey. There was a basketball game down at Big Stone Gap, and a bunch of us went down. Before we went into the gym, someone suggested that we go over to the "nigger" shack and get a short pint. We drove out toward the swimming pool to where a meager shack perched on a slope beside the road. It seemed to be empty when we knocked, but shortly a bass voice asked "Who's that?" It was proper to reply either "CCC" or "orchestra," two organizations whose discretion had been proved. "Wha' ya want?" the voice would rumble, the answer to which was "Let us have a short pint." A large hand would emerge from the dim recesses, a quarter would be placed in it, and shortly a small bottle of a white liquid would be handed over.

Then in a dark place on the school grounds the nectar was sampled. Bob Browning demonstrated the proper technique: take a gulp of lemon pop, then a swig of whiskey, and follow it with a larger swig of pop. A moonshine sandwich. In theory, you hardly tasted the whiskey. It wasn't as bad as I had feared, we all had another nip—a short pint would go only so far—and trooped into the gym. The effect was long dead by the time we got home.

We had more colorful bootleggers, such as John Wiley and Hobert Bell, though both of these worthies fell upon evil days because of their own misdeeds. John boasted that he aged his whiskey in oak chips that gave it its light brown color and distinctive flavor, until Rance Thompson discovered John coloring his booze not with oak chips but with cow pies, which he put into a toe sack and dipped into the liquid until it had attained the proper tint. John's business fell off sharply. The word also got around that Hobert's whiskey beaded so well when shaken because into each batch he dropped a dollop of carbide, a granular chemical used to produce acetylene in miners' lamps.

No such shady doings darkened the reputation of sweet old Widow Carter, on whom we depended for refreshment at dances. At intermission we would drive up Guest River, park and cross a corn field to where a lamp in the window of a cabin heralded the Widow's abode. When we knocked, a cheery, creaky voice would bid us welcome, and we would enter a living room where the widow, looking like the jollier sister of Whistler's mother, sat in a rocking chair in the glare of an Aladdin Lamp.

She would welcome us, ask if she could offer us something to drink, and lead the way to the kitchen, where an earthen crock rested under the sink. She would dip a gourd dipper into the crock, pour the smoky liquid into a glass about the size of a restaurant juice glass, and with each glass hand the drinker a gourd of water to keep the fire from spreading. Each man would get two measures of the smoky stuff, showing good form by exclaiming over its merits. As one departed, one might notice the open Bible on the table by the lamp, and on the shelf beneath a mean looking pistol, reportedly ready for use in the event someone forgot to pay.

But these were small-time bootleggers. Our big manufacturer of moonshine was John Shephard, a tall, wiry, hawk-faced man who lived on the other side of High Knob in a ramshackle white frame. John grew corn which he turned into liquid profit in stills reportedly located down in the lake hollow. He did not sell in the retail trade, except to prominent businessmen such as Ed Osler's daddy and some lawyers in town who would buy by the keg.

We were afraid of John, who had reputedly killed several men. But sometimes when we were camping out on the Knob we would go to his house, sit on the porch and talk, and once he told us about going over into Kentucky in search of work in one of the mining camps. "I was sitting there on the commissary porch one day, listening to a feller play a banjo, and there was this feller sitting next to me, and I noticed he didn't look too good, when all of a sudden he groaned, and said to me 'I been cut bad,' and he just eased over, fell out into the street, and his entrails slid out in the dirt, and I said to hell with this, I'm going back to Virginia." He laughed.

John never had trouble with the law, principally because he was married to the sister of our chief of police, who never saw anything he wasn't supposed to. But in time John's luck ran out. Federal agents caught him, not for moonshining, but for failure to pay tax on it, and sent him to prison for some absurd time. It proved too much for John. He was too much the mountain hawk to stay in a cage, and I heard later that he went crazy, was shipped off to the mental hospital where he confessed to several killings and died. Everyone asked the same question: What the hell did that accomplish?

Virginia went wet along with other states in 1933, but went

grudgingly, permitting only state-operated stores. The whiskey was better, but it wasn't as much fun and cost a lot more, so that a lot of people stuck with the moonshine. No matter who is in office in Virginia, they love to take the fun out of life. If Jesus returns, Virginians will ask who his people are, where they came from, if there are any Catholics in his family.

***

Each fall I went out for football. I never made the first team, partly because I was never very big. At 14 I realized to my anguish that other boys were out-growing me. By the time I was a senior, I was about five-nine, but never weighed over 135. But I played quite a bit because we could not play, or even practice, if we were not passing every subject. I was not a very good player, but I was fast, could run forever and always had passing grades. I recall the first game in which I played. It was against East Stone Gap, and Frank Nard, our quarterback, called my number for an off-tackle run. I dashed down the field, saw the final stripe and lunged dramatically over it. Frank came trotting up. "What the fuck are you doing?" he snarled. I had dived over the ten-yard line. But in my senior year I made my letter, saved up enough to buy my orange, crew-neck sweater, on which Mama sewed the proud black N. And I had one moment of glory. Against Clintwood, we received, Junior Baker ran the ball to the eighteen, and on the first play I took the ball on a split buck and suddenly found only the safety between me and the goal. I feinted right, but cut left and went eighty-two yards for the score. I swear, to this day I recall every step, the name of the safety—Steele. The girl whose body I coveted was in the stands with Robert Osborne, and as I trotted back I hollered, "How you like them apples?" Frank Nard slapped me on the back.

Frank was unusual, black-haired and muscular, with a big Italian nose, loved music, played the clarinet, but tried to hide his sensitive side. In our senior year, Frank and I won the Kiwanis Club Cup for our plaster model of the Panama Canal. I still don't see how we did it. It had everything, locks, dams, lakes, the Chagres River, the mountains. I remember telling Frank "I'm going down there one day." Little did I know.

16

Norton, VA

The summer before my senior year was a high spot. Daddy let me have our blue Ford, and I got five other guys to chip in money for expenses, including mine, and we took off for the World's Fair in Chicago. We had a great time, took a plane ride over the city, went to the Chicago Theater where Joseph Cherniavsky and his orchestra rose up out of the pit playing "Song of India." That was spectacular. So was a girl named Barbara Worth that I met at the fair. One night the fellows followed Bob Browning to a whorehouse. I wanted to go, but was, to tell the truth, afraid, and pretended to be too drunk. We had a lot to talk about when we got home.

A few days after we returned, the city, using WPA labor, finished the swimming pool in the city park, and Phil Porter and I rushed down and got jobs as lifeguards. That was a joke. Phil could swim, at least, but I have bones of lead and sink like a rock. But I was willing to report in the chilly mornings and pull one end of a pool-wide seine, with Phil on the other end, and skim off the leaves and the oil that dropped from the coal smoke from the trains that ran only a hundred yards away. We also had to discourage the small kids from peeing in the pool (you could tell what they were up to by the guilty, wide-eyed look on their faces), and occasionally chase out some ridge-runner who would lather up in the shallow end until we introduced him to the showers. And there was the night when this bosomy blonde came in with two tough-looking characters, all half drunk, and got the idea she wanted to float around with the life-saving ring around her. But the time came and she found she couldn't get out of it. "Get her out of it," Reese Stradley, the desk manager, ordered, and I tried gingerly to show the lady how she would have to ease it up, pushing down one breast at a time. She was giggling, the two men were roaring with laughter. "It's them big tits," one hollered. "You'll have to let the air out of 'em." Finally, I took the bull by the horns, or in this case, the cow by the tits, and pushed her breasts, one at a time, down through the ring. The men howled.

That was the summer I became a fighter. Several of us went to a party at Evvy Taylor's, down at Big Stone Gap. It was a good party. A lot of the boys against whom we played football were there and we kidded each other. Big Stone boys, like the girls, were first class; we were always glad to have them at our parties. I was sitting on the porch railing talking to one of the Horton girls when this boy I didn't know came out and made some remark that I took as a joke. I responded in kind. The next thing I knew, a streak of lightning shot across my eyes, just as in cartoons. The guy had hit me without warning, right in the temple, and almost sent me away. When my head cleared, we were wrestling. I had grabbed him by reflex and held on, and the girls were screaming and hollering. This guy was a tiger. He hurled me to one side, I braced my feet and we went down, with me on top. His head hit the concrete floor with a nice pop, and for a few second he was out of it. John Graber, Bill Potter and some others came out and pulled us apart. "It wasn't John Ed's fault," Evvy said. "Ralph just said something and then hit him."

"Yeah," Bill Potter said, "that sonofabitch starts something every time he gets a drink." I then realized that I had been locked in hostile embrace with Ralph Potter, Bill's cousin and a boxer at a Tennessee prep school. Next day the word was all around the pool that John Ed Pearce had just beat the hell out of Ralph Potter. Yeah, beat his head on the floor. I modestly assured everyone it was nothing, really, that Potter had been drinking.

That was the last summer that I got to spend much time on the Knob, usually with Buddy Conner. We fished a little, swam a little, gigged frogs at night and cooked them for breakfast. If it was a moonlight night we would pop our carbide lamps and hike up the valley to the top of the Knob, just to be doing it, just to sit in the moonlight and watch the mist spread a curtain of haze over the lake hollow, listen to the night wind, now and then hearing a train whistle from down in the Norton yards. We would smoke and talk about girls and what we wanted to do when we got out of school. I was aching to get out of Norton, away from the coal mines and coke ovens and slate dumps piled along the road to Wise, away from the cold house where Mama fought her never-ending battle against coal dust and soot, washing the white curtains every week, hanging them on the curtain stretchers and shaking her head when they got gray before she could get them on the windows; and away, most of all, from wanting things, seeing the family do without, with never enough food in the kitchen, never enough money for clothes and dances. I wanted to get away from the mothers who regarded me as second-level, away from seeing Mama looking so tired and unhappy or lying down with a headache, away from seeing Daddy, who was acting stranger with each day, stride through the house, waving his hands, talking to himself, playing his damn guitar at all hours. I had decided that he was finally over the edge one day in my senior year when we kids were loafing in front of the Esser house during noon recess, and Daddy came slouching down the walk, long underwear, no shirt, and everyone looking at him as at a freak. "Hey, Pearce," Frank Nard yelled at me, "can't you afford to buy your old man a shirt?" I wanted to sink into the sidewalk. Fuck you, I replied wittily. How could he humiliate us that way? I just wanted to get away. I could do better than this.

Not Buddy. He was perfectly content where he was, as long as the town yielded females willing to see things his way, and he had time to get up into the mountains, and wade along the creeks that creamed over their rocky beds between the banks of pine and rhododendron. And I had to admit that I was going to miss the mountains, the Knob and the lake that had become comfort and escape, the quiet places of beauty that every life needs. And I wonder at the tenacity with which those hills cling in memory even today. I can still recall with surprising clarity an afternoon on Eagle Knob, the slightly lower peak just across a gentle swale from High Knob, recall the sweet smell of sedge grass, the purple of the far mountains and the sight of that hawk lifting off from the tall, dead chestnut tree, soaring in graceful defiance of the earth, his wings golden against the dark green of the valley, seeming in his wheeling flight a symbol of all that was free and beautiful, sailing without effort the river of air, still there in my mind, caught like a fly in the amber of memory.

***

But we always had to go back down to reality. And school. Except for getting to play a little football, my senior year was unexceptional. We graduating seniors were not disappointed in our big senior prom, principally because we didn't have one. I can't say that I missed it. I did wish that we could have a yearbook, with pictures and inscriptions, but the Depression was still gnawing at us, and Prof Burton said that the school budget couldn't afford a yearbook, just as our parents couldn't afford class rings. I think it was at the beginning of our junior year that we were called to the auditorium and told that we would have to double up in our studies, since there was enough money to keep school open only eight months.

So when it came time for class night I, being class president, called some of the others together after school and we decided to put on a play, like Mickey Rooney and Judy Garland. I was all for a dress-up deal, where the girls would wear long dresses and the boys would press their suits, but the girls outvoted me, since three of the girls did not have a long dress and couldn't afford to buy one. So we put on a skit and afterwards some of us went up to the Kettle to dance. I don't think anyone got laid. I sure as hell didn't. If it had been left up to the girls of Wise County, I would have entered the pearly gates with the vestal virgins. I was dating a girl who, everyone said, looked like the actress Norma Shearer, and who possessed the most delightfully curved bottom I had ever groped. She drove me mad. I roamed all over that girl, up, down, around and about, pawing and puffing and dying inside, but she refused steadfastly to lower that final barrier to happiness.

The next day Mama saw me off to the Baptist Church, where we donned rented caps and gowns for the final words of hail and farewell. It was a lovely day, with the mountain standing out in green relief, and the scent of blossoms of the locust trees along the walk heavy and sweet on the air. I remember that we entered singing "Holy, holy, holy, Lord God Almighty." Mama said later, "I could hear you singing above everyone." I'm not sure now that that was a compliment. There was a dull address in which we were urged to aspire to greatness, then handed diplomas and left. I gave my lady of the beautiful buttocks a camera, and she seemed pleased, though not enough. That was it. A bunch of us went to the Kettle that evening, then my lady and I went to her house and writhed on the sofa for a while.

There had been the usual talk about what we were going to do now. I surely couldn't expect a scholarship; my grades had slumped after I dropped out half a day to work, knew that my chances of college were slim and seeing little point in getting good grades if I was going to have to stay in Norton. On the day school let out, I went by to pick up my books and say good-bye to my teachers, and Lennie Blankenship snapped "Come in here, John Ed. Sit down." I knew Miss Lennie wasn't as sour as she let on. In my sophomore year she had motioned to me after class one day and handed me a book, saying it was time I started reading something worthwhile. She gave me Sigrid Undset's *Kristin Lavransdatter*, which I loved. I went from there to the Jalna books, to the *Forsyte Saga*, and finally to *Lord Jim* and Conrad.

Miss Lennie looked at me severely, but then her expression softened to a sort of sweetness. "What are you going to do now?" she asked. I admitted I didn't know, since college seemed out of the question. "Don't accept that," she said. "You get out of here. You're not half as dumb as you make out sometimes. Get out and see life, see the world. Don't let these hills hem you in." I have wondered since whether she was speaking to me or to the girl she was at seventeen.

Even dreams that you know must die eventually, can die painful deaths. I still wanted to be a college man, a fraternity man, with autumn leaves crackling underfoot as I walked toward the stadium with a beautiful girl. It didn't take long for that dream to shatter. The day after graduation I walked into the kitchen where Mama was sitting at the table.

"Well, what are you planning to do now?" she asked. I said I thought I'd go down to the pool and see if any of the kids were in from college.

"Ted says Swift and Co. is looking for an assistant bookkeeper," she said, not looking at me. "He thought you might be interested. Jobs are hard to get."

I said yes, I know, but I'd been hoping to go to college. Mama said there was nothing she wanted more, but with things the way they were...The next morning I put on my blue suit and walked down Main Street, through Little Italy with its Bargain Store and Italian restaurants to the squat brick building across from Norton Wholesale Grocery and Norton Hardware.

***

The Swift and Co. branch house had a smell I cannot describe but that I could identify if I smelled it today, the smell of bloody beef and salt pork, soap and cheese and sausage seasoning. Corridors ran between stacks of cartons piled ceiling high, a massive door clanged open to reveal a deep cooler, and to the right of the front door were two glass-enclosed offices. I recognized Neal Blanton, the branch manager who lived up the street from us, a tight-faced man with short-clipped red hair, a cigar in his mouth that he never lit. Behind a wide desk at the other end of the room sat a short, stocky black-haired man with a thick mustache. Ted had told me that he was D.J. McNerny, for whom I would work if I got the job. I prayed I wouldn't get it. He looked hard.

I stepped inside and strode to his desk with my best positive-thinking look. "You looking for somebody?" he snapped. I told him of my mission. "Oh, Jesus," he said. "Sit down." I sat. He asked what kind of job I wanted, and I said I would take anything open.

"You had any experience?" came the expected question. With total aplomb I informed him that I had taken a bookkeeping course in high school and had graduated from Roanoke Business School. He put out his cigarette and looked at me with total disbelief.

"I think you're a damn liar," he said tiredly. "I think I've seen you around town. Tried to play football, didn't you?" We talked about little or nothing, and he finally told me to come back next day, that he had some more applicants to talk to but would consider me. All the while, loud-talking men clumped in and out, and Neal Blanton bellowed into the telephone about the price of "them cheddars." Maybe I could get a job teaching grammar.

McNerney was already there when I reported at eight the next morning, in his vest, sleeves rolled up. He looked at me with fine scorn.

"Take off your coat and sit down," he said in his Yankee Irish accent. I learned that he was from Oil City, Pennsylvania, and had been tossed at random into Norton by the Swift machine. "I don't think you know anything. If you do, forget it. We have our own system. You learn it fast or you won't stay here. I'll try to teach you, but I'm short of time. I haven't had any help for three weeks and I'm up to my ass in work. You get here at eight, you leave at five, with an hour off for dinner. Forty hours, fourteen dollars a week, and we have to come in Saturday morning to make reports. That's about it. You report to me and nobody else. We're separate from the rest of the operation. But try to get along with Blanton. He may ask you to ride with some of the drivers at night or on weekends, and you get paid extra if you do. You don't have to. That's about it."

The job was simple, boring and demanding. The branch house received meat, soap, lard, cheese and so forth by the freight-car load from Chicago, and a half-dozen salesmen sold it throughout Southwestern Virginia and Eastern Kentucky. The salesmen would phone or bring in orders on tickets that would be given to the shipping clerk in back, and he and the drivers would load the ordered goods onto the trucks for delivery. Most of the stuff went to coal camp stores, called commissaries, that sold it to the miners. The miners seemed to eat an awful lot of fat back, salt pork that was kept in dark bins in the basement where Nigger Oscar shoveled salt over it, wet it down and then tried to kill any attacking rats. Rats were a problem, but there was an old dog that hung around that took care of a lot of them. The men would throw him scraps.

When the orders were filled, the tickets were sent up to us, and we would multiply the pounds or cartons by the current prices, which Chicago kept changing to meet the market: Stonega Coal Company, Inman store, 5 cases Silverlead lard at 11 cents, 500 pounds backs at 8. Multiply them out, add them up, put the finished ticket to one side, grab the next. A job not requiring a wealth of imagination or personality.

I didn't mind it too much. McNerney was a prince. Everyone liked him, partly because he would do anything for anyone, never became truly angry, and cursed the salesmen with a colorful flair that they loved. He was patient with me and soon seemed to be satisfied with my work.

***

But I always felt a twinge when, walking home at noon, I saw kids at the pool, or listened at night to the kids home from college speak a language subtly changed. They took trips to visit college classmates, and classmates visited them. I skirted around the edges, not quite one of the bunch any more, though I was probably more aware of that than they were.

Saturdays were rather fun. The salesmen would come in with reports, and Mac would curse at them for getting in the way by sitting in the windows and watching the action across the street. The miners would start sifting in from the camps up the road toward Coeburn or Wise, settling in to Nard's Cafe, which served good food and kept things orderly, or the Silver Moon Cafe and Hotel, which was another matter. I cannot say that the Silver Moon was a house of ill repute, but it was said to house seven tables and seventeen waitresses, and rented rooms upstairs, all of which aroused suspicions. The miners would get hold of some white whiskey, play mournful tunes on the juke box concerning troubling minds and lonesome valleys, and by ten o'clock the fights would start. Sounds of shouts and scuffling would drift across the street, and here would come a couple of battlers, relieving the stress and boredom of their week by beating hell out of each other. Often, the ladies with whom they had been consorting would follow them out onto the sidewalk, trying to part them but sometimes becoming involved themselves, pulling hair, punching and screeching. The salesmen would cheer them on, while McNerney and I tried to balance the sheets or "biffs" on which the sales were collectively recorded for the week.

We were all being screwed, knew it and knew there was nothing we could do about it. We were supposed to work forty hours a week, but after five eight-hour days we had to come in on Saturday morning to "make reports," which took a full half-day. Then two men would have to man the premises during the afternoon, one in the office, one in the back plant, to wait on the walk-in retail trade. There was an unwritten law that the unfortunate who got the Saturday afternoon duty could steal a little, not much, but a little. Meat loses water weight or "shrinks" when left hanging for any length of time, and allowance was made for the difference in weight between what came in to the plant and what went out. We could therefore steal a little and blame it on shrinkage, knowing that if caught we would be fired. A second unwritten rule decreed that if one of the girls from the Silver Moon came over and bought an order costing less than three dollars, the man waiting on her could give her the option of paying or stepping into the cooler for a quickie.

I learned to purloin a little cheese or a little pork loin, but had never tried a transaction with the girls. Whores made me nervous, and I couldn't imagine how the contract was carried out. But one afternoon this tall, emaciated female came across from the Silver Moon and I went back to wait on her. As usual, she asked for ham and cheese.

I got it from the cooler and wrapped it, and was about to make out her ticket when Bob Stallard, who was working on the rear platform called me back.

"How much she get?" he asked.

"Ham and cheese. Three dollars."

"Take her in the cooler," he said, grinning.

"Huh?"

"Take her in the cooler and fuck her," he said, as to a slow-witted child. Terror swept over me.

"How do you know she wants to?" I quavered.

"Sure she does. She doesn't pay the ticket, it's like getting three dollars for it. She never gets over a dollar. Go on. You're not scared, are you?" Oh, God no. Who me, scared? Petrified.

I went back to the fatal customer, who loomed half a head taller than I, and stood leaning against the door in weary boredom. "You like to step into the cooler?" I quavered, praying that she would choose the path of virtue.

She grinned, surprised. "Huh?" she said. "Why, sure." And together we strolled into the garden of love, with beef carcasses adorning the walls, while in the middle stood the symbolic chopping block, on which it was custom, or so I had heard, to lay a sheet of wrapping paper before placing on it the sacrificial virgin.

Now what?

I looked at her in fear and trembling, praying that God would remember all the good things I had done and strike me dead. I knew I could never mount this woman. I also knew that if I didn't I would be the object of scorn and ridicule throughout the branch house on Monday morning. She gave me a sympathetic look.

"That Bob Stallard put you up to this didn't he?" I nodded. "I bet you ain't never done it," she said. I nodded my shame.

"Well, don't worry about it," she said kindly, patting me on the shoulder. "We'll just stand here and talk a while, and he won't know no difference."

A wave of relief swept over me. We chatted. We walked out. She got her ham and cheese and returned to the Moon, in my eyes a blessed lady, if not a blessed virgin. Bob Stallard came up and asked "Well, how'd it go?"

"Better than I expected," I answered truthfully.

Monday morning my fame made the rounds. McNerney

frowned. He was a faithful husband to his lovely, black-haired wife, Alma, and did not approve of such dalliance. I told him the truth. He chuckled. But wherever she is, if she still is, I offer up my loving thanks to my lady of the chopping block.

***

Those women had a hard time during the Depression, and they were not the only ones. I was over at Nard's Cafe one day with Lee Bowling, one of the salesmen, having the specialité de jour—bean soup, ten cents, with maybe some bread thrown in if Katherine was in a good mood—when this pale, thin, ragged-looking little girl, not more than twelve, came up to Lee and said, "Hey, buddy, you want to go with me for a quarter?" Lee just looked at her without expression, as at a kid trying to sell cigarettes for a penny each.

"Hell, honey," he said, "you ain't big enough to be fucking."

"I'm bigger'n yer fist," she said defensively. I felt so sorry for the poor little thing. You wonder what happens to poor creatures like that.

But there were lighter moments. Periodically, the boys in the back would make sausage, Brookfield Pork Sausage that was, I still think, the best I ever tasted. Chicago would ship in barrels of sausage trimmings, pieces of pork not rendered into lard or other delicacies, and tins of sausage seasoning, a blend of spices that, precisely mixed, gave the sausage its distinctive flavor. The boys would shovel the pork onto the sausage table, a four-foot square stainless steel surface slanted slightly toward a hole in the center where the pork, with seasoning splashed on, would pass into the grinder. The extruded sausage would be packed into pound cartons, or larger boxes or buckets. Simple procedure, but now and then a rat, driven to daring by the scent, would manage, while backs were turned, to leap onto the table and grab a hunk of the pork. The poor bastard would then head for home, carrying his loot, only to find the footing slippery with pork fat. He would start slipping, as the boys hollered, "Rat on the sausage table!" and everyone would run out to watch. At first, the rat would cling to his booty, but soon, as his feet ran faster and faster and got nowhere and he slipped ever backward toward the hole of fate, he would drop his pork and lunge toward escape. To no avail. We would shout encouragement, but little by little he would slip backward until, with a squeal, he disappeared into the grinder. Everyone would howl, and watch the sausage coming out, careful not to let any of the suspiciously gray extrusion make it into packages, scooping out the inferior product and throwing it out to the dog.

But for the most part, life at the branch house was a grinding routine. The manager bore down on the shipping clerk, who bore down on the drivers, who hated the clerk, the manager and the job, but didn't dare quit when jobs were so scarce.

I was not asked to ride trucks often, but I recall one Saturday when I was riding with Bob Stallard, or Troy Sturgill and we had the run over into Letcher and Pike counties, in Kentucky. We thought of East Kentucky as mean country, but the people in the commissaries were nearly always good-natured and ready to kid with the drivers; I remember one woman who hollered at Bob, "Hey, Stallard, who's your short-peckered friend?" Everybody laughed. "Show it to her, Pearce," Bob said, "don't let her talk that way about you." I set another blushing record, but rather enjoyed it.

Anyhow, they were having labor trouble over in Kentucky, and strikers were picketing some of the roads. We started down a hill near Virgie, in Pike County, when four mean-looking hayshakers stood up ahead at the ends of a log laid across the road.

"Get down," said one of them. We got out and stood, saying nothing.

"You for the union or again it?" the man asked. This posed a problem. If we said we were for the union and the men were company thugs, we could get the hell beaten out of us. If we said we were against the union, and they were union men, we could get the same.

"Swift doesn't take sides," Stallard said. "We're just delivering meat so you guys can eat." The man glared at me, probably wondering what the hell I was doing there.

"That's right," I piped up. "We're not for or against."

The man standing next to me said "Shut up!" and slapped me with the back of his hand, knocking me down into the ditch along the road. I had enough sense to get up and say nothing. After a minute they removed the log and we went our way. Bob asked me if I was all right, and I said I was. Actually, I found the whole episode rather exciting. But I had a new appreciation for the driver's job and understood why Ted, Katherine's husband, was so glad to quit Swift and get a job in Charlotte as a salesman for a drug company.

***

That winter was long and cold, and the walk from home to the branch house was a long, brutal mile. I would gulp my oatmeal and coffee and brace myself, until one morning Mama said, "Sit for a minute and smoke your cigarette. I know you smoke." That gave us a chance to talk a little. Rose sometimes ate with us, but her taxi usually came before we ate. She had to take the cab clear through Dorchester and up Thacher's Branch to her school. She was paid, as I recall, eighteen dollars a week, and the cab cost her fifty cents a day, but between us we were able to make things a lot easier.

Daddy was still a problem. I had established a charge account at Gillenwater's Corner Store, and Daddy would charge things until I had to cancel the account. And he would get up before daylight to turn on the radio and play along with the country music bands out of Knoxville, waking us all until I screamed at him to turn it down. Sometimes he wouldn't, and I didn't know what to do about it. My romance had me worried, too. Sooner or later, I knew, my love would spread her legs, I would get her pregnant and that would be it. We would get married and settle down to a miserable life of semi-poverty. And all the world out there, waiting, as Miss Blankenship said.

Then the blind hog came stumbling onto the scene. A young man named Sagaser Kash, a University of Kentucky graduate from Carlisle, Kentucky, had come to Norton to work on the *Coalfield Progress* and had been dating Shan Seidel, a friend of Kat's, and one day in late summer he said to me, "Hey. I'm going down to Lexington this weekend. Want to go with me?" I did. I got leave from McNerney, and we took the night L&N, arriving in Lexington just before daybreak, and as we got off the train at Central Station on Main Street, I had the feeling that here was something very unusual about this town. I knew in that moment that I wanted to live in that town.

We walked out across the UK campus as day broke, spent some time at Sag's fraternity house, and then went to the *Kernel* printing office in McVey Hall, where Dave Griffith, the plant foreman asked me why I wasn't in college. I told him that I had no money, but he said hell, that's no excuse; half the boys here work their way through. You can find a job if you want to.

And, oh, I wanted to. Just walking through the college grounds, drinking coffee in a fraternity house rekindled the fires. Somehow, I had to do it. I went home, told McNerney I wanted a week of my vacation, told Mama I was going down to Pineville to see friends, and stuck out my thumb on the road leading west. I got to Lexington without trouble, got a room in the Drake Hotel on Short Street for a dollar a night and started looking. I shook that town from one end to the other, tried to pass myself off as everything but a doctor or lawyer, put on my best pathetic face, young and earnest. Nothing. On the third day I gave up, took a city bus out to the end of the line on Richmond Road and started hitch-hiking home, defeated. I couldn't even catch a ride. All afternoon I flashed thumb and smile without a taker, and finally gave up, realizing that it was too late to get anywhere that day, and went back to the Drake. Sitting on the bed, discouraged, I remembered Dave Griffith and called him. He told me where he lived, a street off of South Limestone, and told me to come on out.

I found the street and picked a house by the sound of voices on a porch. Griffith's voice assured me I had the right place, and I walked up and told him my sad story. He sympathized. Times were tough, all right, but he assured me that I could find a job if I kept looking.

"A shame you can't run a Duplex press," he said. "We've got a new one coming in the first of the month and I need someone on it. It could pretty near pay your way through." He could not hear the Big Lie Special come thundering down the track, as I assured him that I was an old hand with a Duplex, having worked for my father and for Bruce Crawford. Piece of cake.

The next day I hitch-hiked home, catching rides with no trouble; thank you, God, for not letting me catch one the day before. I told Mama I was going to college. She was shaken. "I would be happy for you," she said. "You deserve a chance, but I just don't see how we can do without you."

That was a hard hand to play to, but the next day I hitch-hiked up to Tazewell, and tried, in the family tradition, to put the bite on the Leslies. I did not have Daddy's luck. Uncle Bland, now head of the family, was sympathetic but unyielding. I rushed to explain that I was not asking help for myself, asking only that he give Mama a little help, five dollars or so a week, until I could get out of school.

"Boy," he said, "your Mama's been good to you. Now you get home and help take care of her. In these times we have to put our own wishes second."

But I was determined. Back home, the boys around the drug store warned me that I couldn't do it without help and shouldn't try it unless I could get a loan. I knew I could make fifteen dollars a week at the *Kernel*, but Rance Thompson, who was going to the University of Tennessee, told me that wouldn't be enough.

Sag Kash urged me to go ahead. So did McNerney. A big shot from the regional Swift office in Baltimore had come down to examine our books the month before and had asked me if I would like to come to Baltimore. I told him frankly that a life keeping books didn't appeal to me, but he said a young man like me could progress in a lot of fields with the company. McNerney was impressed, but now he told me to go on to college. And I was gratified when Don and Sue stopped me one morning and urged me to go.

"Don't let Mama talk you out of it," Don said. "You've done your part; we'll do ours. We'll get along."

I didn't need to be urged. I was going. I got a ride with George Botts, a Transylvania student who owned a Packard coupe, packed my fake leather suitcase, gave Mama what money I had saved, keeping a dollar for myself. George arrived, and I hugged Mama good-bye. She didn't cry, but her lips trembled. "Oh, take care of yourself," she said, pressing her hand to her mouth. And I was off.

***

We had lunch at Sanders Court in Corbin, and I arrived in Lexington with fifty-three cents and a joyful heart. George drove me down South Lime, we spotted a room for rent sign on a house next door to Memorial Hall, and a woman named Smith said she would trust me until payday.

I walked across the campus, savoring it. In the small amphitheater behind Memorial Hall an orchestra was giving a concert, and I sat and listened. They played "Deep Purple." Good song. I breathed deeply. A college man.

17

Strange Times

Next to the Braden case, I suppose the most unpleasant episode the *Courier-Journal* faced during my time was the fight over the busing of school children. We bridled editorially when anti-integrationists called it forced busing, but forced it surely was. A majority, or at least a large minority of the people directly involved were fiercely opposed, to the point of welcoming civil violence. Under busing, children from poor sections, in which most minority students lived, were bused to mainly-white schools, while white students were bused across town to create a balance in previously minority schools. It was a rather tortured way to integrate the schools, with buses shuttling children all over the metropolitan area for hours at a time, and thousands of children waiting for buses in the dark.

Parents, even those white parents who did not mind their children attending school with blacks, wanted their children left in their own neighborhoods, where parents could run them to school in emergencies, knew the teachers and principal and could take part in fund drives, parents' nights and games. Many parents, of course, objected to the racial mix in classes, protesting that blacks held bright students back, were coarse and profane in speech and sexually lewd.

We argued that the experience would be realistic training in the real world for whites and blacks, and that blacks would benefit from contact with whites and with affluent white neighborhoods. The theory was and is condescending to black students. And where we got the idea that being driven through wealthy neighborhoods and going to school with children from rich homes and then returned to their usually-inferior neighborhoods would somehow inspire them to study and become rich escapes me. It didn't work, of course. It made a lot of black kids envious and surly. It certainly did not prevent the rise of violence and gunplay among young blacks. And the extent to which anti-segregation became integration is a matter for hot argument. Athletic teams quickly became integrated because many blacks were good athletes, and coaches favored and played any kid of ability, regardless of color. The same equations did not apply in the classroom, where many of the blacks were at a disadvantage. And integration at social events such as dances raised sexual questions that were hard to answer. White parents who did not object to their sons playing ball with blacks did not want their daughters dancing with or dating blacks, and divisions along racial lines continued much as before.

I sympathized with the white parents who felt that they had no recourse to justice, that no one cared about their children, that the playing field had been slanted in favor of the blacks. And they resented being treated like a bunch of rednecks. A nasty time. On the other side of the coin, I got tired of being awakened in the middle of he night by calls for Mr. Nigger Lover. ("Is this the nigger lover?" they would ask. "No," I would reply, "but if you'll wait I'll call Mr. Nigger Lover to the phone." They would usually hang up.)

We had some nasty demonstrations in front of the *Courier* building, which the police managed to break up without too much trouble. But then the riots flared on Dixie Highway, and they were quite another matter, with fires set along the street, windows broken, and men fighting openly with cops. Finally state troopers were called in, and Lt. Ken Vanhoose, an old friend from Bert Combs days, slapped them into riot gear, formed a line across Dixie Highway and gave one terse order: "Clear this street! And take no shit! " They cleared it, but hundreds of protesters were arrested and put into a ball field to await arraignment. It was not a good start toward school integration, and it took a long time for those sores to heal.

The busing plan was the creature of Judge James Gordon. He had approved one plan, but it was appealed, and the Federal District Court told him to try something else; in fact, the court practically blueprinted the busing. It also told Gordon not to talk to the press about the plan and the pending suits, but I called Jim, with whom I had gone to school at UK, and suggested a story for our magazine that would skirt the court's order and still tell his side of the story. He approved, and I had a clear beat. Newsmen from some of the television stations screamed that the news embargo had been violated. Our news room ignored the story when it appeared in the magazine, though it was a clear victory for the *Courier*. An exclusive like that is usually advertised and given a lot of promotion.

***

What did people gain from all this? I am not sure. The grades of black students have improved somewhat, but this may be due in part to improved economic times. Have race relations improved? Again, I am not sure. Twenty, thirty years ago I met a lot of blacks at cocktail parties and dinners and some of the benefit balls. Today I meet almost none. There is some interracial dating in schools, a few two-tone couples, but the lines are still drawn. They are not as distinct, but I have a feeling they are just as strong. I have no idea how many families moved out of the county to nearby Meade, Bullitt and Oldham counties to get away from busing, because there is no way to ascertain why families moved, but while Louisville and Jefferson County lost population, the counties around us gained. Looking back, I think things are better, how much I am not sure. Blacks and whites just don't seem to be comfortable with each other, and we have yet to find a medium where they can mingle enough to find that each is human.

Twenty years ago, my friend Johnny Popham, of *The New York Times*, told me that in time sex would bridge the color gap. Improve the economy and give black women access to dress and make-up now available to whites, and men would see that they are as desirable as their white counterparts, just as opening colleges to them would reveal them as intelligent companions. To a degree, that has worked. The fashion world has shown us that black women can be very beautiful, just as movies and sports have exhibited the handsomeness of black men. Television commercials make it appear that blacks and whites mingle at every level from laundry room to business office, and newspapers, including the *Courier*, relate the most trivial happenings if they occur in black neighborhoods and seem to use any or no excuse to publish photos of blacks. But while commercials may sell soap, they do not sell social change very well, and newspaper Afrocentrism makes readers like the papers less but not blacks more. Nor is the policy always popular among white staffers. In 1995 a respected *Courier* reporter said to me, "If an out-of-town visitor picked up a *Cou-*

233

rier-Journal, he would assume that Louisville was at least fifty percent black, instead of ten or twelve percent. We publish too many black stories that aren't of general interest, too many pictures of no importance. That may be defensible as social policy, but not as journalism."

Despite criticism from black groups, the *Courier* had been making an effort to hire more black journalists, and with school integration the effort was increased. A man was appointed to find capable minorities, especially blacks, and the effort yielded some first-rate reporters, photographers and editors. I don't know how much it changed the community.

***

In 1976 the Belden agency rated our magazine among the three best in the country, and number one in readership. A few months later, Geoff Vincent was forced to resign because of differences with Bob Clark. There's reward for you; why the Binghams let that happen is beyond me. The episode was one of several in which the *Courier* management made no real effort to keep outstanding people on the staff or to utilize the special knowledge that it had helped staff members to gain. Ward Sinclair, the head of the *Courier* Washington bureau, and one of the outstanding capital reporters, comes to mind. Ward could have, and should have been used to furnish the paper, especially the Op-ed page and magazine, with commentary and interpretive stories, a feature on which we were weak from both Washington and Frankfort. But Norman Isaacs insisted that Ward abide by the new ruling requiring all bureau people to rotate periodically, and Ward made it plain that he was not about to rotate. He quit, and we lost.

I am thinking also of Grady Clay, who studied urban planning, land use and architecture intensively at Harvard, and became a nationally recognized authority on land use, landscape architecture, etc., was chosen editor of the *Architectural Digest* and president of the Society of Landscape Architects, among other national honors. His expertise might have made the *Courier* an acknowledged source of news and an authority on these subjects, and given the paper skilled interpretation, but it was never fully utilized. Grady himself complained that while he was trying to develop stories of national import, his city editor complained if he was not always available for local stories of hardly any importance. The contribution of American papers has been diluted by the failure or refusal of papers to pay for and utilize special talent.

The episode might have reflected the strange lack of communication between the Barrys, Sr. and Jr. Apparently, they did not talk, discuss situations on the paper. One day in 1973 I called on Molly Clowes, who had retired as editorial page editor. She told me that Barry had visited her the previous week and that she had expressed to him her distress over what she considered the deterioration of the ediorial page. "I know," Barry had replied. "It's heartbreaking."

Naturally, she asked him why he didn't do something about it, but he replied, wearily, that he couldn't interfere, though he was chairman of the board. Molly asked why he couldn't at least talk to Barry, Jr. and impress on him that the page was damaging the reputation of the paper, and he promised to try. He soon called to say that he and Barry, Jr. had agreed to have lunch at least once a month and perhaps exchange ideas. But he admitted later that, though they enjoyed lunches together, they had never gotten around to discussing the quality of the page or paper. If this seems unusual, and it surely does, I can't forget that George Burt told me one day that over dinner Barry had lamented that, when Barry, Jr. took over, he, Sr. wrote him a note (wrote him a note, for God's sake!) reminding him that he, Sr., had some expertise in foreign affairs and policy, and would be glad to contribute an occasional editorial on such subjects, and would be more than happy to write an occasional editorial notebook. But, he told Burt with a resigned shrug, he had never received an answer.

Shortly after Geoff left, the paper received another Pulitzer, this time for photo coverage of the busing fight. Perhaps that helped management forget Geoff and the flimsy reasons for his departure.

***

At about this time I got a Dear John from M. In person. Very calmly at dinner one night she said she thought it was time we began seeing other people. It was not a total surprise; you can sense restlessness in a woman to whom you are close, and I had seen signs of restlessness for some time. I couldn't blame her; it was natural for her to want men and social company in general, more her own age. And I recalled the day when Ed Prichard, who was also fond of M, said to me, "Watch out for her. Emotionally, she's got the John Brown (our

Governor John Y. Brown, Jr.) syndrome—short attention span." Still, it was not a day to press away in memory's bouquet.

But getting dumped like a wagon-load of over-ripe manure had a curiously interesting effect. I began dating a lot of women, some of them the finest women I have ever known, and over the next ten years enjoyed a whole new social life. Because of the women I was seeing, I was invited to parties, on trips and to various social occasions by people I had never known before, in whose circles I had not been able to move. It was pleasant. I had always liked social life, liked to dance, and now I was invited to dinner dances and attended benefits, such as the Speed Ball, a dinner dance for which you pay an inordinate amount of money for a mediocre meal, some ordinary music and the chance to be seen in the company of people who matter, and who go in order to show that they matter. It got so that I was going to parties all the time. I had to have two tuxedoes. I also went to England, New York, Michigan, the Bahamas and the Virgins, Florida and Mexico and Steamboat Springs. It was a social decade that I remember fondly, and I am grateful to the women who made it possible. I would never have been invited to all of those places and events on my own.

During these years several things happened that I might mention, things having nothing to do with my peripatetic career in journalism, which was flourishing, incidentally, because of the column. I addressed the Kentucky Club of New York, substituting for Ed Prichard, who was too ill to make the trip. It was a purely wonderful evening and, I must admit, a huge success. Peggy Silhanek, Kentucky's commerce representative in New York before misguided politics replaced her, had arranged a perfect dinner. The University Club was packed, the tables beautifully decorated, with enough bourbon on every table to assure a friendly audience, and as I began speaking heavy snow started slanting down outside the tall windows, very dramatic. I got an incredible reception, and afterward John Moremen, Sue Geiger and I went out and drank a bit. It was one of those nights you would like to re-live.

***

Less successful was my attempt to get a sailing education, my second attempt, actually. I had gone once to the Annapolis Sailing

School in St. Petersburg, Florida, with M. We had a fine time, even though the idiot who was supposedly our instructor almost got us drowned. We were sailing with an attractive couple from Cincinnati named Seltzer, when the instructor sent us out into Tampa Bay to sail back to base, though it appeared that a storm was brewing and the sea was becoming very rough for beginners. The storm hit us before we were two miles out, a gust tore the jib sheet rigging out of the deck and almost capsized us. I had a time getting that boat back to harbor and, had I had my way, would gleefully have killed the mush-mind in charge. To prove that some people will not learn, I went back, in company with Rich Nugent, Mary Lawrence Young and my daughter Betsy, for a course in coast-wise sailing. This course almost ended before we got coastwise when three of us, a young woman named Dixie, Mary Lawrence and I went out with a helium-head instructor named Bob who, this time, actually did wreck us. I tried to warn him that the storm on the horizon was approaching faster than he seemed to think, but he told me very archly that there was room for only one captain on a ship, that he knew the weather and that the storm, if it came our way, would be hours away. Ten minutes later a gust almost knocked us over. We could not come about into the wind, and were washed up on the rip-rap boulders lining the approach to the low highway bridge. People on shore spotted us through the rain, caught the lines we heaved and secured us to the rocks long enough for the girls to jump to safety. Our collision with the rocks left a ten-foot gash in the boat's hull, and I had uncomplimentary words for Captain Bob.

***

Meanwhile, back at the ranch, the musical chairs were being played to a mad tune. In turn, we won another Pulitzer for Richard Whitt's coverage of the Beverly Hills supper club fire, I lost my Dinkins Bayou subdivision on Sanibel and Barry, Jr. fired Bob Clark. Don't ask me why. If he had done it a couple of years sooner, Geoff Vincent might have stayed with us. As it was, Paul Neely, handsome and somewhat autocratic, took over as Sunday editor. He was more orderly and methodical than Geoff, but not as much fun to work with and a little curt at times. Paul Janensch was named executive editor, to the surprise of many who had expected George Gill, who had been general manager and was popular with the news staffs, to be chosen.

237

***

At the begining of the eighties, which would prove disastrous for practically everyone associated with the *Courier-Journal,* my life, personal and professional, was remarkably pleasant and placid. Jerry Ryan, a man with a wild and wonderful sense of humor and a world of talent as both writer and illustrator, came up from the newsroom and took the office that had belonged to fashion editor Lana Ellis, and we got Eleanor Brecher as a magazine staffer. Ellie was—and is—a sheer delight, a revised and re-issued hippie of the seventies who had battled back from near self-destruction without complaint or self-pity, and regained both her sense of humor (she did the best imitation of Myron Cohen imaginable) and writing ability. Later Elaine Corn showed up as food editor—strange title when you come to think of it; how do you edit food? She and Ellie, both barely five feet tall and flinty, became close friends, known around the office as the Jewish bookends. Despite Ellie's guidance, Elaine was something of a problem, outraging St. Matthews club ladies with prick jokes, and dabbling in pot and worse. Irene Nolan, as managing editor, asked me to warn Elaine to shape up or be shipped out, and eventually she did, but not before causing a surprisingly patient Irene headaches.

Irene was a sweetheart. She had come from Indiana University, where she graduated first in her class, married and divorced reporter Jim Nolan, and created something of a stir with her blonde good looks. She became a top reporter and feature writer, but drew an editor whom she absolutely despised. She would come into my office, close the door and for five minutes curse the offending editor with a vocabulary remarkable in a woman so gentle-appearing, then go back to her labors. Unlike others to whom I had been supportive on their way up, Irene felt no compulsion to make life difficult for me once she became managing editor, but was always generous and friendly. An interesting thing about Irene: for years she took her vacations on North Carolina's Outer Banks, and you could tell by the tone of her voice that she considered time spent elsewhere time wasted, much as I had felt about Sanibel in its early years. When she was made managing editor, with a substantial salary, I supposed that she would have less time and attention to pay the Outer Banks. It didn't turn out that way. On the Outer Banks, she met a builder and lumber broker who built a house for her. She married him, quit her job and moved to her dream spot. I admired that. Not many people have the courage to pursue their dream.

***

My blind hog was finding a lot of acorns. Colonel Harland Sanders, developer of Kentucky Fried Chicken, died in 1980, and since I had known and written about him for years, a friend of mine, Joanne Watson, suggested that I write his autobiography, which she would publish. Joanne, better known as "PeeWee", knew nothing about publishing, but she took the book to New York and sold it to Doubleday. Sad to say, it did not sell as well as we had hoped, though it was a pretty good book. But I got a good advance.

I liked to write books, even those that required a lot of research, which was often a bore. I had written a commissioned company history for Brown Forman Corporation in 1972 titled *Nothing Better in the Market*, and had enjoyed both the work and the pay, which, after years at the *Courier*, was almost shockingly generous. I was writing other articles, the column was going well and, as a result, I was getting a raft of requests to speak. The trouble was, and is, that every club in the country needs a speaker a week, but few clubs want to pay that speaker, apparently assuming that addressing them after a poor meal is an honor. I was asked to speak one time over in Shelbyville to a group of civic clubs, and after I had stumbled through my remarks the program chairman came up and handed me my check. I sensed that I was in trouble when he kept a tight hold on one corner of the check and, sure enough, said that their recent speakers had handed their honoraria back for the club's improvement fund. I asked what the improvement fund planned to do with its wealth. "Well," said the chairman, "we had hoped to get some first-class speakers." I kept the check.

Another trial that small-time writers face is the Man with the Book. Half the people in the world have a great book in mind, if they can just find someone to take a few minutes and jot it down. Of course, they do not expect to pay for the jotting, though it takes a year or more, thinking you will be glad to take part of the profits when the book is published, as it never will be. It is easy, they declare, to write things down; they just don't have the time. They are worse even than the people who have a great idea for a column and become indignant when the column doesn't show up in print. What madness drives these people?

But I was having a good time and making a good living, free for the time from debt and worry. Some years earlier, in 1978, I believe, Paul Janensch, then managing editor, called me in and asked if I would like to compile some columns into a book. I said I would. He said the company would be glad to pay me $1,100 for my efforts. I declined. But in 1983 I received permission from George Gill, who was always very kind to me, to copyright enough columns to make a book. I picked out a bunch, and Steve Lee, Sunday copy editor, edited them and I published, on my own, a volume entitled *Seasons*. Bill Swearingen designed an attractive cover, and the thing sold like tickets to the promised land. I printed 5,000, sold 5,000. Made a bundle. Even today I get requests for the book and have tried to find a publisher for a similar volume, but have found no takers, despite the example of *Seasons*.

The year before, something happened that seemed inconsequential at the time but proved tragic. Shirley Williams, *Courier* book editor, had to go to the hospital for surgery and asked Sallie Bingham if she would like to take over in the hiatus. Sallie was more than casually interested in books and was herself a writer of sorts, having published her first novel shortly after college. Critics have said that all of Sallie's books were the same book with different titles but one plot— the sensitive daughter of harsh parents growing up in a provincial southern town. I should walk softly here, I suppose. She has always managed to get a national publisher, which is more than I can say.

Initial reaction to Sallie was generally positive. She ran a low-key operation and staffers liked to drop by and chat. Rich Nugent was from the beginning, and still is, very fond of Sallie. And she has ability. Shirley's office looked as though a hurricane would improve it, books everywhere, in no order, correspondence lying about, people drifting in and out. Sallie at once brought order out of chaos, installed record-keeping and proposed to adopt new ideas. Then came the shocker: Shirley returned, but Sallie very blandly announced that she had decided she would like to be permanent book editor. It was rumored that Barry, Sr. urged Jr. to appoint her, to keep peace in the family and on the board of directors, and that Jr. had complied. So much for Shirley and fifteen years of hard and productive work. Sorry, lady. Out you go. Keep in touch.

I am still puzzled that Mary Bingham did not scotch this move. She knew, from having been book editor herself, how much Shirley had achieved. She had built up a sound network of capable reviewers, people willing because of the page's reputation to review for a pittance. She had cultivated new regional writers and had added significantly to the book page with profiles and stories of writers, conferences and the book world. It is hard to believe that an untidy office could cloud this record.

The situation became more irritating the following year when, in response to a highly congratulatory article in the *Washington Post*, Sallie failed entirely to give Shirley credit for having developed the page and added that running the page was easy because, after all, "nobody reads it." It was another indication that the woman knew nothing whatever about the paper and its region. We got another dose of this that same year, when Carl West, editor of the *Frankfort State Journal*, announced that he and some associates were planning a book fair in the state capital. He had attended the big book fair in Washington and decided Kentucky, with all its writers, could do as well. I had hoped that Sallie would welcome the idea and give the fair some needed publicity. To my disappointment, she dismissed it as a joke. Oh, come on, John Ed, they can't do anything like that. She would not even carry a note announcing the date and place, and the failure of the state's main newspaper to mention the event could not have been helpful.

The fair, of course, was a whopping success, so much so that in five years it had outgrown the state library and packed the huge gym at Kentucky State University. The first fair drew about fifty authors, last year's more than 150. More than 5,000 people attended before lunch—and on a Saturday when the University of Kentucky football team was playing 25 miles away. Among the authors recently offering her works was Sallie Bingham. Her attitude was a typical example of people who regard Kentucky as too backward to accomplish anything in the field of the arts. The fair has also attracted writers from Rosalyn Carter and Andy Rooney to Scotty Reston and Jack Kilpatrick. I can attest that it is a boon to Kentucky writers and gives the public a chance to see and talk with people whose names they have seen previously.

Sallie also demonstrated a remarkable ignorance of the paper and its history. In her book in which she slashed at the family for failing to appreciate her, she declared that the *Courier* had ignored women and had never had a woman in an executive position. This was a slap at Molly Clowes, who brought national recognition to the paper as first editor of a major editorial page. Apparently, Sallie had never even heard of Molly. When Molly wrote a letter, praising Shirley Wiliams for her management of the book page and lamenting its feminist emphasis under Sallie, Sallie asked several of us who were sitting around, "Does anyone know who this old biddie is?" She had also brushed off Carol Sutton as "an assistant of some sort to one of the editors, or publisher," though Carol, the bright and attractive protegée of George Gill's had made a reputation as editor of *Today's Living*, a women's section and succeeded George as managing editor of the *Courier*. It is hard to see how Sallie could have missed the acclaim given Carol. She received a flood of national attention as the first female managing editor of a major daily. She was included among *Time's* Women of the Year and appeared on its cover. Unfortunately, Carol was never comfortable in the position and was made assistant to the publisher. At the time it was not known that she was suffering from a cancer that would kill her two years later.

But, again, it did nothing to improve staff morale to know that a woman who knew nothing about the state, the paper or the people who comprised either, was sitting on the board of directors. Sallie further irritated staff people, as well as book lovers and general readers by gradually turning the book page into a vehicle for women writers, especially black women writers. The book page never recovered the reputation it had enjoyed under Shirley Williams. Today, under Gannett, it is a poor shadow of what it was, though Keith Runyon, a knowledgeable and dedicated book editor, has tried to run it on a shoestring. I recently wrote a long review of a substantial book about the converted communist Whittaker Chambers and received a check for $15 for my efforts. It must have been humiliating for Keith to have to authorize such a payment. It was another reminder of how things had gone downhill when Dr. Kenneth Cherry, director of the University Press of Kentucky, at a huge dinner honoring writers, congratulated Art Jester, book editor of the *Lexington Herald-Leader*, for having developed the state's number one book page.

We were given another Bingham surprise when, in the summer of 1984, Barry, Jr. announced that he and his wife Edie were taking leave to go to Northampton, where Edie planned to finish credits for a degree, while Barry studied electronic journalism. That was surprise enough, but then Barry announced that in his absence Paul Janensch, and not George Gill, would be in charge as publisher. That shook up the place.

It didn't shake me. I was doing fine, becoming an author. In 1976 Bert Combs had asked me if I would write a short book, not much more than a pamphlet, on his administration, just something he could put on a shelf that would show his grandchildren what their grandfather had done. I was glad to undertake it, though I knew it was going to mean countless hours in libraries. Bert offered to pay me, rather handsomely in fact, but that proved unnecessary. I had hardly begun researching before I began to suspect that I would have to write of Bert against a background of Kentucky political history. That meant that I would have to go back to Earle Clements and Lawrence Wetherby, and then to the administrations of Happy Chandler. And so on. I finally finished a short version and showed it to Ken Cherry as a possible University Press book. I was a little sensitive about this, since I had been for some time on the Press editorial board. But Ken took it, and Malcolm Jewell, probably the state's main authority on politics and the legislature, read it, recommending several additions and corrections and concluding that it needed to be expanded. As I had feared. I spent another two years on that book, and instead of an essay it became *Divide and Dissent*, which was a pretty good book and got good reviews but did not sell as well as it should have, although at least one community college professor used it as a text.

But then occurred a nasty little incident that caused me a great deal of embarrassment. A group of people, including many of the state's outstanding officials, educators, newsmen and business leaders, planned a dinner in Frankfort for Ed Prichard. Bert Combs was to be the featured speaker of the evening, and I was flattered when asked to introduce Bert. Engraved invitations were sent out, including notation that I would present Bert, but a few days before the dinner David Hawpe, then managing editor, came to my office and told me that if I insisted on taking part in the dinner I would have to quit the paper, since being so identified with Combs constituted a conflict of interest. I could hardly believe he was serious, but he was. I pointed out that this was a private dinner and could hardly make a pubic impression as a conflict. Both he and I, like a dozen other newsmen, had for years talked and consulted with Prich, and I could hardly commit a conflict of interest by introducing Bert, who was the company's chief counsel. No, David said, Bert was still identified with party politics, as I would be if I became even privately and casually identified with him.

This was ironic, for a rather unusual reason. A few years earlier, David and I were in Eastern Kentucky and dropped in to see Jeff and Treva Howell in Breathitt County. As usual, they were deep in a political campaign and were backing a large, stolid man named Bill Farler for sheriff. Treva said, "Now, you fellows are big-time writers. I need an ad to put in the paper, and something to put on the radio for Bill." We threw ourselves into the task. I reminded Jeff that Bill Fields, a relative nonentity, had become governor by becoming known as "Honest Bill from Olive Hill," and suggested that we make Farler, who was from the hamlet of Barwick, "Honest Bill from Barwick Hill." But Jeff called me to one side. "Don't get me wrong," he said, "I never knew Bill to do a dishonest thing, but maybe we ought just call him Big Bill. Nobody can deny that he's big." So Big Bill from Barwick Hill he became, though I thought it lacked a certain panache.

Meanwhile, David was doing the important work. He found an old country-music record of a song called "Old Rattler," stole the tune and wrote a song to fit, which went, as I remember:

Vote for Bill Farler

Get out and vote for Bill.

He'll treat you good and honest,

If anybody will.

Yodellady, hoo. Get out and vote for Bill.

Catchy. Treva found a couple of guitar-whangers from Lee County, they made a record of David's ditty and put it on the radio. It became so popular that people actually called in asking for the Bill Farler song. I regret to report that Bill didn't win, despite our artistry, but he had his day in the musical sun. And when David showed the gall to warn me against conflict of interest, I came within an inch of looking at him and singing: Vote for Bill Farler... But something warned me that this boy was afire with ambition, that someone up the ladder had sent him on his fool's mission, and that he would not hesitate to hang me out to dry if it advanced his career. I had to call the organizers of the Prichard dinner and apologize, profusely but insufficiently.

I knew that David and his wife, principally his wife, had taken a deep dislike to me some time before. I did not know why, since David and I had always been close, and I had done nothing to disturb that relationship. But I heard later that it concerned an episode involving M, though indirectly. As I pointed out earlier, David had suggested, after M. was divorced, that I ask her out, saying, casually, that were he single, he would ask her. Talking to a woman in Louisville who knew us both, I said, again in an off-hand way, that I was glad David was happily married, since I thought M would "eat him alive," she being a very mature woman for her years, and David being rather naive and vulnerable for his. The woman to whom I told this became angry with me, went to a party at David's house and told his wife that I had said that David was fascinated and in love with M. Watch out for angry women, son.

***

But things in general were going along well. In another fine scrap of irony, I became an authority on the Ohio River, which I had seen briefly from houseboats belonging to Jack Matlick and Gene Johnson. I became an authority in this manner: Rich Nugent, who actually did know something about the river, and even had a boat, suggested in the summer of 1987 that we try to sell Jimmy Pope on the idea of a word and picture piece on the river for the *Magazine*. Jim went for it, and Rich and I were off on his bronchitic boat and a *Courier* expense account. We had a time. Starting at Ashland, we followed the river along the entirety of its Kentucky shore, ending at the Mississippi. I usually fixed lunch, mainly sandwiches or salad, and Rich fixed dinner, usually featuring burned potatoes or, as he more elegantly put it, *pommes noires*. We got wet, we got eaten alive by mosquitoes, we survived a breakdown that stranded us for days opposite Cincinnati, but in all we produced a pretty fair story. People liked it.

Not long afterward, John Morgan, film director for Kentucky Educational Television, came over from Lexington and asked me if I would be interested in doing a documentary on the river for KET. He whispered the magic word—money—and Rich and I geared up for a far more ambitious effort, starting at Pittsburgh and going to the Mississippi. Morgan, a good-natured Vietnam veteran who had been an Army Ranger and had only recently beaten back a cancer in his hip, and his crew shot the journey, making it an unusual experience.

And that was not all. Ken Cherry asked me if Rich and I would like to do a book on the Ohio. (What next—a movie?) We got a new boat to replace Rich's old wheezer and started out at Pittsburgh. By the time we got to Cairo and the Mississippi we began to feel like the old river rats we were supposed to be, running around and speaking to river clubs. My life as an old fraud. The book still sells here and there. Pretty good book.

***

Back home, tragedy struck again, and like a thunderclap. Barry, Sr. was struck down by a brain tumor. I had wondered about his health for some time. When writing *Divide and Dissent*, I had to write about the meeting at the Standiford Motel between Clements, Wyatt and their backers. I had not been there and had heard varying versions of the meeting, so asked Barry if he would read that portion and check my facts. He said, rather absently, I thought, that it seemed fine to him. It wasn't. The meeting had not happened the way I had written it and that he had approved, and when the book was published, Wilson Wyatt took exception to it. And it seemed to me that Barry was losing much of the grace and ebullience that had been so much a part his elegance. When he came into the office, he often seemed vague and red-eyed. I was not too surprised when Mary announced his illness. Our mutual friend and city leader, Wendell Cherry, co-founder of Humana, Inc., had recently died of a similar tumor, but Barry was flown to Boston for the best in medical care, and we had reason to hope that he would recover.

18

College Years

It seems that each of my brushes with Lexington has lasted about four years, and I suppose the first was best. It was also the most difficult, as I found out in the first days. Being a college man was one thing, staying a college man was something quite different. I reported to Dave Griffith at the *Kernel* office and was told that the new Duplex press would not be installed for another week. In the meantime there was the delicate matter of eating to be considered. I went up to the Commons, the student cafeteria on the top floor of McVey Hall, but was told that it would not open until after registration. A woman there suggested that I see Dean Jones, Dean of Men. I went to the basement of the Administration Building and found that he would not be in for a couple of days. Also there were two women with two boys that I took to be their sons. They were wondering aloud what to do, and where to find rooms. Genius sometimes flourishes in the dry soil of poverty, and I hurried out South Lime, where I had seen "Student rooms for rent" signs. From there I worked up Maxwellton to Bonnie Brae, and by noon felt I was in business, a simple business, but one soundly based on deception. An empty stomach knows no scruples.

What I did was to ask each landlady if she would give me a dollar for each student I sent her way. Nearly everyone was willing, and I hurried back to the closed Dean's office, and ensconced myself behind a desk in the outer office. Sure enough, in walked a lady with a young man in tow, I tossed out a ray of charm and asked if I might help. What do you know? She was seeking a room for junior and the Dean, to her distress, was not in. Not to worry. I was helping out, I assured her, until the Dean returned. Go to this address, tell Mrs. Kelly (Mullins, O'Neal, etc.) that Mr. Pearce sent you. If you do not like it, come back and I will find you one you do like. They expressed gratitude and left. By next day I had sold six freshman, collected from the landladies and had a little dough. Then an officious woman arrived, asked what I was doing at her desk, and my career as a realtor ended. At registration the next week I found myself in line with one of my rentees. He stared at me, puzzled. I explained that we all had to make a living.

One good thing about living in the state where you go to college is that you are always among friends, or at least acquaintances. Everywhere I go in Kentucky I meet people with whom I went to UK, and it is more comforting and rewarding than I would have imagined. Standing with me in registration line was a boy named Jim Caldwell who was aiming at journalism and became editor of the *Kernel*, a Phi Delt, a member of ODK, the top honorary, and an outstanding student. Jim was a sharp dresser, dated proper girls from the Kappa house and wrote conservative editorials for the paper, which the more liberal among us criticized in scathing terms. He was better behaved than most of us on the paper, drank less, and ran more with the fraternity crowd. But he was a good friend, and still is. A first-rate man.

I decided to take journalism, because I was told it was fairly easy and would allow me to work; after all, my purpose was to go to college, not to get an education. The classes, though, were generally disappointing. I recall that on the first day Neal Plummer, head of the department, fixed us with a happy eye and asked "What is news?" I think the earth was supposed to move under us as we awaited the light. "News," he revealed, "is whatever makes you say 'Gee whiz.'" Harry Williams, sitting next to me, said "Oh, shit!" I felt somewhat the same. Harry, sharp-featured, black hair slicked back, had a curvature of the spine that made him almost hunchbacked, and a cynical sense of humor expressed in a sideways grin. He explained to me later that he had no interest in a degree, but wanted to learn enough to get a job, and didn't think this course advanced him in that direction. I agreed. Other journalism courses were little more inspiring. We spent an entire semester on typography, type faces, which I already knew pretty well. Boring business. At the beginning of my second year, Neal called me in, told me that I could be a good student if I didn't think I knew more than my teachers I thought about it, decided he was right and transferred to political science, with a minor in journalism so that I could write for the *Kernel*, and in rooting around finally found an acorn in a feature writing course taught by Willis Tucker, a delightfully droll, witty man and an excellent teacher, as good as I found.

But I soon discovered the meaning of the term working student. I had to work forty hours a week to make the fifteen dollars I had estimated to be the minimum necessary, and those were forty long, hard hours. The magic press finally arrived, and a *Kernel* printer named Hartzer and I toiled a day and night trying to discover how it operated, how the half-ton roll of paper was lifted to the front of the press and threaded through the angle bars, rollers and cutters. By noon the next day we had printed enough papers for the student mail boxes, and there were doubts that I knew as much about Duplex presses as I had claimed.

But I learned, though it remained a tough, hot job, since the press was located in the basement of McVey Hall, where overhead pipes carried hot air to the building. We published twice a week, and the press run usually took from ten at night to four or six in the morning, but we were on a time clock, so I checked in at around seven in the evening to "get the press ready," which consisted of thirty minutes of preparation and three hours of sleep or study. The forms carrying the type that printed the paper were made up in the composing room and my helper and I carried them, each weighing about eighty pounds, to the elevator and to the basement, where they were placed gently on the bed of the press. I say gently because a jar would cause the form to fall apart, strewing type everywhere and requiring hours of ill-tempered re-doing.

In addition to the two press runs, I cast cuts, a primitive form of stereotyping, on Wednesday night, and one afternoon a week melted lead previously used in printing and poured the molten metal into molds or pigs, carrying it upstairs, eighty pounds a time when it cooled. With ingenuity I could stretch this into about forty hours and fifteen dollars, but soon found that the doubters had been right, and that fifteen a week was not going to support a life of Scott Fitzgerald. I got other jobs, before classes in the morning and at noon waiting tables, a hideous chore, and in my spare time worked in the *Kernel* bindery. This was a fascinating job consisting of putting together pamphlets issued by the Department of Agriculture to show farmers new, improved ways to build hog pens, store corn and such. I tried not to think of what a nice boy like me was doing in a moronic hole like this, and later turned the work to good account by taking the pamphlets, re-writing them into English, and selling the result to farm magazines.

The biggest problem was studying and staying awake in class. Introductory English was tedious, but history under Tom Clark was good. So was introduction to psychology. But I was in the coils of a dilemma; if I worked enough to live, I had too little time for learning. If I insisted on reading, going to class, etc., I was going to have to learn to steal.

***

But help was in the offing, and from an unexpected source. I was working on the press one afternoon when a sharply dressed boy about my size came in, introduced himself as Edgar "Chickie" Penn, business manager of the *Kernel*, and said the fellows over at the PiKA house would like to have me over to meet the brothers. I found he was not joking, accepted gracefully and went with him next evening to the chapter house on Transylvania Park. It was all I had expected a fraternity house to be: affable, smoothly dressed young men stood chatting while soft lights shone on cases filled with cups and trophies won by the brothers in the athletic wars and the pictures of prominent alumni smiled grandly down from the walls. We gathered around the table, the brothers sang fraternity songs and I wondered what the hell I was doing there.

I went back a couple of times, for the free meal if nothing else, and was finally asked if I would like to become a pledge. I told the truth—I would love to, but had no money. Someone said that help might be found, and I was presented to W.T. Bishop, the brother of Wyman Bishop, the chapter president. W.T., I was told, was general manager of Keeneland, and I acted impressed, though I had no idea what Keeneland was. Bishop told me to report to his office Friday at noon and he would see what could be done.

Thus began my four-year, totally happy relationship with Keeneland. On Friday I hitch-hiked out Versailles Road, wandered goggle-eyed through the gorgeous grounds until I found W.T. and was sent to a man named White who gave me a job selling pari-mutuel tickets five days a week, noon to five, at eight dollars a day. That would pay my $60-a-semester tuition and leave a hundred dollars toward lush living. And it interfered with nothing except the excitement of the bindery.

The fraternity required the usual foolishness of paddling, shining shoes, raking leaves, but it also involved introductions to girls, and on an October day I found myself wandering through the autumn afternoon toward the stadium, crisp leaves underfoot and a beautiful girl named Nell Thornbury on my arm. I had done it.

I took my first Keeneland check and bought a tuxedo, a tweed jacket and a pair of covert slacks. If I was to starve, I would do it well dressed. Looking back, I realize that had I been willing to wear the ROTC uniform we were issued and required to wear twice a week to military science classes, stuck to my table-waiting jobs and been content to be a working student, I could have sailed through. But I knew that this was the only chance I would have at the life I had longed for, and I was not going to miss it.

Freshman year whipped by. I played my dual role. By night I was the sweaty, ink-stained slave, then at dawn stepped into the phone booth and came out the suave, if sleepy, fraternity man. The offices of the *Kernel*, the student newspaper, were located across the hall from the pressroom, and I started hanging out there, and soon became more or less accepted by the fearsome foursome who ran the paper—Ross Chepeleff, Geoge Kerler, Harry Williams and Don Irvine. Don wrote a column, reviews and anything else needed and was, I quickly learned, the wittiest, most learned and most irreverent person I had met. The four of us became drinking, dinner (when I could afford it) and weekend party friends. In my second semester, Chepeleff decided I should write a column, and I did, an adolescent bit of trash, but it brought me some recognition on campus, especially at the fraternity house. Irvine got me into Patterson Literary Society, where I delivered a dazzling paper on Conrad. To manage all this I did with little sleep, as well as little food.

Spring of my freshman year brought two notable developments. The PiKA chapters from Kentucky and Tennessee colleges held a conference each spring, with a concluding banquet at which a freshman from one school and a senior from another gave talks, naturally devoted to the glories of Pi Kappa Alpha. I was chosen to deliver the freshman oration. Sensing opportunity, I labored over that thing, making it drip with lofty phrases about brotherhood, loyalty, lifelong bonds, and other edifying qualities, and at the banquet, (let's not let modesty interfere with fact), I wowed them. The brothers pounded my back, alumni came up to congratulate me. So swelled was my head that I paid little attention when two men, Joe Palmer and Simp Estes, shook my hand, asked me what field I intended to enter and told me that they had a little magazine downtown called *The Bloodhorse*, and if I had nothing to do the coming summer I might like to look them up. *Bloodhorse?* A grisly name. Surely I was meant for better things. Anyhow, I had been offered a vacation job as counter man at the Paddock Restaurant on Rose Street, near the fraternity house.

Having pursued the elusive lady fortune through the thickets of life, I had finally found her—and given her a mighty kick in the ass. I later found out what *The Bloodhorse* was, and realized the life I could have had had I possessed the brains that God willed to a bowl of buttermilk. But by then it was too late. Anyhow, I had chosen my path.

I did better in my second notable event. The glory of sex was spread before me and I grabbed it as a starving dog grabs raw meat. I had been dating a blonde girl who danced well and had fine breasts. We were at a party down on Lake Herrington at the summer house of the aunt of Don Irine's girlfriend, and were dancing languorously when I sensed that we were sharing a thought, so we slipped out to the nearby small guest cabin, found a bed and fell into the sweet frenzy of kissing, clutching, moaning, groaning and generally banging away. It was even better than I had hoped. Totally wonderful. To my pleased surprise, I seemed to know exactly what to do, as did she, and my only regret afterward was that I had to occupy hours with other things. She seemed equally pleased, and until she graduated that spring we humped away whenever we could find a little privacy and a place to lie down.

***

The job at the Paddock was a blast. On afternoons when there was little business, we would take off in Pee Wee Lynn's car—he managed the place for the owner, a Mr. Devereaux, who also owned the liquor store next door—and go swimming down at Boonesborough, drinking a little cheap gin and messing with available girls. But the blast fizzled out. One night Devereaux called me over and told me to take a case of Scotch whiskey out to Hamburg Place. I thought it strange that a hamburger joint would want a case of expensive Scotch, but followed directions, and found this elegant horse farm. The car was a two-door job, and when I reached over into the back seat to lift out the whiskey, I felt a strain in my groin. The next morning I could not move without sharp stabs of pain.

I called Irvine, he came and took me to his family doctor who informed me that I had a double hernia that would require an operation. I reported to St. Joseph Hospital, where a young Dr. Combs joked with me as he sliced away. I stayed there over three weeks (today I would have been out in three days). To my surprise, Mama and Daddy showed up and arranged for me to borrow enough from the bank at home to pay my medical bills. I limped out of the hospital, weak from a too-long stay, unable to work and a week late in registering for classes. I went to the fraternity house asked the student manager to carry me for room and board until I was able to work, but he said he was sorry, but the house was full. Irvine came to the rescue, took me to his home for a week until I could return to work at the *Kernel* press, and the admissions office let me register late. But the next few weeks were rough.

***

Sophomore classes were much more interesting, and I began to dabble in campus politics, was nominated for office by the fraternity, and elected vice-president of my sophomore class. When I went home for Christmas, rumors of my campus success had preceded me, and in my sharp tweeds decorated with my brilliant fraternity pin, I was no longer a fringe person but a member of the old crowd again. Mama was proud.

Poverty was still my roommate, but there were ways around it. Cecil Wathen, who owned the Cedar Village at the corner of Limestone and Maxwell, ran a weekly ad in the *Kernel* featuring a male student chosen for Kernel of the Week. When things got thin I would go with hat in hand to Bob Hillenmeyer, *Kernel* business manager, and he would make me Kernel of the Week. This entitled me to two meals at the Village, and they were good meals. For fifty cents you could get a club steak, fries, salad and coffee. That made an impression on a date, although it did not always produce results.

That summer was the usual work and party. We would get dates and go to Joyland, an amusement park north of Lexington and dance. Joyland got some good bands, and for a dollar we could dance to Artie Shaw or Tommy Dorsey. We were great devotees of swing music, and would drive over to Louisville or up to Cincinnati to hear one of our favorites. We also made the run to Cincinnati to attend the opera, *Traviata, Trovatore, Boheme*. Irvine knew a great deal about music, and made it more pleasurable. One time I had a date with Lucy Elliott, who later married the famous Ed Prichard, and we and Irvine and his date drove to Cincinnati. We splurged for the occasion with a pint of Old Granddad, which we placed discreetly on the floor between us, but at intermission Lucy got up, kicked it over and broke it, a tragedy surpassing any on stage.

I also learned a new technique of free-loading. Several of us, in Arvin's car, would drive out to the Lexington Country Club, register as guests of Dick Stool, and dance. Dick, the plump, pleasant son of Judge Richard Stool, gave his permission. We had no money for the bar, but would go out now and then and nip from a bottle in the car. It was at the Club that I met Sue Fan Gooding. Some monument should be raised to Sue Fan for sheer sweet, wholesome beauty and goodness. When I first saw her she was dancing, slender, tan, dark hair falling to her shoulders and the sweetest smile that ever knocked a young lout off balance. She was simply gorgeous. We dated off and on, and though we never did he mattress thing she remains in my memory. Her parents were kind to me. If Sue Fan was not ready when I arrived, Mrs. Gooding would tell me to go on in the kitchen and get what I wanted from the fridge. Her father always put gas in the car and let us have it. I think Sue Fan and I might have made a life of it, but she went off to Finch, and we sort of lost close touch. But we kept in touch until she was killed in an automobile accident years later. After she left, I switched my affections to a plump, pretty blonde local girl whose mother did not consider me Mr. Right, and shipped her daughter off to Sweet Briar. Then there was a girl from Ohio with a wonderful figure who shared my belief that Adam and Eve had discovered everything worth knowing. After a year her parents decided there was no sense spending money to let her play in Lexington.

***

Harry Williams moved into an attic apartment in a building on South Upper Street, and as soon as I had the money I joined him. It was our idea of a romantic, bohemian garret. We had a record player and a hot plate, and we would invite girls up for tea—tea, yet—and lofty, intellectual conversation.

That was quite an apartment building. Downstairs lived a reporter known as the antiseptic typist, who feared germs were after him and spent half an hour each morning dousing himself with smelly potions. Mark Purude, head of the local Associated Press bureau, occupied the front apartment and had a fancy record player on which we played classical music, with Harry screeching his version of Pagliacci. And across the hall from Prude lived John and Sarah Macey, an ideal young couple, smart, vivacious and handsome, John a beginning lawyer, Sarah a clerk in a downtown dress shop—a great deal of flair and a fine cook. On Sundays the Maceys would often invite us for a massive breakfast and good music.

***

In my junior year I did not go home for Christmas vacation, but took a stack of books to my room and went through them one by one. This had a depressing effect, making me regret for the first time that I had not had more time to study. I enjoyed learning, liked to write papers, and was usually good at exams. I had never thought I would actually get a degree, but now I began to wish I could. I had not, for instance, taken the required two years of military science and physical education. I was usually too tired for physical Ed, and considered ROTC rather silly. That brought me some trouble. At mid-semester, I was hauled up in front of the disciplinary committee, and asked why I had not taken the required courses. I replied that the catalogue instructions required that I take two years of the silly subjects, but did not specify that I should pass them. I had an idea I was on shaky grounds when I looked across the table and saw Dean Horlacher, with whom I had an unusual relationship, sitting in judgment. I had reason so to believe.

At the beginning of the year Jim Shropshire, graduate manager of publications, called me in and revealed that the department had a problem. When the editor of *Sour Mash*, the student humor magazine for which I had written, graduated the previous spring, he decided not to give up the magazine, and simply went down town and copyrighted it, in effect owning it. The school moved to block him, and had his Chamber of Commerce accreditation revoked, but if he couldn't publish the thing, neither could the school. Shropshire suggested that I take the magazine, change the name and publish it. The editor had left some debts that I would have to pay, after which I could keep the profits. I adopted all sorts of corny tricks to sell the thing—crude jokes, cartoons lifted from other magazines, radical essays. At Christmas time we printed an edition in pine-scented red and green ink. That sort of thing. Among our specialties was a feature called Your Grade, Professor, in which we profiled and graded teachers, handing out cards to members of his or her classes, asking that they evaluate his skills, and publishing the results. Most of the reviews were kindly, but we felt obliged to publish the almost uniformly critical opinions of Dean Horlacher. He was not amused, and when I appeared before his board I was unceremoniously suspended for six weeks, almost guaranteeing a failure for the semester. But I explained the situation to my professors, and they advised me to keep coming to class and try hard on exams. I did, and nothing more was said about it.

Such trivia did little to interrupt the pleasant flow of life. On Saturdays Irvine, Kerler, Williams and I would go to the Canary Cottage, sit in the bar and drink whiskey sours, after which we would go to Wing's Tea Room, where Wing served the best small steak I had ever eaten, and then stagger off to listen to music.

Sometimes, late at night, Williams and I would go down Limestone to Uncle Johnny Furlong's, an unimpressive hole-in-the-wall eatery serving select roast beef and steaks, and the best bean soup on earth. Uncle John, slightly crippled, carried his head sharply to one side, and seemed to be sizing you up. He had a black helper named Henry, a magician with beef and a favorite with the horsemen who made a bee-line for Uncle John's and one of his steaks when they came to town for the meets. It made no difference that Uncle John carried a limp, soiled towel that he used to swab off the counter and, with muttered irritation, slap at flies that settled on the huge round of beef on the sideboard. John knew that we were cheap-skates, but had mercy, and with a ten-cent bowl of beans he would usually throw in the rye butts that he did not serve good customers. For a dime we wandered out into the night, warm and full.

There were girls around. I had a little money. I had my clothes made by Hank Cowman, at Thorpe's men shop. I recall riding downtown with Irvine one late-fall afternoon, hanging loose, feeling good, when Irvine said, "Pearce, they talk about the golden years. Friend, these ARE the golden years. The days of wine and roses." I thought yes, that's it. I had a feeling it wouldn't last, but I was going to hang on as long as I could.

There is something I should probably add here. From the beginning I had decided there was something unusual about Irvine. He was different, though not objectionably so. I had never known a homosexual, but I somehow figured he was, and when Robin Sweeney, a friend of Lucy Elliott, referred to Don as "that queer," I was not surprised. I knew Don tried to conceal it, had a steady girl, and did all the usual male things. It made no difference to me. He was a fine friend, and as good company as I had ever known. It gripes hell out of me when I hear people such as Jesse Helms, who really is disgusting, refer to gays as disgusting, or hear people condemn them out of hand simply on the basis of their sexual preference. What difference? Every gay meant one fewer competitor for the girls, I figured. I couldn't see why it should make any difference to me. I still can't.

Don was usually around in the summer, though I had less time to play than I would have liked. In order to pay off debts and pile up money for the coming fall, I sometimes worked in the bindery, where students endured tedium to pay for an education. We would come to work on Monday morning, and work until Sunday night almost without pause. At mealtime, one would go out for coffee and sandwiches, while the others filled in. At midnight, we would fall into the piles of paper in the back and sleep until six, when we hit it again. One week I put 112 hours on the time clock, raising suspicions, but it took only a few such weeks until I had money to pay and play, and then it was off to the lake.

There we would mooch from girls' mothers who had lakeside cottages, sit on the dock at night with a fifth of Gilbey's Gin, a couple of lemons and a pack of cigarettes; a pull of gin, a suck of lemon and a drag off the cigarette. Jump in the lake, try to lay the girls, fail, and finally go to sleep wherever possible. We would stay at one cottage until the parent mentioned that someone else deserved the delight of our company, and we would move on. You are young only once, and we were richly young.

***

By the end of my senior year, I didn't have enough credits to graduate, but decided to stay on and try for a degree. I had it almost too good to quit, with some wonderful teachers with whom I had formed friendships—Willis Tucker, Grant Knight, Tom Clark, Amry Vandembosch, Jasper Shannon. But my primary interests were shifting away from the campus. Some of my friends had graduated from their newspaper correspondent jobs to full-time employment in other towns, leaving openings into which I stepped. George Kerler had gone with the Associated Press. Harry Williams had been promoted by the United Press to Columbus, Ohio. Gradually I became a stringer, or correspondent, for United Press, International News Service, *Cincinnati Post, Time-Life* and other papers that took special stories on tobacco or horses during those sales seasons. It was not as hard as it may sound. When I uncovered a good story, or more often re-wrote a good story from the *Herald* or *Leader*, I simply made copies and fired them off by Western Union to any of my papers that I thought could use them, and was paid space rates.

I also got a job at radio station WLAP, the main station in central Kentucky, to provide daily two local newscasts of five minutes each. It was right interesting. I learned the difference between radio and newspaper writing, and covered some good stories, including the murder by two Louisville men of golf champion Marion Miley and her mother, who was manager of the Lexington Country Club. It was a regional sensation and the trial was dramatic. I would sit in the Canary Cottage bar and snow Sue Fan, home from Finch, with my glamorous life.

But I think we have a sentinel nerve in our system that warns us, if indistinctly, that things are too good to last. We were all very concerned, of course, about the war in Europe, and worried that we would get pulled into it. We ran poems in the magazine, that I had re-named the *Wildcat*, decrying war, the Army, and anyone who should suggest that we once more "pull England's chestnuts out of the fire."

Ours was not necessarily a minority opinion. A great many people, on and off campus, opposed any participation in the war, campus opposition naturally being stronger since it was the young men who would have to fight. Congress had already passed the Selective Service Act requiring all able-bodied men over the age of 18 to spend a year in the Army as a precaution against the nightmare, and many of us scrambled to find ways to avoid even that, and hating the popular song "Good-bye, dear, I'll be back in a year." It made the Army sound fun. Something there is about patriotism that brings out the worst in song-writers. And in November of 1941, Congress extended the draft for a single year by one vote.

We had all been called on to register for the draft with passage of the initial act, but we hoped now that our number would not be called for years, or that we would get college deferments, or prove physically unfit. Still, recruiting offices did a brisk business, and a lot of young men volunteered, tired of the uncertainty, wanting excitement or for reasons of patriotism. My former fraternity roommate, Billy Sugg, big, good-looking, loose-hanging boy from Morganfield who had cut a sexual swath through the campus and seemed to be the last man on earth to volunteer for the military, went down and joined the Navy, went through the ninety-day training course and came back to campus in his dress blues, even more of a threat to maidens than before. We went out on a double date and he almost humped my girl's best friend in the back seat. He appeared rather pleased with the Navy, which baffled me.

Then came a Sunday when the Maceys had us down for a late breakfast, after which Harry, Purdue and I went for a drive out Versailles Road; they still did that. It was a rather gloomy day, but we enjoyed the drive out past Keeneland and back, talking and listening to music on the radio. Then the announcer broke in to say: "Ladies and gentlemen, we interrupt this program to bring you the following bulletin; The Japanese have just attacked the American Naval base at Pearl Harbor. Stay tuned for details."

We didn't need to. "That," said Mark, "was the sound of the shit hitting the fan."

All illusion was shattered. We knew then that there would be no escape. We just waited to be drafted. Each day, gathering human interest items, I would make the rounds of the recruiting offices, getting thrilling tidbits about fathers and sons volunteering together, ten-year olds trying to join up, and other such sickening details. Every time I saw a man in Army uniform, I sweated. I had one small hope; I would soon be in my last semester at UK in search of a degree, and thought perhaps I would be spared until graduation. There was also my physical condition. I had worked and played my body down to a skeleton, and when faced with the need to take physical ed and ROTC in order to keep the deans off my back, I got Dr. Rather, campus doctor and a friend, to write me an excuse, saying that chronic bronchitis prevented too much exercise. Maybe that would keep the uniformed menace at bay.

Then one fateful day I strolled into the Navy recruiting office, seeking human interest stuff for my WLAP newscast, and spoke to the chief petty officer in charge. "Hey, kid," he said, "ain't they gonna draft you?" I said it appeared so. "Don't let 'em do it," he growled, upon which I uttered what I still consider the greatest straight line in history. "How," I asked, "can I keep them from it?"

My feet barely hit the floor as he jerked me through a doorway and plunked me in front of a life-size poster of a heroic Navy flier, resplendent in his whites, gold braid on his hat and blue shoulder boards, his eyes, bright with manly courage, on far horizons. "That's for you, kid," said the chief. I said, in all seriousness, that I didn't think they would take me.

"Sign here," he said.

I walked out of the building a member of the U.S. Navy. That morning a screaming protester, four hours later a volunteer, a patriot. Ever since, when asked, I declare that I did not have to be drafted, but volunteered. A fraudulent truth. Two days later they called me down, gave me some preliminary tests and told me to go home and put on at least eight pounds; I weighed a strapping 132. They also gave me some books on physics and trig. I went back to South Upper Street and started grazing. I ate everything I could swallow, all I could buy, specializing in a half-dozen bananas a day, having heard that they piled on the weight. I couldn't understand my fever to get into the Navy, but had to admit it looked better than the Army.

Then, irony. I received from my draft board a notice to report for a draft examination. There were about two hundred of us in line in the basement of the federal building, naked and feeling awkward. "You'd think they would at least give us a doily or something," said Irvine, obviously uncomfortable. They gave us some routine tests, which I regarded sourly, until I came to the psychological probe, conducted by a smirking ghoul. He started asking questions about whether I liked girls, and I told him to save it, since I was not going into the Army. Oh, that brought a glitter to his beady eyes; he almost drooled as he bore in, determined to find what quirk led me to believe escape was possible. I kept assuring him that I was not about to, and he finally snapped, "What makes you think so?" "Because," I said archly, "I just joined the Navy Air Corps." He wilted like hot lettuce.

A few days later, John Carrico and I accompanied a poor, flabby friend of ours (one of the louts, incidentally, that I had sold into a rooming house that first week of school), down to the federal building to enter the gate of sighs. Poor guy, he had been drunk for six weeks, either in dread of the draft, or in hopes that his alcoholic condition would excuse him. It was not to be. At the federal building he stood on the steps and delivered a diatribe against Hitler, Roosevelt, God, the Army and whom it may concern. To no avail. A sergeant came out, and with a huge hand led him away. We never saw him again.

I got orders to report to a building in St. Louis, checked into the specified hotel, slept nervously and the next morning started drinking water. By the time I got to the Navy building I was so full of water, I sloshed. I took off my clothes, down to underwear, and stood praying that they would weigh me before I had to release my bogus weight. They finally got to me, just in time. I was five feet nine, the petty officer intoned, and weighed 142. I then peed with hideous relief into a container. I could have filled a dozen.

The mental exams were pretty much a snap, but then the fiends put us through physical tests designed to make enemy prisoners talk. I took one look around the room of recruits and wilted. There was one plump boy, one pathetic guy about my size, and twenty or so ads for body-building, college athletes, all muscles and confidence. I told myself I didn't want to be in the Navy, anyhow.

They put us in a chair and whirled us up and down and around the room, made us run backward, jump off a platform, take color blind and depth perception tests. They told us to wait in the outer room again, and finally an officer came in, handed out a sheaf of papers to each man and explained that those who had not passed could apply for re-examination, and that those who had should stand by. To my astonishment, I passed. So did the plump guy, and my pathetic look-alike, along with a half-dozen muscle men. The rest, looking shocked, got silently into their clothes and left. The officer had us sign some papers, and told us to go home and await orders to active duty. Active duty. I didn't know whether to be excited or terrified.

Back in Lexington, I tidied up affairs as best I could, saw that my credits were registered, gave my books away and sent my beloved clothes home to Don. UK issued a notice saying that any male student drafted in the final semester of his senior year would be granted his degree. I checked to see if that applied to volunteers and was assured that it did. I had nothing to do but wait. Then my orders arrived, in an official Navy envelope, and on the night before I was to march off to glory, Irvine and I went down to the Cottage for a last couple of drinks. He said, with a note of genuine grief, that he envied me, that he would be going too if it were not for the fact that "I am, you know, what they call queer." I said yes, I knew. He seemed surprised.

"How long have you known?" he asked.

"I don't know," I replied. "Years, I guess."

"Be damned," he said. "Thanks."

The next day I packed what was allowed into my even more battered fake leather suitcase and walked down to the station. I had told no one I was going. There weren't many left to care. The train pulled in, I got aboard, stashed my bag and walked to the rear platform. I had arrived alone, I would leave alone, but the weight of all the years and memories between was a pain for mind and body. The train eased out of the station. I stood and watched Lexington and college and all that slip past. So much for the days of wine and roses.

19

No Way to Win a War

The U.S. Naval Air Station at Lambert Field, Mo., was an orderly collection of neat white buildings, a neat street and a sentry box manned by a sailor who seemed too casual for the backdrop. He looked at my orders said, oh, yeah, most of them are already there, and motioned up the street where a Marine sergeant faced two lines of civilians who gazed upon him in bemusement, as though they did not quite believe he was real. I walked up, stood in the front line, affirmed that my name was Pearce and asked what I should do with my suitcase. The good sergeant, whose name was Coleman, looked at me scornfully, and told me in a rasping voice that as far as he was concerned I could stick it up my ass. I had never heard the expression before, and it struck me as funny. I laughed. He glowered and asked me if I thought that was funny. I admitted that I did. He looked at me as though he did not believe I was real.

The man next to me, about my shape and size and with a casual air, said, out of the corner of his mouth, "Poor sense of humor." I agreed. The man's name was McCormick. We are still friends today.

A variety of officers put us through the usual routine of paperwork, shots and instructions, and we drew bedding and uniforms that turned out to be leftovers from the CCC, since our Navy uniforms had not arrived. They were drab, but sufficient, and we felt the Navy close in around us.

We lined up for meals that were surprisingly good, slept in comfortable bunks that we made up each morning to rigid specifications and were inspected by officers. Classes began at once in physics, engines, principles of flight and meteorology, most taught by civilians. The only unpleasant thing was morning exercises in front of the barracks, led by a former school teacher who was despised by all. It says in the Bible, or should, that you will fill the tank before you start the engine. We did the tedious calisthenics in a haphazard fashion. This was known as the Tunney program, named for the boxer. We loathed it. After the joy of jumping, we were permitted to shower, dress, and eat.

After we started flying, we shifted to the Hamilton program, designed by Commander Tom Hamilton, which was fine. We would fly in the morning, then take ground school and have a couple of hours for exercise—a few calisthenics, and then touch football, cross-country or obstacle course. Then the morning fliers would switch off and fly afternoon and the ground schoolers would fly mornings. I fell in with three other cadets, W.C. "Chug" McCormick, a fledgling architect, Joe Kingsbury, an osteopath who had decided he wanted to fly, and Ken Bellile, who was strong, handsome and had played football for the University of Wisconsin. Kingsbury was short, wiry and seemed in constant motion, just as the dark-haired McCormick appeared totally relaxed, never in a hurry and viewing the Navy, the war and the world with wry amusement. He was good at everything, classes and flying, and was the only man in the company who could beat me at rifle drill.

McCormick tended to regard rules rather casually, too. I think he had trouble sleeping. In the middle of the night, he would shake me awake, motion to me and we would go into the head (men's room) and smoke and talk and then return to bed. Several times he awoke me and said, "Get dressed." Out of curiosity, I would, and then he would show me a way he had discovered to get out of the barracks without having to encounter the officer on duty—up a ladder into the attic, down an outside stairway and down the street to the gate. I feared the sentries would stop us, but as Chug said, they didn't. They didn't know we weren't supposed to be up and out, and we would stroll down to Moon's, a beer joint with a waitress who had a fine body. Legend was that she had lent the body to a cadet who wandered off and left her weeping, with the result that she would have nothing to do with cadets.

After a couple of weeks of nothing but ground school and close-order drill, we were put on a bus and shipped to a small airfield at Merimec, where we flew Piper Cubs, which seemed pointless, since the instructors did the flying and would not let us take the things up alone. But then, back at Lambert, we were put into the Stearman or, as the Navy designated it, the N3N, the world's greatest airplane. Anyone other than the aged, the infirm or mentally disadvantaged could fly the thing, and after ten hours of instruction, most of us were cut loose on our own.

If it had not been for the specter of war lurking in the background, we could have had a fine time at Lambert. Flying the Stearman was a joy, and once we had survived aerobatics, we were convinced that we were hot pilots. Our uniforms arrived and, gorgeously arrayed, we went into St. Louis to stun the girls, which we seldom did. Our social life was lively. Nearly every weekend the bulletin board carried invitations from St. Louis matrons: six cadets invited for dinner and dance. Ten cadets for lawn party, etc. We were magnificent in our whites, or so we thought, although I must say this: if a man does not look good in Navy dress whites, he should give up trying. He will never make it.

***

It was too good to last. We piled aboard a southbound train for Corpus Christi, Texas, a trip featuring a massive crap game at which I lost money. Worse, I got off the train with a high fever and was soon in sick bay with what turned out to be infected tonsils. These were pre-penicillin days, it took a while to make me whole again, and by that time my class had gone on before me. We still met on weekends in Corpus, got rooms at the Driskell Hotel, and McCormick and I would go to dinner, then take a bottle down to the waterfront for a quiet evening of talking and drinking. We found that there was no use in hunting for girls. Corpus at the time had about 35,000 population, and there were 40,000 sailors on the Navy base. But I enjoyed McCormick's company. He was one of the most intelligent, witty and decent men I have ever known. After he shipped out to another base things were never as good again. The strong bonds welded in wartime seldom carry over into civilian life. People change, as do political and social interests, and the shared concerns of wartime disappear. But twenty years later, I got a call from McCormick; he was passing through Louisville and wondered if we could share a drink at the airport. Dreading the disillusionment I felt was likely, I went out, and it was as though it had been, really, only yesterday. We still keep in touch.

At Corpus, I was sent to Rodd Field, still flying the Stearman, took night flight, formation flying, and got under the hood for the Link trainer, then flew the Vultee Vibrator, a quirky plane. I was a pretty good flier, with one small exception: I had trouble compressing. In the pressure chamber I experienced sharp pains in my forehead and ears. The officer in charge decided that the test was inconclusive, and might have been due to an ear infection, but in flying I found that while I could go up without discomfort, I had to come down gradually or experience excruciating pain in my sinuses. Being unable to return to earth was a drawback. I had trouble flying the Vultee, partly for that reason, and was relieved when the Navy decided to make me a ground person and gave me an ensign's commission. Bellile busted out, too, was commissioned and sent to Kodiak, Alaska; Kingsbury got his wings and shipped off to carrier duty. McCormick went on to multi-engine bombers in the Pacific.

***

After that my career became bizarre. I was shipped first to—would you believe it?—a preflight school at Murray, Kentucky. The command there had no idea what to do with me, so made me a regimental and athletic officer, my chief duty being to teach cadets military tumbling and track. In brief, we ran. Murray is a good town, the people were hospitable and the cadets were no problem. They were all college men, many of them varsity athletes with good records, probably the finest bunch of men I have seen. They wanted their wings, and weren't about to foul up if they could help it. I became pretty good at the job, found I could still run all day, and became fairly adept in the gym. Again, I knew it was too good to last, and, again, it was. Soon, I received orders to the USS *Barnegat*, AVP-10, a seaplane tender based in Coco Solo, Canal Zone.

I caught a transport out of Norfolk, at once became seasick and vomited my way to Trinidad, where I was put ashore to await transportation to Recife, Brazil, where my ship had strayed. In Trinidad I was assigned to a comfortable BOQ (Bachelor Officers Quarters) set on a lovely hillside looking toward the sea, with nothing to do but wait. I met some British Navy officers running submarine patrol, and went out with them one day, promptly becoming sick. Eventually I caught a seaplane to Recife where, on a steaming morning, I sweated my way down the dock to a strange-looking ship with a big 10 on its front. My home away from home.

The first week aboard the *Barnegat* was a portent of things to come. I had no idea where or what the gangway was, knew I was supposed to salute the quarterdeck but didn't know where it was, either. Finally, carrying my luggage, I staggered aboard, the enlisted man at the head of the gangway saluted me and I returned it, and in a few moments a sharp-faced, small-mouthed man with red hair came out, took my orders and asked where I had been. The officer I was relieving had been ordered to another ship, leaving the *Barnegat* short an officer. An enlisted man got my bags, and the officer, named Fish, led me forward, down a flight of stairs, a ladder in Navy parlance, and showed me to a bare room with two double-deck bunks where, he said, I would bunk until a room became available topside.

***

I met the Captain, a handsome Prussian type named Deitrich, with a trim mustache and bags under his eyes, who viewed me with what seemed amusement, and welcomed me. I was the new air officer, I learned, though I had no idea what that meant. Chief Warrant Officer Smith was to be my assistant, though, again, he knew everything as surely as I knew nothing, and I was and would be more his assistant than he mine.

We got underway the next afternoon to tend planes off an Island called Fernando de Naronah, and by dinner time I was so sick I had to ask to be excused from the table. Sounds of merriment followed me as I rushed down to the head opposite my bunkroom and vomited up anything that happened to be around. It was several days before I could eat normally, but I stayed on my feet, stood my junior-officer watches on the bridge and tried to learn the fueling and storage systems from Smith. The systems, like the ship itself, were a total mystery. The blueprints I was given to study showed a maze of rooms, spaces, storage areas, pipelines, ladders, tanks, pumps and CO_2 outlets, etc. that made no sense whatever. All I wanted to do was lie down and, if possible, die.

The process of tending was both simple and difficult. We would anchor in a fairly quiet bay, where we would set out mooring buoys.

The planes, huge PBM seaplanes, would land, i.e. up to the buoys, the crews would come aboard to eat and sleep, and we would send boats out to fuel and provide the planes with bombs and such. In the more difficult procedure, in case we had less mooring room, the planes would approach the fantail of the ship, we would heave the crew a line with which they would make the plane fast to the ship, and then pass them fuel hoses. This was tricky. The air officer signaled to the pilot when to come forward toward the ship and when to cut his engine. If the pilot miscalculated and came in too fast, he would hit the fantail, damage the ship, ruin the plane, and provide material for a court martial. We had such an accident in Tagus Cove, in the Galapagos Islands, and it was unpleasant.

Most of the time, however, we transported men and materials, especially aviation gas, bombs and torpedoes to out-of-the-way Pacific ports no one had ever heard of, and where few people existed. It was a joke aboard ship, but not a very funny one, that if we were ever hit, we would all draw flight pay. But the *Rockaway*, a sister ship, took a bomb between fuel tanks off Alaska and steamed home for repairs.

The Captain was unusual. Each morning his steward's mate went to his cabin with orange juice, coffee and benzedrine pills. With these put away, the Captain was ready for the day's challenge. A strict and knowledgeable officer, he could also be unconventional. In Bahia, I think it was, or Rio, he had a lady friend and at lunch one day announced that the lady would be glad to have us for drinks that evening. Those not on duty went. The friend had a beautiful home in the suburbs, waiters running around and expensive clothes. We wondered how she afforded all this until she pulled the Captain to one side and whispered to him, whereupon the Captain shouted, "Gentlemen, follow me!" and out we went through any available exit, since her husband was approaching.

But the Captain seemed to like me, or feel sorry for me, and I was sorry when, after only a few weeks, he was transferred to a carrier. In his place came Lieutenant Commander Charles Robertson, whom I think was manufactured by the Navy as the ideal officer— dark-haired, handsome, ramrod straight and absolutely correct in appearance and conduct. Within days he knew not only every officer in his wardroom but most of the enlisted men and the location and function of every piece of equipment aboard. The perfect officer and gentleman.

I got off on the wrong foot with Capt. Robertson for a mistake, an understandable mistake but a mistake. I had been made third division officer and had responsibility for the stern spaces and fantail of the ship, and I fear my division was the worst on the ship, mainly my fault. Upon being given the division, I called the men together and told them, in effect, that I was aware that I knew very little about the division or its duties, but would learn, that I was there to work with them to make it a good division, and that I hoped they would come to me if I could help. That was the mistake. I had been accustomed to cadets who liked their role, wanted to do right, and appreciated good treatment. These sailors were tough, cynical, suspicious of all officers, and eager to get away with what they could. They took one look at me and figured they had a patsy. Within six weeks, they were almost out of control. Boodry, my excellent boatswain's mate, was struggling to keep our spaces up to snuff, but he and I were constantly appearing at Mast (Captain's disciplinary court) to speak for third division men who seemed persistently in trouble. On his first formal inspection the Captain found many of our spaces below par.

Finally he called me in and advised me in quietly measured words that if I didn't get my division in line, it would be taken away from me, a black mark. I called a muster of the division on the fantail and spoke to them in the most scathing terms I could summon, admitting that I had made a mistake in treating them like men and warning that from then on they would be treated like the bums they were until they showed they were otherwise. I revoked liberty for the entire division, and for weeks afterward handed out extra duty and loss of liberty with abandon. I knew that I was punishing them for my own error, but I had little choice. Slowly, they came around, and we gradually achieved a decent working relationship. And I had learned the wisdom of the Navy rule that an officer can be friendly, even intimate with his men, but never familiar, always preserving the line of command between them.

***

I know I was not a good officer; I knew it then. And it was largely my fault. I had entered the Navy with the cynical aim of evading the Army and finding the easiest way possible to live through the war. I still nursed a simmering rage against the fates that had brought

269

me into the service, resenting with all my being that the country had made me sweat through high school, Swift and Co., then college and, just as I was starting to enjoy the life I had worked for and to begin a career that I found enjoyable, the government which, as far as I could see, had done little for me, ordered me to go out and get killed. With that attitude, I could hardly have been a good officer.

But I cannot assume all of the blame. The Navy deserved a share, too. It is unfair to expect a man to perform difficult duties while nauseated, light-headed and weak; seasickness is no joke. But the Navy made no effort to find remedies until late in the war, and then used them experimentally on shore personnel. I was not the only seasick man aboard, or the worst one. Lt (jg) John Sepic was so sensitive to ship motion that he became green one evening when we were tied up to the dock in Norfolk as the sea outside became rough and we moved slightly. He had to be put ashore, and I probably should have been, but fought to stay aboard.

More important, I had absolutely no training in shipboard life whatever. The other officers, who regarded me with condescension, had either had years in the Navy and aboard ship, or had had the usual ninety days of officer training and were fairly familiar with shipboard routine, nomenclature, function and duties before they reported. I had flown a Stearman airplane and had run the legs off cadets, not the ideal preparation for a shipboard officer. The other officers gradually were promoted to positions of importance. Bill Snyder became navigation officer and then Exec. Gene Callan took over gunnery. My roommate Warren "Flea" Fellabaum, a bright, conscientious and morally upright officer who drank little and refused to chase girls, proved to be the best ship-handler aboard. He was an excellent man, and I now have a daughter named for his wife, Marnie.

***

I realize that I have failed (probably significantly) to mention that back in the States I had married a girl I had met at UK, a pretty, vivacious girl who followed me from station to station, was eager to get married and seemed like a good bargain. Men away from home in wartime tend to do such things, as do women. Something in our nature.

There was no disguising the fact that I didn't know much, yet was expected to know the most esoteric terms and functions. Once, at anchor in a Pacific harbor, we got underway, and the word was passed from the bridge to slip number six line, which was fast to a buoy. I relayed the order, not knowing what it meant. Unfortunately, even Boodry didn't know its meaning, nor did any of the petty officers around. We threw over number six line, and it at once got caught in the starboard propeller. A diver had to be brought out from the beach to cut it out of the screws, after I dived down repeatedly in an effort to make up for our error. I never did learn what the term meant.

I did learn enough about radar, sonar, the electric recorder and basic plotting board to serve as combat information center officer, but even there bad luck seemed to dog me. Just east of the Sargasso Sea in the South Atlantic, we got a sonar contact that indicated a submarine dead ahead, and went to general quarters. I checked to see that my crew was on station and took my place on the electric recorder, which would show where the submarine was in relation to the ship, and from which I would give the order to drop depth charges from the fantail. I called the torpedomen on the depth charges racks and they replied that they were ready. Suddenly the recorder came to life. There on the white sheet of paper unrolling before me, was an electrically burned black mark—a German submarine, trying to torpedo us. My knees were shaking so badly that I had to hold on to the recorder, but I kept the information on the sub going to the bridge, so the Captain could maneuver to attack. The order came to fire on the recorder. When the burn mark crossed the vertical line, I called to the men on the fantail, "Stand by!" and was horrified when the reply came back "Fire one!" "Oh, hell no," I screamed. "I said stand by!" Too late. "Oh," said a voice from the fantail, and then the ship shook from an explosion aft. Not only had we dropped prematurely, but somehow the men had set the charges for a depth too shallow. They had almost blown us out of the water. Bill Snyder, the executive officer, came running in. "What the hell happened?" he demanded. I tried to explain, as Rogers, the sonarman, and Fitzpatrick, on the plot, supported my story. Then the Captain appeared. "Are we hit?" he shouted. The exec tried to explain, as the ship came around and we prepared for another run on the sub. We didn't find it again.

Later, in the wardroom, the Captain shook his head resignedly. "Gentlemen," he said, "if any Germans died down there today, it was from laughing." We felt poorly. The quick-triggered torpedoman got busted. I was not guilty, but the sin had been committed by my men, and it was my duty to train and drill them so that such mistakes were not made.

***

It would have been nice could we have remained in the South Atlantic, where we even got as far south as Rio de Janiero, and got ashore in time for Carnival, the most exuberant festival in the world at the time, before Rio became a dangerous town. The women of Rio were gorgeous and hospitable. It is a wonder we got out of there with a full crew. I was willing to stay if needed. But then we shipped out for Boston for re-fitting, and from there ran the icy North Atlantic, which was usually stormy for good measure. I was never so cold in my life, and it was not warming to know that German U-Boats liked the waters between Iceland (where the people were as cold as the weather) and England.

***

From Portsmouth, England we returned to Norfolk and then sailed for Casablanca, which may have seemed a romantic town in the movie, but was a hole as far as I could see, with a harbor full of half-sunken French ships, scuttled by the Vichy government rather than have them become part of the Allied fleet. They were beautiful ships, the battleships *Jean Bart* and *Richelieu*, and some smaller craft—war is madness. From there we headed again for England, but hit a hurricane that tossed us like a cork for two weeks before we limped up the Bristol channel. The trip was not made easier by the fact that the night before we shoved off, Lt. George Bunch and I had fallen in with some Air Corps fliers, had almost gotten shot in the Old Medina, where we were not supposed to be, and had gotten wasted on a vicious drink known as a flip, made of brandy, chocolate syrup and something else lethal. I died many times leaving Casablanca. I really didn't care for Morocco or North Africa, though Rabat was a far better town than Casablanca.

Going up the Bristol channel, I got this overpowering sense of deja vu. I am not joking. I felt—I knew—I had been there before. I recognized every landmark, including the scenic Clifton Bridge, and in Bristol I got the feeling that I was coming home. I don't for a minute believe in that sort of thing, but that is how I felt. The town had been hard hit by German bombers, and the whole center of town flattened, but the people were up-beat and friendly. We unloaded our cargo of torpedoes and fuel and had some time to look around. We had power lines to the ship, but no phones, and every time a call came for us, the bobby in the booth at the head of the dock would come marching down the way, properly stiff, arms swinging and deliver the message in crisp tones. When we left, Bill Snyder, the executive officer, asked him if there was any gift we could give him, and he broke our hearts when he said he would love an egg or orange for his children, who had never had a fresh one. We made up a crate of fruit, eggs, canned meats, candy and whatever goodies we could find, feeling fat and selfish, and presented it to him. His lips trembled. So did ours.

Two small incidents marred our stay in Bristol, or made it more interesting, according to your viewpoint. In the blackout, we could see only vague shadows on the dock, but could hear the babble of young females at the foot of the gangway, where they waited for the sailors to come ashore. One chilly night —I had the gangway watch —Bill Snyder, always a man of good impulses, came out, heard the girls twittering in the dark, and said it might be a nice gesture if we invited some of them aboard for the movie in the wardroom. I agreed, went down in the dark and asked if anyone would like to come aboard for the movie. I almost got trampled. Up they came, and Bill was hard put to steer them into the wardroom. The stewards mates had made up two huge platters of sandwiches and fruit, and our guests went through them like locusts in Egypt. We started the movie, but when we had to turn on the lights to rewind the reel, we saw that half of our guests had left. Where did they go, asked Snyder. How should I know? I replied. Find them, he said. I did. With the sergeant at arms, I found the ladies happily bedding down in the crew's quarters, and not happy with the prospect of being chased out. To the crew's huge amusement they struck out at us, calling us unladylike names. For God's sake, said Snyder, get them off before the old man gets back. I did, and had bruises and scratches to show for it. And I didn't even get a medal.

I don't know whom to blame for the second fiasco. The Captain felt hands across the sea dictated that we should make a gesture and decided to give a ship's dance. We engaged a cavern called Columbia Hall, hired a band and made up a mound of food. Ed Kodys, assistant engineering officer in charge of the festivities, put a notice in the local paper of the affair, but the paper made the unfortunate error of saying that all single girls were invited. What Ed had said was that girls with escorts were invited. But never mind. When the hour arrived, so did a small female army that at once swamped the floor, the sailors and the food. It was a near riot, as the sailors saw what the girls had in mind and rushed to comply. Finally, Kodys got to the microphone and announced that all unescorted ladies would have to leave. Up your bum, they screamed, not about to obey. One leggy female came rushing across the floor to where the Captain sat on a slightly raised platform with some of the local dignitaries, and with a flying leap, hurled herself into the Captain's lap. "I'm with you, luv," she shouted happily. You're mistaken, the Captain said stiffly, and put her back onto the dance floor, where she was quickly carted off by a sailor. Everyone except the Captain laughed about it for days.

Two days later, we sailed again for Norfolk, where we took on fuel and supplies, wives came down and some men were given brief leaves. Funny thing: a group of sailors came to me and said they thought we ought to have church on board. Father Pearce. I went over into Norfolk and tried to bum some hymnals and perhaps a small, used organ, but the Christians there were as cheap as ever. I finally found a Navy supply center that gave me a few songbooks. I was hoping that the men would not expect me to preach, and they didn't. Instead, a pharmacist mate whose name I have forgotten, said he wanted to do it, adding that he had done some free-lance preaching back in civil life. The Catholic sailors hooted a the idea of such informal salvation, but on the following Sunday, word was passed that church would be held on the fantail, and when we had struggled through a couple of old dependable Protestant hymns, the pharmacist mate came to the front, faced his congregation and delivered a thumb-buster. He preached on THE MILLION DOLLAR INSURANCE (pronounced "inshernce") POLICY. I have heard worse, much worse. His point was that you could buy a million dollars worth of life insurance, but it wouldn't do you a bit of good when it came time to die. But God would give you, absolutely free of charge, not a penny, forgiveness of your sins and a place in heaven for all eternity, and you didn't have to do a thing but accept him as your savior and lead a good life. The Protestants were quite pleased, and they later told the Reverend what a good job he had done. The Catholics, who can't speak to God without a priest or pope around, said "Shit!" The Rev preached several times after that, and got a good audience, though I don't know that he saved any errant souls.

We took on fuel and supplies and sailed for Coco Solo, on the Atlantic end of the Panama Canal, and arrived in a downpour of hot water. On cool days it was steaming and the men had something new to gripe about, but I liked the weather, and thought the duty made to order. We ran from Coco Solo to Balboa and Panama City, delivered cargo to Pearl Harbor and various ports, none memorable, and tended planes in Tagus Cove of the Galapagos Islands. That was fascinating duty. When the planes were vectored out and we had no pressing duty, the Captain let us take a boat for fishing or exploration of the island. Remarkable island, with marine iguanas, flightless cormorants, giant tortoises and all kinds of birds. The water was full of fish, and the Humboldt Current, which runs up from Antarctica, flows around the Galapagos and returns south, was incredibly cool, and we would rig a boom out and throw a cargo net over the side so the men could swim. That could have been a poor idea. The next day I went up with one of the planes, and when we flew over the ship I noticed a dozen large, dark shapes in the water where the men were swimming. Sharks! The men, when told of the situation, shrugged. If the sharks hadn't attacked already, they probably wouldn't, was their feeling.

We returned to Coco Solo for air-sea rescue duty, which meant we didn't do much of anything. We made many side trips for one reason or another. It was customary for carriers approaching the canal to launch planes in a practice attack, to give the pilots practice and the Army defense crews a drill. On one occasion, two fighter pilots became lost in a storm and crash-landed on a beach up in Costa Rica, and we were sent to pick up the pilots and salvage or destroy the planes, supposedly to keep them out of German hands, though the only opponent we faced were local kids who played war in them. One of the kids, who said his name, in English, was Charlie Lewis, attached himself to me, and I became attached to him, grieving inside when we had to leave. Another time we sailed up the Cartagena River to Barranqilla, Columbia, where a lady named Regina also became attached to me and vice versa, though at a different level. I will not say that Regina was a lady of many talents, but her few talents were well developed.

***

One evening in Coco Solo, while the Captain and most of the crew were ashore, orders came from headquarters to get underway at once. An Army P-38 pilot had gone down about thirty miles offshore, his wingman had circled his parachute and radioed back his position. Two smaller ships were sent to accompany us in our search for the man.

I had gradually gained some skill on the bridge and was glad to find myself as officer of the deck. Indeed, I was the commander of a small fleet, as I maneuvered not only the *Barnegat* but the two frigates stationed to port and starboard, keeping contact by radio, following seaplanes that came out and dropped flares ahead of us after sundown. With the pilot's downed position plotted, it seemed a simple task to find him. We never did, but for eight hours I stood on the bridge, saying nothing when no one came to relieve me, feeling for the first time a pride in my performance and wishing I could have done as well from the beginning. It was a marvelous feeling, and I knew a rush of respect and affection for the Navy that surprised me.

Captain Robertson was promoted to commander and transferred, relieved by an easy-going, much be-ribboned flier named Roberts. Then came news of the German surrender. It was wonderful news, but we knew that a bloody test in the Pacific lay ahead. The word had trickled down that ship losses to Japanese kamikazes were much heavier than had been reported in the press, and we did not relish the idea of facing the die-hard fighters from Japan with the slow, lightly-armed *Barnegat*. Mama had written that my brother Don had been wounded with the Marines on Saipan, and I gathered that he was back in ranks and on Okinawa. I felt guilty, but still hoped a way could be found to end the war before it got us.

I had just returned to the ship for dinner one evening, after a drink at the Coco Solo officers' club and was standing on the fantail, talking to some sailors, when a ship out in the harbor fired some pyrotechnics. We remarked on it, figuring that someone would catch hell for a breach of security, when another flare went off, then another. The bay was full of ships, loaded and waiting to transit the canal, heading for the Pacific, and suddenly it seemed that every one of them lit up, started firing star shells and guns. We looked at each other, not daring to think what we were thinking, and then Bill Snyder came running down the passageway, waving a sheet of paper. "It's over, Pearce!" he exulted, hugging me, pounding me on the back. "But God, it's over!

We made it!"

We had made it. The government had developed a bomb that could wipe out a whole city in a second, and the Japanese had surrendered. Curiously, I felt no elation at all. A few days earlier a sailor on watch had come into my cabin, awakened me and handed me a wire saying that I was the father of Susan Leslie Pearce. I would not be going back to the days of wine and roses. I was going to have to make a living for a wife and child, and God only knew how. As the celebration raged around the base, I walked up to the bridge and sat in the Captain's chair, looking at the outlines of the ship that had become so familiar, smelling the odor of metal and electrical instruments, realizing that I did not really want to go home, that I didn't exactly want to stay with the ship, either, that what I wanted was to go back to yesterday, knowing that yesterday is never there.

***

The point system was announced, I had more than enough for discharge and was soon aboard a merchant ship bound for New York, where I caught a plane for the Glenview Naval Air Station, near Chicago. I had been given my second stripe, and got some deference from the young Lt (jg) who looked at my orders, agreed there was no use giving me duties, since I would be leaving soon, and assigned me to a comfortable room with a two-stripe flier. We played a little golf in the morning, went into Chicago by night, and in general took it easy. Then I was ordered to Great Lakes Naval Base, where an enlisted man stamped my orders, said "That's it," and set me free. He did not say, "That's it, Sir." I was now Mr. or hey, you. A van took me to the train station and without fanfare or farewell I was on my way back to Lexington, whence I had come. In my uniform, I felt a fraud. And, strangely, I was struck by a deep longing for the ship, my room, the men, the life that had become familiar. I was never so lonesome in my life.

I was returning a far different man, and found that Lexington and UK were far different, too. I got a room on South Lime and started looking for a job, writing letters, making phone calls, putting on a happy face and sucking up to men I wouldn't ordinarily speak to. I hate to look for a job. I went back to the campus but found no one I knew, or who knew me, went to the radio station and found that my job had long been abolished, and finally called at the offices of the

Bloodhorse, where Simp Estes, to my amazement, remembered me. He said he had no opening just then but that, if I could stick around a few months, he would have. I couldn't wait, of course. I had obligations.

By chance, I ran across Margaret King, whom I had known in the UK administration. She asked if I had a job, and mentioned that a Mrs. Williams, from Somerset, Ky., was looking for someone to run her paper, which had been left to her by the death of her husband. It did not sound promising, but I had to face the fact that I was one of ten million job-hunters. I had tried the *Courier-Journal,* the *St. Louis Post Dispatch*, the Cincinnati papers and, at Estes' recommendation, had called Joe Palmer, now on the vaunted *New York Herald-Tribune.* Nothing. I caught a bus for Somerset.

Mae Williams proved to be pretty, sweet and badly in need of an editor. I looked around Somerset and had the dull feeling that I was back in Norton, in a small-town, side-street printing office. But I had to get a hold, a start, somewhere. Mrs. Williams offered me fifty dollars a week. I accepted. I didn't feel like it, but I was a civilian.

20

Trouble in the Boardroom

The decade beginning in 1984 proved to be a depressing one for the Bingham papers and a depressing time for those of us who had known the papers in their days of prominence and influence. The Bingham family had always been considered by those on the papers as the epitome of dependability and steadfast dedication. But now the family seemed to be faltering, without an Ethridge or even an Isaacs around to shore up the operation. Barry, Sr. was obviously tired, in uncertain health and apparently taking little part in management. Barry, Jr. seemed solid enough, but his decision to go off with his wife and leave the paper in control of a controversial leader made us wonder about his commitment. George Gill might have righted the ship, but he had been side-tracked in favor of Paul Janensch. Further, Sallie's open contempt for her brother was worrisome, considering that she was a member of the board, support of which Barry needed (though Sallie's contempt, like the Duchess' smiles, seemed to go everywhere) and her callous treatment of Shirley Williams and her lack of knowledge of the paper's history were disturbing. The staff was hearing persistent rumors about antagonism between board members, particularly between Barry, Jr. and Sallie, but never doubted the basic unity of the family. Then one evening I met George Gill coming from a meeting of the Board of Directors, looking as distraught as George can look. He shook his head. "The bitterness!" he said (almost reminiscent of Conrad's Mr. Kurtz and his deathbed "The Horror!"), "Johnny, you wouldn't believe the bitterness." I didn't question him, knowing the discretion required of his position. But if George Gill was disturbed, we had reason for concern about the future.

279

In 1985 Sallie left the book page, and the paper. A more momentous event occurred when it was announced that the news staffs of the *Courier-Journal* and *Louisville Times* would be merged. Both papers would continue publication, but with some changes designed to improve profits. This was a sign of financial problems unusual for the company, and it was recalled that one reason given for Barry's dismissal of Bob Clark was Clark's alleged lack of concern for profits, and his contention that the bottom line was not the primary concern of the executive editor.

For several reasons, these developments did not concern me directly. For one thing, I had decided to retire. David Hawpe had been made editor, a satisfying climax, I trust, to an exemplary career, but I knew I was not in his good favor. I was asked by a journalist group in Atlanta to go on a junket to China and I accepted. It was fascinating, and upon my return I wrote a long article on China's changing culture and its tentative moves toward a market economy. The paper would not publish it. Six weeks later, Tom Brokaw made the same trip and came up with basically the same story that was made into a series for NBC.

I was making more money than I needed to live on, what with a fairly substantial salary from the *Courier*, Social Security and my Navy retirement pay, royalties from several books and speaking fees. Irene assured me that there would be a place for my column as long as I wanted to write it, whether or not I retired from the paper, and that pretty well decided the matter. I had been with the *Courier* for forty years, had not achieved what I had hoped and knew I would not. So I was not eager to stay.

***

An incident occurred in the first months of the decade that fed my desire to leave. I received a letter from Erwin Keikefer, a former Nieman who had for several years been the *Courier's* farm editor, enclosing an article from a Chicago-area journalism trade paper. "I thought this might interest you," Kiekefer wrote. "I have wondered why you weren't editing that paper or a least running the ed page, and wondered if this explained it."

The enclosed article pertained to conflicts of interest among journalists, pointing to Barry, Jr. as an example of publishers determined to establish and maintain high standards. "When Bingham took over control of the *Courier-Journal*," the article explained, "he found, incredibly, that an editorial writer, John F. Pierce, was managing the campaign of a man running for governor. 'Naturally,' said Bingham, "I had to get rid of him."" I could hardly believe it. So that was what had caused my woes!

I still have a hard time believing it. Everyone on the paper knew that Barry was obsessed with matters of ethics and integrity and was determined to prevent not only conflicts of interest, but the appearance of conflict of interest, though the latter is not possible. No man can control what someone thinks of him. But that was really beside the point, at least as far as I was concerned. The fact is, of course, that I never managed anyone's campaign, or took part in any campaign except at the direction of Barry, Sr. When Barry, Jr. took over I neither had nor wanted any part in any campaign. You would think that a man so devoted to ethics would be ethical enough to check his facts. You would think that a man of common decency would check with a man before trying to destroy him. Incidentally, it does not speak well for Chicago journalism that the trade paper not only did not check its sources, but did not even spell my name correctly. Perhaps I should be glad that they did not libel me but someone named John F. Pierce.

I wrote Kiekefer a detailed letter setting out the facts, already recounted here, of my involvement with Bert and the Combs administration, and sent a copy to Barry, Jr. I quickly received a reply saying "Oops!" (Oops! for Christ's sake? Sorry, here's your head back) and offering to have lunch. We had lunch, but we did not discuss the letter, his accusations or my crippled career. Strangely, I found him still a pleasant man, possessing many of the better Bingham qualities. And while I admit that his actions and my subsequent transfer bruised my pride at the time, it was probably the best thing that happened to me on the paper. My years on the *Magazine* and with the column were easily the best.

***

The *Courier* and *Times* continued to be quality publications; from the product you would not have suspected that the infrastructure was shaking. Under Barry, Jr. the *Courier* won an unprecedented number of Pulitzer Prizes, circulation continued high despite television, and the *Magazine* was very popular, though I heard rumors that it might be headed for the bottom-line guillotine. I still had my column and it brought in bundles of mail. Rich and I completed our book on the Ohio, it received good reviews and promised to sell well. My girls seemed fairly content (if girls ever are content) though age was beginning to tell on my siblings.

But where the paper was concerned, I think we all felt that we were being borne along on an irresistible tide of misfortune. Then the feared misfortune began to take shape. In March, 1984, it was announced that Barry, Jr. had summarily reduced the board of directors, and in the process had removed the women members—including his sisters, wife and mother. This was bound to raise hackles, especially on Sallie, with her strong feminist views. He explained that he had received no support but constant objection and harassment, from Sallie, more than anyone else. Sallie replied that she had repeatedly asked for information about the financial condition of the papers as well as other details of the operation and had been refused. Barry and his backers on the Board insisted that Sallie had been kept informed, especially through official reports and financial statements, of the firm's condition. But it was now open warfare. I was told that Barry, Jr., and Paul Janensch, his chief adviser, urged George Gill to side with them against the women but George declined, and wrote an official letter to Barry, Sr., chairman of the board, pointing out that he, Gill, was president of the company, and thus legally as well as ethically obliged to represent all of the stockholders, and would be legally liable if he took sides in a fight of stockholders. He asked and received official recognition and approval from Barry, Sr.

It was at this point that Sallie put her stock up for sale. This did not concern the staff too much, since we assumed that the family would buy it, or get a friendly third party to buy it for future transfer. That was not to be the case. Sallie offered to sell to the family for a reported $32 million, which seemed a more than reasonable price, but Barry, Jr. countered with an offer of $26 million. Tim Peters, Sallie's husband at the time, told me that Sallie was willing to split the difference at $29 million, but that Barry, Jr., on the advice of Janensch, who feared the drain of capital and thought the company could not risk the added burden of a multi-million dollar loan, again refused.

Cyrus MacKinnon, president of the company before Gill, told me at our luncheon club that met every Friday that this version was

basically correct. That the Bingham half-billion dollar empire was sacrificed in a dispute over three million dollars is another of the incredible events of that daft decade. Sallie, of course, finally received for
her 13.4 percent of the company stock far more than she had asked
and been refused.

Then Barry, Sr. made a landmark and, in my opinion, disastrous decision. Fearing that the children, on the basis of their bitter
and adolescent bickering, would tear the paper apart and doom it to
mediocrity or failure after he and Mary died, he announced that the
papers, stations and other corporate entities would be sold. If nothing
else, the proceeds would make the heirs financially comfortable. The
word had apparently been out for some time, for Dick Harwood, rep-
resenting the *Washington Post*, turned up one day to talk about a possible purchase, but told me later that *Post* publisher Katherine Graham was unwilling to engage in a bidding war. We had hoped, of course,
that Barry Sr. would still step in and, as chairman of the board and
chief stockholder, save the day. We also expected him and Mary eventually to back Barry, Jr. in his battle with Sallie, as they should have.
They didn't. We then hoped that the papers would be purchased by
some firm like the *Post*, *The New York Times*, the *Baltimore Sun*—
some paper with a sound and relatively liberal reputation. We reck-
oned without Gannett.

The very name sent chills through the ranks of employees.
Gannett was known as a strictly bottom-line chain that had little or no
regard for journalistic standards or anything but profit. Its chief product and point of pride was *USA Today*, more or less the Ross Perot of
newspapers, full of graphs and charts, bells and whistles, a shallow
thing of no visible policy or philosophy, of capsulated news that was
easy to read, and little of that. Eager to own a paper of long and un-
questioned reputation for excellence, Gannett simply outbid everyone
else to get itself a "flagship" it could point to. The Binghams had no
choice but to take the high bid; had they not done so, Sallie was ready
to sue, in order to get the largest amount possible for her stock, as she
had a right to do. Barry, Sr. announced that the papers were for sale on
January 9, 1986. On May 18 of that year, he announced that they would
be sold to Gannett for an estimated $300 million. The companies as a
whole brought approximately $436 million.

***

We heard the news with shock, then resignation and depression. It was as though Buckingham Palace had been sold for a pool hall. Then a black limousine pulled up out front, and Al Neuharth, Gannett CEO, arrived. Beautifully marcelled, shiny in a gray silk suit and looking so slick that Super Glue would not stick to him, Neuharth mounted a desk in the newsroom, said he knew what a fine paper they were getting, and promised to maintain its quality and staff. I leave it to others to judge how well he kept his word.

In January, 1987, the Gannetteers took over. Barry, Jr., to his credit I suppose, took care of those who had been close to him with golden parachutes; the rest were told to stand by the door and await the signal to jump. Needless to say, I was not among the favored few, but had not expected to be, and it made little difference. I had already planned to retire, and Irene, true to her word, gave me a contract to continue my column, and after forty years with the *Courier*, I retired, renting a small office in the Starks Building at Fourth and Muhammud Ali. I still occupy it and like it. The building offers practically anything you could want, from banks to eating places to men's shops and barber shops, and is connected to the Galleria. It also offers a gaggle of unreconstructed Republicans who come in each day, eager to show me the error of my ways. I do my generous best to set straight these poor, benighted souls.

***

Gannett took over control in January, 1987. Shortly afterward, the *Louisville Times* ceased operation. This probably should not be blamed on Gannett's reputed appetite for profit; it was generally assumed, even before Barry, Jr. left, that the *Times* was headed for the cemetery.

It affected me only peripherally, of course. Still, it was a blow. The death of a paper is a curiously sad thing, and not just because of jobs lost and hopes abandoned. A newspaper, more than almost any other business, is a thing of emotion and dedication as well as a reflection of those whose efforts, sacrifices, ideals and hopes gave it personality and character. It was hard to think of the *Times* as simply a thing when one remembered all the fine, devoted and talented people who had given it life.

But then came a blow that was like a knife in the gut. In August, 1988, Barry died. We had not been permitted to see him during his final weeks, but I had written to him. Mary replied with a fond note. I'm afraid the end was painful in every way; we had heard that he had protested that he did not want to live, despite Mary's anguished pleas. It was good to know that Barry, Jr. and Eleanor had been with him often. He was a great man, a fine citizen and a symbol of the best in American journalism. Personally, I will never forget that suave, handsome, charming man I met that first day in the old *Courier* building. Sad to say, his breed among American publishers is also dying.

I think that all of us who were close to her were concerned about Mary. She and Barry had been so close throughout their lives, we wondered how long she would survive without him. Indeed, one of the things we resented most about the semi-biographies written about the family were the somewhat derisive remarks about the continuing physical and emotional love between the two, their absolute devotion to each other. Somehow, the authors seemed to take seriously the complaints of the children, especially Sallie, that their parents loved each other so much that they neglected their children, spent too much time together, went off on trips without the children, and when away from each other wrote frequent, loving letters. Such enduring love is a rare and beautiful thing in modern marriage, or modern relationships in general, and is a tribute to two unusual people.

Incidentally, we could not have been more mistaken about Mary. It was as though she felt she had to compensate for Barry's death by doubling her activities. She directed the affairs of the Bingham Foundation, managing before her death to select beneficiaries and give away nearly all of the money that she and Barry had set aside for the purpose. She was in constant demand to address some group or other, and was forever being feted by state and local organizations. She led an active social life (I was privileged to escort her on many occasions to concerts at the Center for the Arts, and to luncheons and dinners at the River Valley Club) and entertained frequently. But she still harbored a lingering bitterness toward both Sallie and Gannett. "That Neuharth sat right there at the table with me," she told me one evening, and said, 'Mrs. Bingham, I know what a fine paper you are handing us, and I promise you that we will keep it that way.' And of course," she added, "they didn't."

Mary Bingham was unusual in many ways. She had a fine sense of humor and loved a good laugh. She often lunched with John

Richards and Leon Tallichet, who handled the nuts and bolts of the Bingham Foundation, and Sam Thomas, who had become something of the family historian, and though she had passed ninety, she would traipse up and down the long steps to the Colonnade cafeteria in the Starks Building, and carry on sprightly conversation. We often referred to her as "The Queen," and I still think that was fitting. She was regal.

Then in August of 1988, a man from the Louisville Rotary Club asked me to be the master of ceremonies for a dinner honoring Mary. There would be several speakers, the presentation of a gift, and the formalities that go with such an occasion, and I was asked to write introductory notes for each speaker, make opening and closing remarks, etc. I called Mary to ask if she had any advice or requests, and she said she asked only that I try to keep it short, adding that she loathed such events. I told her that I did, too, and that I would suffer with her. But on the afternoon of the dinner, I began having serious pains in the region around the small of my back, went to the doctor and was sent immediately to the hospital to pass a kidney stone. After the doctor gave me a merciful shot to dull the pain (a kidney stone is more painful than you might think) I got in touch with the man in charge of the dinner and explained my difficulty, recommending that he ask Baylor Landrum, who is expert in these matters, to take over, explaining to him my condition. Baylor, may the Lord reserve him and his pretty wife a special space in heaven, did his usual, impressive job, and the program went off smoothly, with one speaker after another heaping praise on Mary. Perhaps the most welcome words were the words of love and admiration spoken by her daughter, Eleanor Miller.

Then Mary rose, smiled that beautiful smile and said she felt humbled by remarks so kind that she would not be surprised if a little pink cloud came down and carried her away. Whereupon she dropped dead. Thus stopped a noble heart, ending a lovely life.

***

Of course, my life was not ordained to run smoothly. And my nature, I fear, decreed that my blind hog should eventually find not an acorn but a club with which I could beat myself. In 1989, I took my wares to the state Book Fair in Frankfort. I love the Book Fair. It gives me a chance to see people I haven't seen for years, people from whom I have received letters, people who just want to say hello, or talk a while. I did pretty well that year, sold quite a few books. Then, as the afternoon waned and the crowd thinned, who should walk up, smile and sit down, but M. I had seen her once or twice in the twelve years since we had gone separate ways, and once, before a dinner for Harry Caudill, we had a very pleasant conversation. She looked heavier and not as vibrant, but much the same. We talked when no one was buying a book, and the conversation seemed surprisingly relaxed and natural, and when the Fair closed I walked her to her car.

She suggested that we go down to the hotel and join some friends involved in the Fair for a drink, but instead of joining the others we sat in the bar and talked. As usual, I did most of the talking. Talk had never been her strong suit. She was more intelligent than I and had better judgment, but she seldom expressed it. I often wished she would talk more, for I enjoyed it when she did. After all, communication is what a good relationship is about, though perhaps it need not be verbal. One time on a drive from Frankfort to Louisville, I determined I was not going to speak until she did. We drove to Louisville without a word.

She seemed somewhat dispirited, but reluctant to leave and when I took her to her car she said, "I want to see you again." Just like that. Curiously, I was not terribly surprised. I had always nurtured a bat squeak of belief that she would come back. I told her that, for reasons of survival, I did not do married women, but she said she was taking care of that, and would call me.

A month or so later, she did, and like a Pavlovian dog, I responded. I knew what I was doing. I remembered Prich's warning about her short attention span, and it occurred to me that I had served and was again about to serve as a convenient fill-in between marriages until she again found a proper mate. But I went running back, eagerly, happily, destroying the placid, pleasant social life I had built in Louisville. I have no one else to blame, and have but little regret. The ensuing four years were good, up to the inevitable end of the relationship. We did a great deal of traveling, to San Francisco, Monterey, the Big Sur, Mendicino, Boston, Maine, Costa Rica, England, and to St. John with Bert and Sara Combs, whose wedding we attended on his farm in Powell County.

***

I saw a great deal of Bert in those years, and I think they were also the happiest years of his life. Sara treated him like a king, and he luxuriated in it. He was fascinated with the farm, and was easing his way toward retirement so that he could spend all of his time there. It gave him a chance to raise his beloved roses (the Flower Clock and beautification of the Capitol grounds were among his proudest accomplishments as governor) and to get back to his country-boy roots with a big garden, a fish pond, and horses, including some miniature horses that he bought from Cawood Ledford. Dogs and cats crawled all over the place, and Sara put bird feeders around the lawn. Bert would spend four or five days a week in the Lexington offices of Wyatt, Tarrant and Combs and then head for Powell County. He had become a most treasured friend, and I loved to visit him on the farm.

A major acorn fell my way in the summer of 1990 when John Carroll, the new and much talked-about editor of the *Lexington Herald-Leader* called and asked me to lunch. I was curious about the often praised, often condemned Carroll and jumped at the chance. When the Knight-Ridder chain bought the stodgy *Herald* and *Leader*, it sent John down to put vitality and meaning into the combined paper, and he had done just that. The editorial page, under David Holwerk, became a free-swinging, usually liberal voice, featuring the brash editorials of Bill Bishop, son-in-law of my long-time friend, Philip Ardery, and the sometimes vicious, usually controversial cartoons of Joel Pett, while the news department slaughtered the familiar herd of sacred cows, even taking a closer look at the University of Kentucky and exposing skullduggery in its basketball program, for which it earned the Pulitzer prize and the condemnation of hordes of Big Blue fans.

I found John Carroll charming, humorous and very low-key. He asked me to write a Sunday column for the *Herald-Leader*. I regarded the offer cautiously since, as I told John, I was afraid the *Courier* would not carry my column if I wrote for the *Herald-Leader*, and that while I was established in Louisville, I was an unknown quantity in the bluegrass, and at my age was not eager for a failure.

But it was a tempting offer. In the fall of 1940 Andrew Eckdahl, who roomed in our South Upper apartment house and was a *Herald* reporter, asked me if I would like to do some feature articles for a tobacco special edition the *Herald* was planning. It was not, as I recall, prize copy, but it was my first time in a real daily paper, and very satisfying. And now, fifty years later, I had a chance to return to the scene of my youthful glory, or crime, as your literary taste may dictate.

I finally accepted Carroll's offer. We signed a very generous contract for a column per week, and in September I wrote my first column for the *Herald-Leader*.

As I feared, Hawpe was furious. I did not know it at the time, but Carroll was David's bête noire, partly, I suppose, because John had so revitalized the *Herald-Leader* and successfully invaded the *Courier's* Eastern Kentucky circulation area. The *Courier* now had real competition for the first time, and apparently did not like it. For months David did not speak to me. M and I were at Spindletop one afternoon for a program saluting Bert, and David, after speaking to M, simply turned his back on me. I asked him why, and he said it was because I was writing for "that paper." John Carroll, having coaxed me into the water, walked out and left me blubbing away, leaving in the spring of 1991 to become executive editor of the *Baltimore Sun* papers. I was happy for him, of course, but was truly sorry to see him leave, not only because I liked him personally, and found him and his wife good company, but because he was good for Lexington and for Kentucky. I wish we did not have to lose so many men of his caliber.

***

About the time Carroll left, John Morgan, television director with Kentucky Educational Television, asked me if I would like to do another documentary, this one on Highway 80, which runs from the Virginia border at the Breaks of the Sandy Interstate Park to the Mississippi River at Columbus—Belmont State Park. Remembering our experience with the Ohio River documentary, I grabbed the chance and, again, had a wonderful time, though I caught a slight cold standing for hours in Mammoth Cave. I was getting to be quite a ham. Morgan was a fine director, and a joy to be around. I am sorry to add that he died of cancer a few years after we completed Down Highway 80.

For several years I had been working, when other duties permitted, in an attempt to trace the origins and causes of the feuds that racked Eastern Kentucky in the years following the Civil War. It was a much longer task than I had anticipated, and entailed hours and days in the Filson Club, the Kentucky Historical Society Library in Frankfort, the Kentucky Room of the UK Library, the State Archives, the Louisville Free Public Library, and days with county courthouse records. Happily, it also led me to dozens of wonderful people such as Stan DeZarn, Tom Walters, Pauline Logan, Jess Wilson, James Klotter —to list them all would take up a book. Georgiana Strickland, of the University Press of Kentucky, nagged, hounded and harassed me until I had the manuscript in some state of accuracy and generally put it in readable condition. It was published in 1992, received mostly good reviews and has sold fairly well, though not as well as it should. It is a good book, and tells of an important and interesting phase of Kentucky history.

But you don't stay on a roll forever, and in 1992 my luck began to run out. That is not to say that my life turned sour, but that bad things began to happen. Molly Clowes, that wonderfully sweet, intelligent woman died, largely, I think, because she was tired of living as a semi-invalid. She had suffered a severe stroke that partially paralyzed her, and though she fought back, regained her speech and was mentally sharp, she slowly lost interest in the things that had mattered most—books and magazines, conversation, cooking and her greenhouse. In her last year, she did little but watch television, which she had never done before. She grieved about what had happened to her beloved *Courier-Journal* and would just shake her head wordlessly when the subject of the paper or the Binghams came up.

And in that year, age began to lay an increasingly heavy hand on my shoulder. Before, I had not thought seriously about age and aging. I still felt young, fairly virile, was still active. But I was visiting the men's room more and more frequently, and finally underwent the old man's fright—a prostate operation. It was a simple operation, with a complex result. The doctor had warned me beforehand that there was an even chance that it might reduce my sexual potency and even leave me impotent for a while, but I don't think I gave it much thought. Impotence was one thing that had never occurred to me; I might have been better off if it had slowed me a little earlier in life. But now it struck. The doctor said that with time, and possibly testosterone shots, I would again take my place in the old stallion barn, but for the time it was clear I was not a major threat to maidens. Each morning when I shaved, I regarded more closely the face looking back at me. It had never occurred to me that I would get old, and I was reluctant to face the possibility now. I resolved to get back to the YMCA.

21

Hauling Down the Flag

The *Courier-Journal Magazine* folded in 1991, and Jimmy Pope decided to retire. It was a painful development for many of us. I never understood how the *Magazine* could have such solid readership and not attract advertising, but was told that it had to do with department store sales, which had to be announced on short notice, lest the opposition see the prices in sales ads and jump in and undercut them, and copies of the *Magazine* were available days in advance of distribution, making it almost inevitable that prices carried in the ads would be leaked. Clothes merchants wanted fashion stories to carry the fact that the clothes were for sale at such and such stores, but that was ruled a violation of separation of news and advertising. Barry, Jr., incidentally, almost drove Shirley Williams into the mental hospital with a decree that we should pay publishers for books sent us for review, especially those that were reviewed. Shirley tried to explain this to the publishers, who thought she had lost her grip on reality. They told her they had no means of billing for such books, that they had no way to set a price on them, that they could not do it for one paper only, and that their accounting system took into consideration a percentage for books sent out for review. Shirley was also told not to give out to company employees books not sent out for review, which left her wondering what the hell to do with them. That place could get nutty.

But under my contract, I continued to write for the Sunday Forum section. It was not like the old *Magazine* column; there was little room for nostalgia or humor, and I was again thrown back into politics and official affairs. But the pay was the same, and I soon gained some readership, though not what I had writing for the *Magazine*. Those columns were different, personal, and off the beaten path, something readers could not get elsewhere and relief from comment on current affairs.

Then I received from David Hawpe a cold, formal letter–by registered mail, yet–saying in effect, we don't want your column every week any more; your contract allows either party to cancel or revise the contract at any time, with thirty days notice, and beginning thirty days from now on we will take only two or three columns a month, since we want space for columns by our own editorial writers. Keith Runyon will be in touch with you to discuss a revised contract. Yours truly.

For a while, that threw me. The letter made sense only if I assumed that David was looking for a way of getting rid of me by degrees. If he needed Forum space for editorial writers, he had from six to eight syndicated columns running on Sundays that he could run or hold as he wished. None of them was local, and I knew the Forum section needed a local columnist besides Bob Garrett, who carried the ball alone on state politics. I waited. I had about made up my mind to refuse the proffered contract, but debated because I knew that if I did the paper could explain to any reader who might protest that I had turned down a contract of my own volition. Keith called, we had lunch at Vincenzo's, and he handed me a manila envelope with neatly-typed pages enclosed. I read to the second paragraph, put the papers back into the envelope and said, "You and I have been and are still, I trust, friends. Let's not spoil a nice lunch discussing a contract we both know I won't sign." It was a nice lunch.

I heard that someone had seen David's letter to me on his desk, and had told Billy Reed, *Herald-Leader* (and former *Courier-Journal*) sportswriter, who had told the people at the *Herald-Leader* (I hate to be involved in that sort of back-fence tattle). David Holwerk called, reported this and told me that if I would sign an exclusive contract with the *Herald-Leader*, they would let me write two or three times a week, and pay me more than I was then getting from both papers.

I then got a call from Ed Manassah, the round-faced, smiling new publisher of the *Courier-Journal*. We met in the Brown Hotel cafe for breakfast and talked for more than two hours. He insisted that the contract the *Courier* offered was a good one for me and the paper. Ed Manassah is a very quick and bright man, and persuasive, but his proposal made little sense. I told him, honestly, that I had already talked with the *Herald-Leader* people, and of their offer. Totally open about it. I pointed out that if I didn't sign with the *Courier*, I could make more in Lexington than I was making from both papers. If I signed with the *Courier* I would be getting the same pay from Lexington and reduced pay from Louisville. It was hard to see how that could be translated into a good deal for me. We parted on friendly terms–Ed has always been cordial–but with no contract.

And here is the remarkable aspect of the roundelay: I did not know where we stood. Each week I would call Keith and ask if he wanted a column, or he would call and ask if I had a column for him. I would send him a column. Each month I would get a check. That went on for years.

***

As you might gather, 1994 was not a year for memories that I would remember with fondness on long winter nights. Bert Combs died. I do not yet understand what happened, and probably never will. The known facts of his death make no sense at all. He left his office in Lexington one Friday afternoon, went by his apartment and shortly after four o'clock drove to Powell County, arriving in Stanton a little after dark. He turned left on Main Street and drove to a grocery store, where he bought a few things for the farm. The woman who waited on him said he seemed completely normal and good-natured, showed no signs that he had been drinking or did not feel well.

But then he did an inexplicable thing. He knew that the Red River, which runs between Stanton and his Lower Cane Creek farm, was in flood. In fact, in leaving the farm that morning he had taken a longer route into Stanton from the west, apparently to avoid the flood waters. But instead of taking that safer road home, he left the grocery and drove east, and when he reached the bridge across the Red, for some reason he drove into the water covering the approach to the bridge. He certainly knew the road well. He may have misjudged the depth of the water on the bridge approach and felt he could ford it. It had started snowing, and he may have been unable to see clearly. None of these reasons is sufficient to explain why he drove into the swift, muddy water until his car stalled, got out, and was carried downstream. His body was found the next day by state troopers. The coroner said he had died not of drowning, but of hypothermia, the cold, indicating that, still alive, he had managed to catch hold of a tree, but was unable to reach the bank.

In any event, he was gone. Kentucky had lost a great man, a governor who left his footprints indelibly on Kentucky history, and I had lost a great and good friend, to whom I am so indebted. I was asked to deliver the eulogy over his body when it lay in state in the rotunda of the state capitol. I wanted to do it, felt I owed him that, at least, but it was sheer torture. I barely got through it. Then we took him home and buried him on a hillside in Clay County.

I will tell you something, if I can express it without sounding pompous or melodramatic. The worst part of growing old, the real pain and hurt, is not in the shrinking body, the shriveling skin, not in the white hair or lined face that reminds you every morning of time's toll; it is not in the blurring eyesight, the veined, freckled hands, the joints that have lost their spring, the flabby muscles, the ebbing sexual power or a memory that slips and stutters. No, the pain is in the loss. The loss to some minor extent of places—of houses, stores, schools, swimming holes, mountain trails gone—but mainly of people, of voices and tears, expressions and laughter that made up life and gave life substance and meaning, the memory of whom is heavy now with love because we love life and they were part of life. We stand with Housman "by brooks too broad for leaping, beside fields where roses fade, and long for those whose smiles, now gone, could light up the evening of life."

***

Only months before Bert left I had buried Mama among the scenes of her girlhood in Tazewell, Virginia, and then Katherine in a field near Charlotte. And now Bert. I was really not in a positive frame of mind, if such there could be, to have M slip away again. But she did. Again, our relationship had lasted just about four years. After the final words were spoken, I took her out a couple of times, to dinner and a performance of *The Phantom of the Opera*, but it was words without music, half a song. I wondered if she would again come back, but this time I had the feeling she would not.

I went to see my brother Don in South Carolina, but something happened that didn't help. I had been meaning for some time to go by Greensboro, North Carolina, on my way home, and see my old high school friend and quarterback Frank Nard. We had a few days to talk over. I got his number and called his home. Billie, his wife, also a high school friend said, when I identified myself, "Oh, John Ed, Frank died last summer." I had waited too long. And I had a conversation with Don that shocked and saddened me. We were discussing Joe, and the hardships he had encountered, when Don mentioned that the congregation of the Episcopal Church in Norton had arranged for Joe to receive a full scholarship to the Episcopal High School in Washington, D.C., after which he would almost certainly have been given a college scholarship leading to the ministry and a comfortable, rewarding life. But Joe was not of age, and Mama, for some reason, would not sign the papers allowing him to accept. She never explained her refusal. Once, Don said, she had told Joe that he could enjoy religion without making it his whole life. But, Don added, both he and Rose believed it was simply that she did not want to be left alone. I could hardly accept it. Such utter selfishness, such disregard for Joe's happiness and welfare baffled me. My mother, the one person I loved and trusted above all others, had flaws like the rest of us.

I felt very tired. And then John Moremen, my friend who had established and was doing very well with The Sulgrave Press, told me he wanted me to write the text for a word-and-picture book on Kentucky, with Dan Dry doing the photography. I didn't want to. I didn't feel that I could drum up the energy and interest such an undertaking demands. And I doubted that such a book would sell. Jim Archambault already had a beautiful pictorial history of Kentucky, with text by Dr. Thomas Clark, and I had enough sense left to know that I was not going to surpass Tom Clark. But John nagged me until I finally agreed. I was afraid I was attempting more than I could do well, and did not want, at that stage of the game, to do poorly. But writing the book proved easier than I had anticipated, and more fun. Laura Lee Brown, a wealthy, bright and attractive Louisville woman, agreed to underwrite most of the cost, and she accompanied us on a trip through part of the state to give her an idea of what we would try to show. She proved fine company, and the trip was going well until Dan Dry caught a kidney stone. John drove him to Middlesboro, rented a plane and flew him back to the hospital. But we finished the book on schedule, it was a beautiful volume, and it sold as though it contained the map to the lost gold mine. It is still selling, and we may soon have to risk a third printing.

***

By this time I was really tired. I got a card from Betsy, living in Cape Coral, Florida, containing a shot of North Captiva Island, a small spot of sand about 25 miles north of Sanibel that has to be reached by boat, since there is no bridge or ferry. This is understandable, since there are no roads and thus no cars, and everyone gets around by golf cart or bicycle, as in pre-war Bermuda. Betsy had circled on the photo a cottage near the end of a sandspit where, she wrote, she had just spent the most wonderful week of her life. She insisted that I come down and see for myself. I called her, she rented the cottage, belonging to Gary Walker, a local realtor, and I drove down.

She was right. The island was quiet and pretty, with lots of birds and marine life and few people. The cottage was perfect. I found it relaxing and restful. Gary Walker, owner of the cottage, drove me around the island in his golf cart, as he did most newcomers, and we passed a house on White Pelican Drive that had a For Sale sign out front. To condense, Betsy and I bought it. I had always loved the region, and now I loved the island. I wished that Buddy Atkinson could have been with me when I bought the house.

So I started 1996 working on the house, beach-walking, bird-watching. We made some major changes in the interior of the house and, if I must say so, improved it greatly. It does not attract hordes of fans by the outside, but the interior has a lot of charm. If I must be alone, I can think of no better place.

But 1996 proved to be a depressing time. I probably should not burden you with these glum details, but I am trying to make a true accounting. On the way to the island, I stopped by to see Rose, and was horrified to see her condition. I knew she had had a stroke, but the reports understated her illness. She had always been such a tough little thing, but now she was little more than a shadow, pale, in and out of a coma. She smiled weakly when she saw me. I held her hand and gave her the usual malarkey about this being a fine way to greet me, and that I hoped she would be up and about when I came by on my way home. I am not sure she heard me. Once she opened her eyes, turned toward me with a wistful look and said, "John Ed, Mama was so proud of you."

I was on the island about ten days when Don called to tell me Rose had died. I went up to Columbia, and we drove to Charlotte and buried her. She was a good little woman, spunky and feisty, with a fine laugh and a loving heart.

I went on home, but planned to head for the island again, when I got a call from Buddy Conner's niece, Deanna, saying that Buddy had died. I felt bereft. All the memories of High Knob and the Lake, Stoney Creek, and high adventures and girls came flooding back. Bit by bit, life was taking my past. I drove to Norton and went to the funeral parlor, parking in the lot that was once our sole tennis court, and we buried Buddy within sight of our old house. Deanna told me that my last letter to him was on his bedside table when he died.

Time had taken the last reason I had for going back to Norton, but it was still, in some obscure way, home. Strangely, Norton is a clean, rather pretty little valley town, now. The railroad yards are not as busy as they were, and the locomotives burn diesel, not coal. You can hardly see the traces of the coke ovens that once blackened the sky. Nearly all of the coal mines are closed. I talked with Robbie Tate, publisher of the old *Coalfield Progress*, and she agreed that it was hard to see what was holding up the economy. But there is a new Holiday Inn on the road to Wise. The Copper Kettle is still operating, but now as a restaurant, rather fancy. There are some fine new homes, the streets are neat, and the spindly trees that used to line them are tall and graceful. But much of the vibrant life has ebbed away.

I went back to Louisville, but the year was not through with me. (There I am wallowing in self-pity again. Well, what the hell; if I don't feel sorry for me, who will?) A few weeks later I was in my office when M called. I was amazed to hear her voice and wondered about the reason for the call. She asked about the island and we chatted for a minute. And then she said, "I wanted to call you. I'm getting married." I mumbled felicitations, wished her luck and hung up, thinking, well, at least I won't have to speculate about chances of her returning. It was a shock, but I had for some time been dating a very nice woman, and could now get on with a different life.

On the island when Don called again. Sue, our last sister, had died at her home in Lexington, Virginia, where she had lived since World War II with her husband, Wilfred Ritz, a law professor at Washington and Lee. After her husband died, Sue showed less and less interest in life, became more and more reclusive, and finally just left. Don told me not to try to get to Lexington, that Sue had left instructions that she was to be cremated immediately, without funeral or memorial service, her ashes buried in an urn alongside those of Bill, as Wilfred was known, just down the hill. That had already been done.

As Don said, our family, all of those sweet, tough, witty people, had left us.

***

I stayed on the island for another month, writing my columns, reading, doing a little planting in my weed haven of a yard, then drove back to Louisville. I got in late one Thursday night, tired from the drive and was about to drop into bed when the phone rang and Helen Jones-Pike told me that Jimmy Pope, my long-time friend and magazine editor, was dead. I could hardly believe it. Jimmy, who was partially crippled thirty years before by a tumor near his spine, had gone to the hospital two weeks earlier for an operation on his knee, but, as I told Helen, I had talked to him the day before I left the island, and he seemed in good spirits, though disappointed that his rehabilitation was not yielding faster results, and discouraged at having to walk around the house with a walker. Anne, his wife, told me that he was actually doing as well as the doctor had predicted, but was just impatient. Then Helen added that Jimmy had killed himself, gone into the garage while Anne and one of their sons were at the movies and turned on the car's engine.

Jimmy was one of the sweetest humans ever born, universally loved. I can't imagine what impelled him. Edie Courtney, a close friend of Anne's, said that Jimmy was afraid he would never really recover, and that he had a horror of being a burden on Anne.

Helen said that he had left a note stating he did not want a funeral and, if there was a memorial service, no sermon, no prayers, no injection of religion. That did not surprise me; Jimmy was not religious in the accepted sense of the word, did not believe in prayer or the rituals of church, heaven and hell. But his note, according to Helen, had specified that if there was a memorial service, he would like for Helen and me to say a few words in remembrance. Helen preached a sermon, with two prayers. I tried to keep my remarks as close to Jimmy's wishes and as unemotional as possible. It was not easy. Jimmy was a fine, dear man. My heart was becoming heavy from delivering eulogies over my departed friends.

I went back to the island, where I expect to spend quite a bit of time from now on. By that time, I had begun, at Moremen's insistence, on this book. I arrived the day after Thanksgiving, and a week or so later, Ed Manassah called to say that the *Courier* would discontinue my column the first of the year, which would allow me to say that I had written for the paper for fifty years. I suppose they considered that generous. They had finally decided, for what reasons I don't know, not to debate the matter any more, and just drop me. They later referred to me as having retired. That is misleading, if not downright dishonest. I did not jump. I was pushed. I liked that column.

***

I spoke to God about all this. I said, now is the time to show that what goes down comes back up. You owe me. He didn't respond. But there mostly have been fifty good ones. I would gladly live any of them over. There have been so many wonderful people, so many wonderful events along the way. Like most people, I suppose, I have known disillusionment. Many of the idols of my youth have proved to be only men. The newspaper I revered is a thing of only paper and ink, no better or worse, in the final analysis than the talents and dedication of those who produce it, but also of the goals and purposes of those who control it.

I suppose I have not gotten to the top of the hill I intended to climb, but the climb was fine, and in its way satisfying. Several times I have sat in Whitney Hall of the Center for the Arts, listening to the marvelous sounds of Beethoven or Brahms, watching a classical ballet in its beauty, and it has seemed that I have come a considerable way from the cold and smoky confines of Norton and Swift & Co. I have seen the corners of the world. I have known love, and the satisfaction of work done to the best of my ability. And I am not yet through. The idea of retirement is not attractive. Eighteen holes of golf are enough to last a normal person at least six months; fish are dull creatures, and are best eaten in a restaurant. As long as I can match wits with a woman, why try to outwit a fish?

There is a lot of world I haven't seen, music I haven't heard. I want to learn to tango, go to Paris, return to Vietnam. And there are words yet inside me. Perhaps I shall try a novel, write travel articles.

Somewhere down the road I know my blind hog will find an acorn for me.